Marxism and Criminological Theory

Marxism and Criminological Theory

A Critique and a Toolkit

Mark Cowling
Reader in Criminology
University of Teesside, UK

palgrave
macmillan

First published 2008 by
PALGRAVE MACMILLAN

Palgrave Macmillan in the UK is an imprint of Macmillan Publishers Limited, registered in England, company number 785998, of Houndmills, Basingstoke, Hampshire RG21 6XS.

Palgrave Macmillan in the US is a division of St Martin's Press LLC, 175 Fifth Avenue, New York, NY 10010.

Palgrave Macmillan is the global academic imprint of the above companies and has companies and representatives throughout the world.

Palgrave® and Macmillan® are registered trademarks in the United States, the United Kingdom, Europe and other countries.

ISBN-13: 978–1–4039–4599–0 hardback
ISBN-10: 1–4039–4599–3 hardback

This book is printed on paper suitable for recycling and made from fully managed and sustained forest sources. Logging, pulping and manufacturing processes are expected to conform to the environmental regulations of the country of origin.

A catalogue record for this book is available from the British Library.

Library of Congress Cataloging-in-Publication Data

Cowling, Mark.
    Marxism and criminological theory : a critique and a toolkit / Mark Cowling.
        p. cm.
    Includes bibliographical references and index.
    ISBN 978–1–4039–4599–0 (alk. paper)
        1. Communism – History – 20th century. 2. Communism – Philosophy. 3. Criminology – Philosophy. I. Title.

HX44.5.C68 2008
364.01—dc22   2008029983

10 9 8 7 6 5 4 3 2 1
17 16 15 14 13 12 11 10 09 08

Transferred to Digital Printing in 2010.

To Amani

Contents

Acknowledgements

The author would like to thank the following:

Lawrence and Wishart for kind permission to reproduce passages from Karl Marx and Friedrich Engels, Collected Works in 50 volumes, London, 1975–.

Pluto Press for permission to use my chapter of *Marx's Eighteenth Brumaire: (Post)Modern Interpretations*, London, 2002, which with minor changes forms Chapter 6.

Preface

The origins of this book lie, paradoxically, in the workings of the market in higher education in the United Kingdom. The University of Teesside introduced various degrees in Politics in response to student demand, but then was forced to close them when this demand waned again. From a lecturer in Politics I was therefore transformed into a lecturer in Criminology. I was delighted to discover that my long-standing interest in Marxism fitted well with my new role in teaching criminological theory. However, although there has been a substantial interest in Marxism amongst writers on criminological theory, it has been relatively unsystematic and usually mixed with other theories such as symbolic interactionism which are founded on assumptions dubiously compatible with Marxism. Hence this volume, in which, after some preliminary reflections on the continuing usefulness of Marxism and the best ways of linking it with types of crime, I start by reviewing the main existing work in the area of Marxism and criminological theory, and then move on to discuss the repertoire of Marxist ideas available for enhancing our understanding of crime and criminal justice systems. I do this in the hope that others will find my elaboration of these useful for further work.

In the course of writing this book I have incurred debts to several people. First and foremost come members of the criminology group at Teesside, who made me welcome and have provided a congenial and stimulating atmosphere in which to work. I am also grateful to the management of the School of Social Sciences and Law for providing me with a modest amount of teaching relief. I have presented some of the ideas in the book at various conferences where other people have offered constructive criticism and support. These include several sessions organized by the Political Studies Association Marxism Specialist Group; a seminar at the British Society of Criminology Annual Conference, University of Keele, 2002; a conference to celebrate the 150th anniversary of the publication of Marx's *Eighteenth Brumaire of Louis Napoleon Bonaparte*, held at Tulane University, New Orleans, 2002; a session at the 32nd Annual Conference of the European Group for the study of Deviance and Social Control, University of Bristol, September 2004; and a presentation at the December 2006 meeting of the American

Philosophical Association, Eastern Division, held in Washington, DC. Various people have been kind enough to read and comment on portions of the manuscript: Dave Morland, Craig Ancrum, John Carter, Mike Teague, Terry Hopton, Daniel Chadwick and Paul Reynolds. I would like to thank Access to Work, the British government agency which provides support to keep disabled people in work for the purchase of the Collected Works of Marx and Engels on CD-ROM – everyone disabled should be supplied with a copy! The staff at Palgrave are delightful and extremely tolerant people to work with, particularly in view of how late the manuscript was presented to them. Very much in keeping with the themes of this book, the copy editing was carried out by an agency in India, and I would like to thank Vidhya Jayaprakash, the agency manager, and Deepa C., the copy editor, for their very efficient and courteous work. Finally, and most of all, I would like to thank my wife Amani for keeping me sane and fed while working on this book, and for checking the manuscript. She is the love of my life and this book is dedicated to her. I am, of course, responsible for opinions and any errors in the book.

Part I
Setting the Scene

Introduction

There is a long but unsystematic history of attempts to use Marxist theory to explain crime. Marx and Engels themselves mention crime quite frequently, but in a relatively casual way. For example, in *Outlines of Political Economy* and *The Conditions of the Working Class in England*, Engels takes a conventional definition of crime and argues that the appalling conditions suffered by workers lead them to commit crime.[1] Marx basically takes this approach in articles for the *New York Daily Tribune*,[2] and in *Capital*.[3] Marx and Engels see the lumpenproletariat as a major source of crime, again conventionally defined.[4] Marx recognizes that changes in legal definitions can produce changes in statistics of crime which do not reflect changes in behaviour.[5] Marx also includes in his economic writings the famous passage which appears at first sight to be a functionalist account of crime.[6] These passages provide several interesting suggestions but by no means amount to a developed theory.

As early as 1905 Willem Bonger produced an account of crime based on the analysis in *Capital*,[7] and despite their affiliation to the Frankfurt School Rusche and Kircheimer constructed an account of punishment which also follows strictly economic lines based on *Capital*.[8] The revival of Marxism in the 1960s and 1970s led to interesting work in the United States notably from William Chambliss[9] and Jeffrey Reiman,[10] and in Britain to the flowering of the National Deviancy Conference and the critical criminology of Taylor, Walton and Young and the work of the Birmingham School and others.[11] Subsequently specific interest in Marxist criminology has declined, but has certainly not disappeared as witnessed in the work of Ian Taylor and John Lea.[12] Some of this also draws inspiration from work on Marxism and law, notably from Pashukanis.[13] However, writers on crime typically wear their Marxism

3

relatively lightly, mix it with other approaches such as symbolic interactionism without worrying too much about compatibility problems, and, of course, need to devise their own ways of rendering previous, limited approaches more general.

It is therefore worth attempting a more systematic account of the possibilities of analysing crime using Marxist theory, and it is the purpose of the present book to do just this. Part II of the book, the critique, is devoted to a critique of existing attempts at analysing crime which make some use of Marxist theory. Part III, the toolkit, works in the opposite direction by considering aspects of Marxism which appear to be promising as explanations of crime.

Part I is devoted to a preliminary discussion of Marxism on the one hand and crime on the other. Chapter 1 comprises a discussion of some of the main concepts of Marxist theory. Even the most superficial acquaintance with Marxist theory, with political groups with Marxist affiliations or with the history of officially Marxist states will show anything between vibrant debate and murderous rivalry invoking varying interpretations. There is no way in which a single author could hope to resolve these divisions in a few thousand words. However, by setting out some of the main Marxist concepts, together with some preliminary comments on the strength or weakness of differing interpretations, the reader will be able to form an idea of my overall approach. This chapter also tackles, in an outline way, the issue of whether Marxism has become outdated with the collapse of the Soviet Union and the capitalist turn in China since 1978. I argue that at a fundamental level Castells' concept of informationalism provides a way of understanding of the forces of production which in turn allows us to grasp many features of the globalized economy that has been emerging since the 1980s. The other necessary preliminary is tackled in Chapter 2. The concept of crime is much contested. I argue for an interpretation and five-fold classification appropriate for an attempt at Marxist explanations. In particular I contest the approach to crime which emerges from symbolic interactionism, namely that crime is simply a matter of the sticking on of labels by the powerful. I argue that there is a core of consensus crimes which are widely recognized in an extensive variety of societies. They may be explained in various ways but cannot simply be defined out of existence.

Part II, the critique of existing Marxist criminology, starts with Chapter 3 on the work of Bonger and Rusche and Kircheimer. Because of my acceptance of the existence of consensus crimes I am more sympathetic to Bonger, who has been criticized for accepting the official definition of such crimes, than many subsequent commentators. I argue that the ideas in Rusche and Kircheimer about punishment comprise an interesting initiative but their attempt at an exclusively economic explanation of punishment is simply not plausible. Chapter 4 is a discussion of radical US criminology. I start by considering some of the background. Merton's strain theory, although its most obvious origins are the theories of Durkheim and of the Chicago School, is also capable of being adapted towards a Marxist perspective if it is assumed that US culture is an extreme capitalist culture. The second major background theory is symbolic interactionism. Because this was very influential on subsequent radical criminology I explore ways in which it is not readily compatible with Marxism. I then move on to discuss theorists who specifically make use of Marxism. The Marxist work of Richard Quinney is seen as rather one sided and simplistic, which may well be why he has subsequently moved to rather different perspectives. Although Frank Pearce has worked in Canada and the United Kingdom I include him as a US theorist because his discussion is almost entirely about the United States. I credit him with opening up the discussion of corporate crime from a Marxist standpoint, but also argue that aspects of his work have (not surprisingly) become dated since 1976. The longest section of Chapter 4 is a discussion of William Chambliss and Jeffrey Reiman. They both provide a trenchant critique of corporate crime in the United States and of the way in which the US criminal justice system focuses on street crime as a way of diverting attention from the crimes of the powerful. In my discussion of Chambliss and Reiman I raise the question of why the U S criminal justice system has expanded so massively when other capitalist states cope with much fewer prisoners. This theme continues in the discussion of Christian Parenti. Finally in this chapter I make some adverse comments about constitutive criminology, which has some claims to being a postmodern replacement for radicalism based on Marxism.

In Chapter 5 I move on to British radical criminology. I start by summarizing some of the dramatic changes that have occurred between the early 1970s when radical criminology originated and today. These partially account for the drifting of interest away from Marxist theorizing towards ideas drawn from postmodernism, feminism and Foucault. The first generally recognized text of British critical criminology was *The New Criminology*. In my discussion of this book I follow through the discussion of Chapter 2 by noting how its authors were influenced by symbolic interactionism and the effect that this has on their use of Marxism. I argue that part of their commitment is to a libertarianism which is now largely acceptable within a capitalist society. They have a naive confidence in the abolition of crime in communist society which derives from the symbolic interactionist influence on them. Nonetheless, their work and that of their contemporaries continues to inspire many criminologists up to this day. The work of critical criminologists came closest to Marxism in the collection *Policing the Crisis*. I accept that this had many strengths, particularly a socially situated use of the concept of a moral panic. However, its authors were pretty clearly expecting the emergence of a neo-fascist corporate state instead of the victory of neo-liberalism under Mrs Thatcher. A right realist approach to crime was an important feature of Mrs Thatcher's regime. The failure of the left during her years in office led to the development of left realism. It was argued by some that this involved erstwhile critical criminologists selling out, but my analysis of crime as including consensus crimes leads me to consider left realism as a worthwhile pragmatic approach to street crime, which can have very bad effects on working-class communities.

Moving on to discuss Taylor's *Crime in Context*, I argue that it is quite subtle in some respects but that overall it is too complex and too under-theorized. John Lea's *Crime and Modernity* provides a much more coherent account of capitalist societies today, but I argue that it is seriously exaggerated in some respects. He describes the increased polarization between wealth and poverty that has arisen both within states and between rich and poor states. He goes on to paint a picture in which the wealthy retreat into gated communities and look after their own welfare to the exclusion of the general social good, whereas outside the poor are abandoned, crime proliferates and welfare states crumble. I argue that this is belied by falling rates of crime since the mid-1990s, increased welfare spending in many states, and some patchy but spectacular development in erstwhile Third World countries.

In Part III I move on to the toolkit, the concepts and approaches drawn from Marxism which can be used to analyse crime and criminal justice systems. The first two of these are not in my view very promising. The obvious place to start is with the lumpenproletariat, the grouping which Marx and Engels considered to be the focus of crime in capitalist societies. Unfortunately, as I show in Chapter 6, Marx's definition of the lumpenproletariat may be entertaining but is lacking in rigour. This degenerate grouping functions mainly as a way for Marx to condemn workers who fail to behave in a properly proletarian manner and side with finance capital or the political right. In fact, however, there are many historical examples of displaced members of other classes who have sided with the left. For Marxists today this concept is particularly dubious because of its similarity to Charles Murray's conception of the underclass, which has been used as a stick with which to beat people thrown out of work by the neoliberal economic policies of Reagan and Thatcher.

Chapter 7 comprises a brief discussion of the possibilities of the concept of alienation. Although this concept is associated with some quite poetic language in the younger Marx, it is doubtful to what extent it is compatible with the main concepts of mature Marxism. A major worry with this concept is that it can easily be interpreted as pointing in opposite directions, for example taking either an abolitionist or a sex worker view of prostitution; it is not clear, considering women, why we should prefer a Marxist theory of alienation to one based on radical feminism. Alienation could be seen as the reason why workers turn to crime, which could be justified if it is acquisitive crime directed against capitalists but not if it is directed against fellow workers. Would overcoming alienation from nature point more towards human domination of nature as found in the Soviet Union and China, or to some sort of green politics? Overall I argue that this concept adds little to our conceptualization of crime, our understanding of why it occurs or our ideas of how to reduce it.

In Chapter 8 I consider a variety of ways in which an analysis of crime might be linked to the idea of the reproduction conditions of capitalism. I start by analysing the much-quoted passage in which Marx sarcastically presents crime as a productive activity. Having pointed out that it is a satire, I show that the distinction between productive and unproductive labour is not valid. I move on to thinking more generally about the idea of reproducing the capitalist system and the role that either crime or the criminal justice system might play. Some of the reproduction conditions of capitalism are those of human life more generally, and consensus crimes recognized by most societies can be seen as crimes because they make any social reproduction more difficult. There are particular strains in setting up a capitalist system, and the criminalization of displaced peasants or discontented recent recruits to the working class helps to set capitalism in motion. Once capitalism has become established, there is a widespread view that it develops towards Fordism, linked to a well-funded welfare state. With the rise of globalization and post-Fordism these secure conditions collapse, leaving a much greater need for the criminalization of parts of what had formerly been the working class. Various versions of this account are considered. The idea that mass imprisonment is essential to profit-making in the United States is rejected on the grounds that it is too marginal. It is certainly not essential to the running of all modern capitalist economies, as can be seen from the much lower rate of imprisonment prevalent in Europe and elsewhere. It is more plausible to see mass imprisonment as one possible capitalist option, and arguably a rather poor one in that it fails to make the best use of the talents of all the population for profit-making.

Chapter 9 is a brief discussion of Marxism and law. It starts by introducing the classic problem in Marx's account of historical materialism that law appears in both the base and the superstructure. Having pointed out that Cohen attempts to solve this problem by removing the law from the base, I indicate that I accept criticisms of this view, notably that law can strengthen or weaken aspects of the base; that we need an explanation of why law appears in the superstructure; and that aspects of law seem to have more to do with consensus crimes than with the mode of production. I then move on to briefly discuss the view in Pashukanis and others that criminal law is an instrument of class terror. I dismiss this on several grounds: it provides some protection for working people from capitalists and from white-collar criminals; this view conflicts with other aspects of Pashukanis's analysis; and the law has a degree of autonomy. This last view fits well with the idea that the capitalist state has a degree of autonomy and, with the empirical researches of lawyers and socialist historians. It also opens up the possibility of using the law as an arena of socialist struggle.

Chapter 10 deals with various issues relating to justice. It starts by giving a brief account of a major debate about the interpretation of Marx concerning whether or not he had a theory of distributive justice. I argue that it is not possible to conclusively resolve this, but that there are strong reasons for believing that socialists today need a theory of justice given that the apparent inevitability of the coming of communism in Marx does not look remotely inevitable today. Much socialist struggle today is carried on by advancing arguments for justice. Some of these are in the context of the welfare state, which in some aspects introduces a peculiar element of communism into a basically capitalist system. I move on to consider criminal justice. White-collar and corporate crime essentially make an unjust distribution of property even more unjust. Criminologists have rather neglected corporate crime given the massive scale of damage that it causes, and Marxist criminologists can join with others in documenting it and arguing for more effective prosecution. Some Marxists have argued that street crime can be seen as a way of evening up relations between the workers and the capitalists. I argue that this idea should be approached with extreme caution as it undermines respect for the law, which is generally helpful to socialists, and also because street crime can be very damaging to working-class communities. I finally briefly consider the issue of political lawbreaking.

In Chapter 11 the discussion moves on to consider the political goal of Marxist activism: communism. Several of the criminologists discussed in Part II welcome the prospect of a communist society without crime. I start by sketching Marx's limited account of communist society, and then go on to argue that there are powerful reasons for believing that a communist society would require principles of distributive justice. This in turn makes it likely that such a society would generate crimes perpetrated by people who want to circumvent such principles. Moving on to consensus crimes, although acquisitive motives for such crimes would recede, there is no particular reason for believing that other motives would disappear. Indeed, the better recognition of some consensus crimes is arguably a sign of greater civilization. Communism might be expected to accelerate the decline of religion, and hence of crimes based on religious principles, but crimes based on moral principles, together with disputes about moral principles, would be likely to persist. Offences linked to maintaining the authority of the state might actually become more prevalent in the early stages of communism. A brief discussion of the experience of existing or recently existing communist societies follows. Not surprisingly, they tend to generate some forms of crime and diminish others.

1
Marxism in the Twenty-First Century

Marxism developed over the lives of Marx and Engels, although with considerable ambiguities in several areas. Up to the First World War, Marxist orthodoxy was largely represented by the theorists of the German Social Democratic Party, who upheld the likelihood of revolution against the revisionism of Eduard Bernstein.[1] A major schism opened with the October Revolution of 1917. Lenin argued that the German Social Democrats and most other Western Marxists had disgraced themselves by supporting their own governments in the war, rather than by attempting to overthrow them. He particularly claimed that Western socialists had come to represent an elite group of workers who benefited from the fruits of imperialism, and that they were now lining up workers behind their respective national capitalists in a war directed to redistributing colonies. He split the Western socialist movement between the social democrats on the one hand and the newly formed communist parties loyal to Moscow on the other.[2] An originally unquestioned and undebated belief that revolution in one major country would spread fairly rapidly to the other leading capitalist countries proved false. Stalin developed the doctrine that the former Russian empire, which became the Soviet Union, was so large and had sufficient resources that it could aspire to socialism in one country.[3] This led to the subordination of the communist parties to the foreign policy of the Soviet Union, on the grounds that the absolutely vital need was the survival of socialism. The Russian working class was decimated during the First World War and the civil war that followed the revolution. The Communist Party of the Soviet Union claimed to represent an aspiration to socialism in a society mainly comprised of peasants. Stalin was denounced by Trotsky, who held that he represented an increasing bureaucracy which had come to dominate life in the

Soviet Union. For this reason, said Trotsky, he had lost interest in encouraging revolution elsewhere.[4]

Trotsky also warned of the danger of the rise of fascism, particularly in Germany. He argued that Soviet policies in the face of fascism were disastrous.[5] He did not expect the Soviet Union to do well in the Second World War, but did not really have the time to come to terms with this before he was assassinated by a Stalinist agent. The Soviet Union played the major role in the defeat of Nazi Germany, and emerged from the war with its form of socialism extended across Eastern Europe. In 1949 China became a Communist country in a revolution led by Mao. Despite a split between Russia and China following the death of Stalin, revolution on a broadly Soviet model followed in a number of countries up to the mid-1970s, and seemed at least possible in several others. In the years immediately following the Second World War, Western Marxists were largely divided between followers of Trotsky – who in turn tended to have internecine disputes – and followers of Stalin. However, in the late 1960s Marxism was rediscovered by a generation of student radicals inspired on the one hand by the Vietnam war and on the other by the ideas of the young Marx and those of the Frankfurt School, most notably of Herbert Marcuse.[6] Although there were further revolutions in the 1970s, Western Marxism gradually declined as Marxist concepts were felt to be inadequate for the explanation of advanced Western capitalism. This decline accelerated with the rise of the New Right in the 1980s under Reagan in the United States and Thatcher in Britain, culminating in the demise of the Soviet Union in 1989, which was felt to demonstrate the death of Marxism.

Marxism, however, has refused to go away. Western societies are increasingly divided by a gulf between the income and wealth of a small group of executives and entrepreneurs on the one hand and workers confined to low paid and unstable employment on the other. The spread of capitalism around the world matches the descriptions of Marx and Engels in the *Communist Manifesto* very strikingly. Western Marxists now tend to be less fissiparous and more open to ideas from other intellectual currents than when they felt they had to defend Trotskyism or the Soviet Union.

The above brief history indicates that the rise and decline of Marxism played a central role in the history of the world during the twentieth century.[7] We will now consider some of the main concepts against this background.

Historically, the first appearance of ideas considered by many to be part of Marxism is the theories based on alienation developed by Marx and Engels between 1843 and 1845. The immediate source for these ideas was the philosopher Ludwig Feuerbach, who argued that the human essence becomes alienated in religion. Man creates gods or God and projects his own essence into the divinity. He then becomes dominated by his essence in this alienated form. Feuerbach also applied this idea to the development of philosophy.[8] Marx most famously applied the same basic idea to labour. He obviously had in mind someone involved in stultifying and repetitious labour such as sharpening pins. The labourer would not be working for his or her own satisfaction, nor for the delight of friends, but under the domination of the market and in order to gain enough money for subsistence. The labourer would thus be alienated from the act of labour,[9] the product of labour,[10] fellow labourers (because they are in competition with each other)[11] and his species-being,[12] meaning his non-alienated human essence. Marx also accepts that man is alienated in religion[13] and citizens are alienated from the state.[14] People are essentially communal,[15] loving and creative,[16] but in a market economy these qualities are realized only in the alienated form of a person's capital. Alienation and poverty become extreme, which leads to a revolution in which man reappropriates his alienated essence.[17]

The theory of alienation carries a strong moral claim that we have a particular sort of human nature which we *ought* to be able to realize. A social system which does not allow us to do that is wrong. Several theories characteristic of the older Marx and of Marxism more generally are missing in the *1844 Manuscripts*: the labour theory of value, the theory of the state, the use of abstractions as found in *Capital*, and the role of the Communist Party as the vanguard of the working class.

At this point it is necessary to mention briefly a major controversy in the interpretation of Marx. In an influential book the French philosopher Louis Althusser argued that there is a break in Marx's work in 1845, and that the alienation theory belongs to his juvenilia.[18] The majority of interpreters of Marx in the Anglo-Saxon world disagreed, and argued that the alienation theories are the foundation of the later Marx's views, and are still to be found in the older Marx. In my view they are wrong.[19] There would, however, be fairly general agreement that the alienation theories are much less prominent in the older Marx.

If there is any one central perspective in the older Marx which takes the place of the alienation theory, it is the account of historical materialism. Marx's most succinct account of this theory is found in the Preface to his *A Contribution to the Critique of Political Economy* (1859):

In the social production of their existence, men inevitably enter into definite relations, which are independent of their will, namely relations of production appropriate to a given stage in the development of their material forces of production. The totality of these relations of production constitutes the economic structure of society, the real foundation, on which arises a legal and political superstructure and to which correspond definite forms of social consciousness. The mode of production of material life conditions the general process of social, political and intellectual life. It is not the consciousness of men that determines their existence, but their social existence that determines their consciousness. At a certain stage of development, the material productive forces of society come into conflict with the existing relations of production or – this merely expresses the same thing in legal terms – with the property relations within the framework of which they have operated hitherto. From forms of development of the productive forces these relations turn into their fetters. Then begins an era of social revolution. The changes in the economic foundation lead sooner or later to the transformation of the whole immense superstructure.[20]

The exact interpretation of this theory has been very controversial. A particularly influential interpretation in recent years has been that of G. A. Cohen in *Karl Marx's Theory of History: A Defence*.[21] Cohen argues for technological determinism, in other words that the forces of production determine the relations of production, which in turn determine the ideological superstructure of society. Cohen's account is a subtle and well-argued elaboration of the famous quotation from Marx's *The Poverty of Philosophy*: '[t]he hand-mill gives you society with the feudal lord, the steam-mill, society with the industrial capitalist'.[22] A number of other interpretations are possible, however. It can be argued that the relations of production determine the forces of production, at least some of the time.[23] In this version, for example, capitalists who have assembled handloom weavers together for convenience find out about powered looms and set about introducing them in order to out compete their capitalist rivals, who of course also introduce powered looms to avoid going under. Alternatively Marx can be seen as advocating economic determinism in which the economy as a whole, including both the forces and relations of production, determines the other features of society.[24] A sceptical position is also possible: sometimes Marx argues for technological determinism, at others for economic determinism, and on other occasions agrees with the classic formulation of Engels that amid an 'endless host of accidents...the economic movement finally asserts itself as necessary'[25] – but then, perhaps, 'finally' never comes, in which case the claim seems to be that the economy is jolly important but that you can never be sure in any particular situation that it is going to determine anything else.[26]

Something like this sceptical position has entered into the general culture of Western societies since Marx and Engels' day. Historians and social commentators whom no one would describe as Marxist place much more emphasis on the role of the economy in determining or influencing or constraining politicians and statesmen than would have been the case for their nineteenth century equivalents. Similarly historians write about the role of ideas in social development, but recognize that their influence is constrained by the economy. A problem of interpretation also surrounds Marx's idea that the relations of production become fetters on the forces of production and that this leads to revolution. Does he really mean that increases in productivity under capitalism have to grind to a halt? Baran and Sweezy argue this position in *Monopoly Capital*, offering the example that the US auto industry had not made any real advances between the Second World War and the 1960s but had simply made cosmetic changes such as adding exaggerated tailfins to cars and then taking them off again.[27] However, in recent years the forces of production have increased spectacularly. The most dramatic development has probably been the increase in power of computers and their application to virtually every sphere of life. Coupled with the growth of the Internet our whole approach to knowledge is altering dramatically. We are becoming accustomed to having a massive range of information at our fingertips. The human genome has been mapped, and we seem to be on the brink of dramatic medical advances. Consumers in Western countries at least are being plied with a whole range of new devices enabling them to choose between 50 channels of television or carry around thousands of tunes. We have all become used to communicating with each other on mobile telephones. There is no need to expand the range of examples; it is abundantly clear that the ability of capitalism to expand the forces of production is not remotely played out. Commentators wanting to argue that capitalism is acting as a fetter on the forces of production need to rely on the failure of many of these forces to meet human need or on the wastefulness of military spending, both of which are deplorable, but neither really shows that capitalism is a fetter in any general way.

Marx sees history as a succession of 'epochs', primitive communism, slavery, feudalism, capitalism and in the future communism. These are probably best interpreted as a series of social formations each of which includes a number of different modes of production but which is dominated by one particular mode. Thus Russia at the time of the October Revolution had a substantial capitalist sector featuring large factories developed as copies of those in the West, much agriculture which was basically feudal despite the emancipation of the serfs, numerous petty commodity producers who were neither employed by anyone else nor regular employers of labour, but who made their living by selling goods on the market, and finally, in the more backward eastern areas, nomadic herdsmen who lived under something akin to primitive communism. It is very debatable whether the onward movement of history, even accepting this pattern, is simply powered by the dominant mode of production becoming a fetter. Other relevant considerations would be the extent to which a more productive alternative had emerged, and contestation for power between social classes based upon particular modes of production.

Ironically, probably the best example of revolutions brought about by the failure of the forces of production to develop are the revolutions of 1989 in Eastern Europe and the Soviet Union. A major factor in these revolutions against existing socialism was economic stagnation, particularly stagnation in the production of consumer goods, compared to the advanced capitalist countries. Soviet consumers traditionally carried a string bag in their pockets, ready to purchase anything that happened to have become unexpectedly available. Leonid Brezhnev, general secretary of the Communist Party of the Soviet Union from 1966 until his death in 1982, was popularly supposed to wear Western shoes because they fitted better than those made in Russia. In a famous television broadcast in the early Gorbachev years, a foreman at the Japanese Sony factory was asked by a Russian journalist, 'What do you do about faulty goods?' 'Faulty goods?' he replied, 'What are faulty goods?' In contrast, in the Soviet Union, a television had to need repairing five times in the first year after purchase before the consumer was entitled to a new one. In the mid-1980s, as Soviet consumers became more aware of this contrast, the Ekran electronics plant paid more attention to quality control with the result that 70% of its output was classified as substandard.[28] The widespread feeling that the Soviet system would never match the Western production of consumer goods was certainly one factor fuelling discontent.

Marx's concept of class linked directly to the mode of production: people's class position is basically determined by their ownership and control (or non-ownership and non-control) of the means of production. Capitalism is increasingly dominated by the two classes that this mode of production generates: 'Our epoch, the epoch of the bourgeoisie, possesses, however, this distinctive feature: it has simplified the class antagonisms. Society as a whole is more and more splitting up into two great hostile camps, into two great classes directly facing each other: Bourgeoisie and Proletariat.'[29] The capitalists own and control the means of production; the workers possess only personal property needed for day-to-day consumption but lack property in the means of production. In order to live they are forced to sell their labour power to the capitalists.

Apart from capitalists and workers, however, Marx recognizes, particularly in his account of the 1848 Revolution in France and subsequent rise of Louis Napoleon Bonaparte III, a range of other groupings and fractions which can be found in capitalist societies.[30] There are thus the petty bourgeoisie, who own sufficient means of production to produce goods and services for the market but do not regularly employ other people and are not themselves forced to work for capitalists. Most of them are destined to end up as workers, but a few will grow into capitalists. Politically the petty bourgeoisie will side with the workers if they think that their position is insecure and that they are about to lose the ability to produce independently, but they are not reliable allies because they will side with the capitalists if their prospects look better. There is also the lumpenproletariat, who are displaced members of other classes who have not yet accepted working for capitalists as their main way of subsisting, and lead a hand-to-mouth existence. They are seen as a major source of conventional street crime, and will be discussed thoroughly in Chapter 6. The capitalists are divided economically into fractions including manufacturing capital, finance capital and commercial capital. Although these will side together against the workers, their interests clash to some extent. For example, the immediate interest of finance capitalists is that rates of interest should be high, whereas manufacturing capitalists need them to be low.

In the countryside there is a set of divisions which parallel those already seen, but with their own complexities. At the top there are landowners who live off rent; they lease land to capitalist tenant farmers, who are rural capitalists and employ propertyless agricultural workers. If the countryside is less developed the landowners lease land to big peasants, who employ propertyless workers to work on the land alongside them, middle peasants who correspond to the petty bourgeoisie in the towns, and small peasants who farm some of their own land but also work some of the time for big peasants. The small peasants basically share the same interests as workers in the towns and landless agricultural labourers, but may not recognize this. Rural relations are further complicated by varying patterns of land tenure. For example, a small peasant may own his plot but be crippled by mortgage or loan repayments; a landowner may also function as a tenant farmer; and any of these rural groupings may be involved in mining or manufacturing as a sideline.

The problems of class analysis in modern capitalist societies have been a major source of difficulties for subsequent commentators. Bernstein[31] pointed out that the petty bourgeoisie had failed to disappear in the prescribed manner and offered reasons for thinking that they were unlikely to be eliminated. Some forms of production are amenable to being carried out on a small scale, notably specialized market gardening and the niche production of components needed by larger manufacturing concerns. Service industries typically offer opportunities for small businesses, for example in hairdressing, restaurants or the repair of houses and cars. Technology does not always point to large-scale production: consider the proliferation of printed magazines since the application of computers, or the development of specialized businesses on the Internet. In addition to the persistence of the traditional petty bourgeoisie there has been the rise of the new middle class: people who depend on work for their living but whose conditions of life are considerably better and more stable than those of the traditional working class, thanks to their professional or technical expertise. Examples would be teachers, lecturers, social workers, technicians, accountants, lawyers, journalists, public relations experts, computer professionals, designers, external consultants, physiotherapists, occupational therapists. Such people are typically trained to graduate level, may or may not be involved in supervising other staff, and are difficult to dispense with in an efficient business or the welfare state. There is thus every reason to expect the continuance of a large and mixed social grouping somewhere between the working class and the capitalists.[32]

Marx sees the interests of the capitalists and workers as antagonistic. The capitalists extract surplus value from the workers by getting them to work for longer than is needed to pay for their subsistence. This corresponds to the obvious everyday observation that workers want wages to be high and employers want wages to be low. Beyond this trade union struggle, however, lies the role of the working class in ending the capitalist system: 'What the bourgeoisie, therefore, produces, above all, is its own grave-diggers. Its fall and the victory of the proletariat are equally inevitable.'[33]

The twentieth century undoubtedly saw major confrontations between capital and labour. Aspects of the October Revolution in Russia in 1917 can be seen in this way, as can the attempts at revolution in Germany at the end of the First World War, the General strike of 1926 in Britain, aspects of the Spanish civil war, the events of May 1968 in France. More generally, one feature of the life of capitalist countries has been the struggle between capital and labour in the form of strikes over pay and conditions. In addition, the main persistent political divide in most European countries has been one loosely based on capital and labour, be it between Conservatives and Labour in Britain, Christian Democrats and Social Democrats in Germany, Christian Democrats and their successors on the right versus Communists and Socialists in Italy and so forth. Marx and Engels have been vindicated in the sense that they identified the most persistent fault line for the next century, whereas issues to do with religion or race or the environment have tended to be sidelined.

However, it has to be said that the class struggle in Europe, and still more so in the United States and Japan, between them the most advanced capitalist societies, has typically been relatively gentle and has usually resulted in some form of compromise. The really bitter struggles have been more obviously based on nationalism, as in the two world wars where the working class in each of the combatant societies lined up behind national governments to slaughter the workers of other countries. Since the Second World War the more bitter struggles have also been based on some form of nationalism or ethnicity, be it Basque separatists, Northern Ireland republicans or the ethnic cleansing between Serbs Croats and Muslims in former Yugoslavia. Various Marxists have written extensively on nationalism, generally with the objective of diminishing the effects of nationalism on the class struggle.[34] There have been attempts to reinterpret various national struggles as class struggles, but none of these looks plausible as a general explanation of nationalism.

In addition to the failure of class struggle to develop to an acute stage, various social divisions and issues have developed since the 1970s. These tend to link to claims that Marxism does not provide a very useful account of the issue in question. Nationalist struggles tend to shade off into divisions of race, and some struggles around race have arguably been as bitter and hard fought as those based on the class struggle. Second-wave feminists argue that patriarchy is a more pervasive and long-standing source of division than is capitalism, and again that Marx and Engels' account of gender divisions is very inadequate. Sometimes linked to this have been campaigns based on sexuality, for example those for gay and lesbian rights/liberation. There has also been the rise of various forms of green politics which are sometimes linked to versions of Marxism. However, a straightforward reading of Marxism is that it broadly endorses the capitalist subordination of nature but aims to use this for the benefit of humanity at large rather than for the benefit of one particular class.

Marx's analysis of the state is linked to this view of the class struggle. Under capitalism the ruling class is the bourgeoisie, and 'The executive of the modern State is but a committee for managing the common affairs of the whole bourgeoisie.'[35] This bold statement from the *Communist Manifesto* raises several issues. It becomes plain that the bourgeoisie typically does not rule directly but in some way gets the personnel of the state to rule in its interest, for example in England in the nineteenth century making use of some members of the aristocracy, and, following the development of mass democracy, sometimes makes use of social democratic parties. In the *Manifesto* Marx and Engels assumed that most European states were not democracies, but subsequently liberal democracy has become the norm in advanced capitalist countries. This raises obvious major issues. Marx basically assumed that some kind of armed revolution would be needed in order to displace the bourgeoisie as the ruling class. The proletariat would then control the state and start to transform it in order to start building communism, resulting eventually in a society run under the slogan 'from each according to his abilities to each according to his needs'. Something approximating to this arguably happened in the October Revolution in Russia in 1917, although the revolution failed to spread in the manner expected by Marxists generally. This route to revolution can now be regarded as dead. People in Third World countries were arguably attracted to the Soviet route to revolution up to the 1970s, but today, following the collapse of the Soviet Union in 1989, the idea of facing bloodshed, intervention, heroic efforts at socialist construction leading to eventual ... stagnation and reversion to capitalism is not likely to appeal widely.

This leaves us with the other road to socialism, hinted at by Marx occasionally. If the proletariat and other groupings such as poorer peasants and some members of the petty bourgeoisie come to form a numerical majority, it looks as though it ought to be possible to turn the proletariat into the ruling class by electoral means. The rise of liberal democracy has coincided with the development of the welfare state and increasing state role in managing the economy. The classical Marxist picture of the state emphasizes its repressive features, but although the criminal justice system would basically be part of these they need to be understood against a background where the state has benign features which workers genuinely value. Socialist parties have won electoral victories from time to time in most of the Western European democracies, but this has not led to the installation of communism. More typical has been limited nationalization (not seriously attempted in Western Europe since the 1960s) and the development of running of the welfare state. The various socialist parties have been genuinely democratic and have ceded power to parties of the right when these have won elections. As time has gone on the socialist parties have tended to drop commitments to expropriating the capitalists and replace them with pledges to foster social justice, as in the German Social Democratic Party's Bad Godesburg Programme of 1959 and the British Labour Party's dropping of its Clause 4 commitment to nationalization in 1995. Instead of providing a consistently loyal electoral base to socialist parties, working-class electors have engaged in class and partisan dealignment. In other words they may vote for socialist parties as in Britain in May 1997, but may also desert them as happened in the British Conservative electoral victories of 1979, 1983 and 1987. Communist parties in Western Europe have generally dispersed or transformed themselves into social democratic parties in the wake of the collapse of the Soviet Union.

The 'inevitable' victory of the proletariat thus looks pretty shaky from the perspective of the twenty-first century. To the extent that Marx himself managed to back up this claim of inevitability the most hopeful arguments would probably be drawn from his economic analysis in *Capital*. It is hardly possible to attempt a full exposition and critique of this theory here, but it is worth noting that Marx's major economic claims of inevitability are also flawed and at best present a picture of an unequal and unstable society rather than a doomed one. Marx follows and defends the approach of the classical political economists, notably Smith and Ricardo, which attempts to explain the major features of capitalist economies in terms of the labour theory of value. One persistent line of criticism of this approach is that Marx's analysis in terms of value in volume 1 of *Capital* fails to match up with the analysis in terms of price in volume 3. Debate on this transformation problem continues. One of the most plausible defences of Marx is developed from the work of Sraffa, but leads on to conclusions which undermine Marx's major claims that the system is doomed.[36]

Leaving this debate to one side, the major claims in *Capital* of inevitable doom are generally seen as the problem of underconsumption, the problem of disproportionality and the declining rate of profit.[37] The fundamental idea of underconsumption is that the subsistence pay of the workers is inadequate to purchase the commodities produced by the capitalists. This idea led to claims by Rosa Luxemburg that the capitalists were impelled to constantly expand the market, and thus to imperialism, and eventually to their doom when the entire planet was colonized.[38] Another claim is that this problem was solved in the West following the Second World War by the recourse to a permanent arms economy.[39] However, the problem is arguably spurious: the capitalists could mop up underconsumption by spending money on investment, by their own bloated consumption, and if all else fails by stimulating the consumption of the workers. Claims about disproportionality are based on Marx's analysis in *Capital* volume 2 of the reproduction of the capitalist economy. Following the techniques of the French physiocrats, Marx argues that the wages and surplus generated in the production of the means of production must equal the constant capital (meaning capital not spent on wages) of the capitalists involved in producing the means of consumption. Marx argues that if one looks at fixed capital (i.e. machinery etc) and thinks of how more of it might easily expire in one year than the next, there is an unevenness between cycles built into the system, and hence a ready potential for crises. However, he is demonstrating that, at most, capitalism is an unstable system. Moreover, a degree of flexibility is built into modern capitalist economies through the availability of credit and through the possibility of government intervention.

Even on Marx's account, problems in the capitalist economy rectify themselves after a while. A general crisis occurs when goods are produced which cannot be sold. It is rectified by either the devaluation of the goods, so that they are sold off cheaply, or in the extreme through the physical destruction of goods which cannot be sold. Once this has happened it again becomes profitable to produce commodities. The point is that an economic crisis of this sort can trigger a political crisis because workers thrown out of work become convinced that a socialist alternative would be better.

The third problem which needs to be discussed is the declining rate of profit. Marx argues that as capitalism develops, each worker is matched by an increasing mass of machinery. This means that the value of the machinery outstrips that of the workers' wages, but according to the labour theory of value the sole source of value is labour. The rate of profit therefore tends to decline over time. Although this looks plausible when one thinks about each worker typically being linked to an increasing quantity of machinery, the relevant issue is the relative *value* of the machinery. The role of computers over the past 50 years or so illustrates this point dramatically. Back in the 1960s, computers were so expensive that it was felt necessary to operate them 24 hours a day. This is now less necessary. The most commonly quoted way of expressing this advance is Moore's Law, which states that the number of transistors on an integrated circuit will double every 18 months, and which also translates into a rapid advance in computing power per unit cost.[40] The cost of hard drive space per megabyte fell from US$ 10,000 in 1956 to about 1 cent by the year 2000, and has continued to fall rapidly since that time.[41] This rapid fall in the cost of computing power has also reduced the cost and enhanced the efficiency of a wide variety of machinery used in production. Thus the common sense idea of the increased role of machinery leading to a falling rate of profit not merely has a logical flaw, but has also dramatically failed to work in the real world for the past 50 years or so.

This review of Marx's theory also needs to briefly mention his account of ideology and of the dialectic. One version of the theory of ideology which is specific to Marx is found in the *German Ideology* and argues that because of their class position the ideological representatives of classes other than the proletariat produce an inverted and distorted set of social theories.[42] Alternatively, in the Preface to *A Contribution to Critique of Political Economy* Marx talks about social revolution and distinguishes between

> the material transformation of the economic conditions of production, which can be determined with the precision of natural science, and the legal, political, religious, artistic or philosophic – in short, ideological forms in which men become conscious of this conflict and fight it out.[43]

This second formula suggests that all ideological forms are to be treated with suspicion, but does not seem to make any sharp distinction between proletarian truth and bourgeois illusion.[44] Theories of ideology play a relatively minor role in criminological theories related to Marxism, so there is no need for an elaborate discussion here.

One way of looking at the dialectic is to say that Marx stresses conflict change and struggle rather than harmony and continuity. This is undoubtedly true, but carries no major theoretical commitment. Alternatively, Marx can be seen as having adopted a version of the dialectical method from Hegel. Some theorists see this as a central feature of Marx's ideas. I am inclined to agree with Engels, who responded to Dühring's claim that Marx relied on a 'dialectical crutch'[45] in *Capital*:

> Thus, by characterising the process as the negation of the negation, Marx does not intend to prove that the process was historically necessary. On the contrary: only after he has proved from history that in fact the process has partially already occurred, and partially must occur in the future, he in addition characterises it as a process which develops in accordance with a definite dialectical law. That is all.[46]

By proving that the validity of Marx's claim does not rest upon a dialectical law, Engels is also showing that the dialectic is unnecessary. I realize that there is a much more substantial argument to be had on this question,[47] but for the present purposes this form of bracketing off will suffice.

Preliminary conclusion on the main concepts of Marxism

Because the above theories are so wide-ranging and so amenable to competing interpretation and reinterpretation they retain a perennial fascination. It will be seen that my own approach to them is that the basic idea that the relations of production, or more generally the economy, determine(s) the other features of society looks plausible as a general view of the world, although it should be understood more as a rule of thumb than as a formula which will explain every feature of society. Marx's account of capitalism as a dynamic and revolutionary mode of production which breaks down barriers and conquers the world remains thoroughly plausible. The idea of acute class antagonism between workers and capitalists looks less plausible now than when Marx was writing, and other divisions such as those of race, nationality and gender are more important than he realized. However, his picture of capitalism as a mode of production based on the realization of surplus value rather than on human need continues to make considerable sense.[48] Socialism remains worthwhile as an ideal which emphasizes human need rather than profit, and which juxtaposes the possibility of creative and fulfilling activities for all in a world where everyone's needs are treated equally. These general conclusions are sufficient to make the enterprise of the present book worthwhile. I want, however, to briefly suggest that Manuel Castells' account of informationalism offers a way of bringing Marx's central insight about the determining role of the mode of production up to date in a way which offers as good a social theory as any other available today.

Informationalism: historical materialism for the age of the Internet?

Castells started as a political exile from Franco's Spain but soon sprang to fame as a lecturer in Paris specializing in urban issues. He subsequently became a professor at the University of Berkeley, California, and has recently moved to the University of Catalonia. The high point of his theoretical trajectory and 25 books is undoubtedly the trilogy: *The Information Age: Economy, Society and Culture*.[49]

Informationalism

Castells undoubtedly started from a Marxist framework, but it would be a matter for debate as to whether the analysis he now offers would count as Marxist. He does not claim that it is Marxist, and does not particularly try to draw Marxist conclusions from it. However, the central logic of his approach is to link a change in the mode of production to widespread general change in society, which is a distinctively Marxist way to look at things. His basic idea is that in the past 30 years or so of the twentieth century, there was a fundamental shift in the way in which the capitalist mode of production operates. The new social structure he terms informationalism.[50] In the industrial mode of development the main source of productivity lies in introducing new energy sources or using them in different places. In the informational mode of development the source of productivity lies in knowledge generation, processing and communication. Information processing is focused on improving the technology of information processing. There the chief aim is the production of knowledge.[51]

Informational capitalism has two fundamental distinctive features: it is global, and it is structured to a large extent around a network of financial flows. Capital works globally as a unit in real time.[52] 'Financial capital needs...for its operation ... knowledge and information generated and enhanced by information technology. This is the concrete meaning of the articulation between the capitalist mode of production and the informational mode of development.'[53]

This new form of society is based on networks. 'Networks are the fundamental stuff of which new organisations are and will be made.'[54] The networked enterprise is 'that specific form of enterprise whose system of means is constituted by the intersection of segments of autonomous systems of goals'.[55] 'The network enterprise makes material the culture of the informational/global economy: it transforms signals into commodities by processing knowledge.'[56] 'My hypothesis is that, as the process of globalisation progresses, organisational forms evolve from *multinational enterprises* to *international networks*.'[57] Information processing is central to the new configuration of the mode of production:

> Computer software, video production, microelectronics design, biotechnology based agriculture, and so on, and many other critical processes characteristic of advanced economies, merge inextricably the informational content with the material support of the product, make it impossible to distinguish the boundaries between 'goods' and 'services'.[58]

Who are the capitalists in this new set-up? Not the legal owners of the means of production. Some actors at the top of this global capitalist system are indeed managers, as with Japanese corporations. Others could be identified under the traditional category of the bourgeoisie as in the overseas Chinese business networks. In the United States there is a mixture of traditional bankers, nouveaux riche speculators, self-made geniuses turned entrepreneurs, global tycoons and multinational managers. Some public corporations are capitalist actors. In Russia we have the survivors of the Communist nomenclatura competing with wild young capitalists. 'And all over the world, money-laundering from miscellaneous criminal businesses flows towards this mother of all accumulations that is the global financial network.'[59] There is not a global capitalist class, but there is an integrated global capital network. 'While capitalism still rules, capitalists are randomly incarnated, and the capitalist classes are restricted to specific areas of the world where they prosper as an appendix to the mighty whirlwind which manifests its will by spread points and futures options ratings in the global flashes of computer screens.'[60]

Castells sees this new economy as inimical to organized labour, and says relatively little about a working-class response to the changed situation: 'Under the conditions of the network society, capital is globally coordinated, Labour is individualised. The struggle between diverse capitalists and miscellaneous working classes is subsumed into the more fundamental opposition between the bare logic of capital flows and the cultural values of human experience.'[61]

The central role of information processing in the new development of the capitalist mode of production makes it possible for money to be shifted around the world with extreme rapidity and also for technology and manufacturing to move between states and to be coordinated at a distance. What is developing is no less than a global economy: *'A global economy is ... an economy with the capacity to work as a unit in real time on a planetary scale* [Castells' emphasis].'[62] An illustration of this development is that share of trans-border financial flows for major market economies increased by a factor of about 10 in 1980–1992.[63]

Castells acknowledges that the economy is not yet fully global:

> Markets, even for strategic industries and major firms, are still far away from being fully integrated; capital flows are restricted by currency and banking regulations (although the offshoring of financial centres and the prevalence of computer transactions tend to increasingly circumvent such regulations); the mobility of labour is undermined by immigration controls and people's xenophobia.[64]

Market penetration is not fully reciprocal. The American and, to a lesser extent, European economies are relatively open but the Chinese, Japanese, Korean, Taiwanese, Indian and Russian economies are highly protected.[65]

> It is obvious that the core of the global economy is a tightly interdependent network between the USA, Japan, and Western Europe that is becoming increasingly so ... in 1990 the G-7 countries accounted for 90.5% of high technology manufacturing in the world and held 80.4% of global computing power.[66]

In order to seriously come to terms with Castells' analysis it would be necessary to get to grips with his use of the term 'network'. It makes sense when applied to rapid computerized exchanges of information as part of financial dealings or of dispersed manufacturing and design across the globe or of lateral exchanges of information and ideas between people at the same level in different enterprises. There is also nothing wrong with arguing that the core of the global economy is located in the United States , Japan and Western Europe, although with the rise of China and India this will doubtless change. But to describe this triadic dominance as a 'network' seems inappropriate. However, Castells is much more plausible when he claims that this new economic pattern based on information is having enormous effects on advanced societies, and on what would have been described as Third World countries, played a major role in the fall of the Soviet Union, and is linked to substantial changes in class structure, the decline of the patriarchal family, the role of politics and the media, the form taken by social movements and new opportunities for organized crime.

Many of the developments since 1970 that Castells is analysing have featured in the work of other writers, frequently described as a shift from Fordism to post-Fordism, or as the ineluctable rise of globalization. Ian Taylor, whose book *Crime in Context* will be discussed towards the end of the critique of existing Marxist analyses of crime, uses the shift from Fordism to post-Fordism as the organizing concept for many of the changes noted by Castells.[67] Many other writers give an account of globalization which incorporates substantial outsourcing, rapid financial flows, increased inequality within the advanced countries matched by increased global inequality, power exerted over thousands of people in one continent by decisions made in another and the triumph of neoliberalism.[68]

The effects of the rise of informationalism in the advanced countries

There are very strong differences between the occupational structures of societies equally entitled to be considered as informational. Japan and the United States represent the opposite ends of the comparison although in all the advanced societies theory is a 'Common trend toward the increase of the relative weight of the most clearly informational occupations (managers, professionals, and technicians)'.[69] Crudely there are two informational models: the service economy model represented by the United States, the United Kingdom and Canada with a rapid phasing out of manufacturing employment after 1970 and with an emphasis on capital management services; and the industrial production model represented by Japan and largely by Germany which reduces the share of manufacturing employment but continues to keep it at a relatively high level. Producer services are much more important than financial services in this second model.[70]

Skilled workers in the North greatly benefited from global trade because they took advantage of higher economic growth, and the international division of labour gave their firms a comparative advantage. Unskilled workers in the North considerably suffered because of competition with producers in low-cost areas.[71] Braverman argued that automation and computers transformed workers into second-order robots. This is to do with the social organization of labour. The broader and deeper the diffusion of advanced information technology the greater the need for an autonomous educated worker able and willing to program and decide entire sequences of work.[72] 'There is no systematic structural relationship between the diffusion of information technologies and the evolution of employment levels in the economy as a whole.' High unemployment is mainly a European problem caused by state policies. In the Asian Pacific, overall employment has expanded substantially.[73]

Although the above is true at the global level, the consequences for particular people in particular countries may be dramatic. 'The emergence of lean production methods goes hand-in-hand with widespread business practices of subcontracting, outsourcing, off shoring, consulting, downsizing, and customising'. The social costs of labour flexibility which this precipitates can be high, but on the whole there are improved family relationships and greater egalitarian patterns between genders.[74] The ramifications of informationalism are accelerating the decline of the patriarchal family, which is now a minority form.[75] The direct consequence of economic restructuring in the United States is that in the 1980s and 1990s family income has plummeted. Wages and living conditions continued to decline in the 1990s in spite of a strong economic recovery in 1993.[76] By the early 1990s the top 1% of the population owned 40% of all assets, double what it had been in the mid-1970s, and at the level of the late 1920s, before the change wrought by progressive taxation.[77] The ratio of total chief executive officer to total worker pay increased from 44.8 times for 1973 to 172.5 times more in 1995. Some 80% of American households saw their share in national income decline from 1977 to 1999 by about 6%.[78] The Gini coefficient rose from 0.4 in 1967 to 2.45 in 1995.[79] Poverty has increased. The percentage of persons with income below the poverty line increased from 11.1% in 1973 to 13.3% in 1997. Some 14.6 million Americans in 1991 had an income below 50% of the poverty level. Basically the informational economy and globalization has caused this.[80] In 1999 the new economy comprised 19 million workers, whereas the old economy employed 91 million workers. Education had become a critical resource. In 1979 the average college graduate earned 38% more than the average high school graduate, but in 1999 the difference was 71%.[81] In 1999 only 13.9% of the American labour force was unionized.[82]

The change to an informational economy has put a downward pressure on welfare states. Because firms can relocate freely there follows 'the downward spiral of social costs competition'. In the past the limits to this have been the productivity and quality gap between protected workers from the advanced economies and less developed competitors and the role of protectionism. Both of these are withering away, pushed onwards by the World Trade Organization.[83] Mexican workers' productivity in automobile factories lags only about 18 months behind that of American workers. Now there are similar trends in Asia. American labour productivity is still the highest in the world.[84] 'In an economy whose core markets for capital, goods and services are increasingly integrated on a global scale, there seems to be little room for vastly different welfare states, with relatively similar levels of labour productivity and production quality.' A global social contract would be required to preserve the better welfare states, but in the liberalized, network, global economy this is very unlikely and welfare states are being downsized to the lowest common denominator. Finland has been an exception to this.[85] To survive in a globalized economy the welfare state needs to be connected to productivity growth in a virtuous circle by a feedback loop between social investment and economic growth.[86]

The new economy generates new forms of social exclusion, notably of black Americans. Castells argues that there are what he calls 'black holes' of the informational economy: 'The fourth world has emerged, made up of multiple black holes of social exclusion throughout the planet ... . It is inseparable from the rise of informational global capitalism.'[87] He says that black men don't take up low-skilled, low-paid jobs because they are less willing to accept the conditions, and are therefore seen as difficult.[88] As is well known, there is a very high rate of illegitimacy in the ghetto, which may well be related to lack of economic prospects for marriage.[89] Very many of these superfluous black males end up in prison. In 1996 there were 600 prison inmates in the United States per 100,000 residents, a rate which had doubled in about ten years.[90] Of these 53% were blacks. In addition, blacks were 40% of death row inmates. This is largely due to discrimination in sentencing rather than because of the frequency of crimes.[91] In the 1990s the rate of incarceration in California was 626, which was twice that of South Africa or Russia, both societies with a very high rate of imprisonment in global terms. It was 215 for whites, but for blacks it was 1,951. One major explanation for the rise of imprisonment was the war on drugs.[92] The state of California in 1990s spent 9% of the state budget on prisons and 9% on the education system.[93]

The fall of the Soviet Union

Castells describes the Soviet system as statism, and argues that the crisis of Soviet society from the mid-1970s onwards was the expression of the structural inability of statism to ensure the transition towards the information society.[94] Statism worked well in an industrial society. In the 1950s until the late 1960s, the Soviet Union generally grew faster than most of the world. The annual growth of Soviet national income was 7.2% from 1950 to 1960. It was 4.1% from 1965 to 1970, 3.2% from 1970 to1975, then something close to stagnation settled in.[95] This is because the Soviet Union missed the revolution in information technologies that took shape in the world in the 1970s.[96] There was a situation close to parity in computer design in the early 1960s but by the 1990s there was a 20-year difference in design and manufacturing capability.[97] In the USSR, typewriters were rare, carefully monitored devices, two signatures were required for access to a photocopier, or three for a non-Russian text. There were special procedures for using long-distance telephone lines. The notion of a personal computer was objectively subversive.[98]

Castells does not say this, but there is good reason to think that the fall of the Soviet Union is responsible for several of the well-known features of globalization. The Soviet Union functioned as a counterweight to the capitalist West and as a sort of welfare state for Third World countries, offering them an alternative pattern of development and source of help. The demise of the Soviet Union has left us with a single superpower. The challenge to neoliberal globalization now rests with an assortment of relatively small and powerless social movements. The rampant growth in inequality, both within advanced states and between the advanced states and others, which has characterized the period since about 1980, would have been much more subject to challenge if there had been an alternative ideology and power base.

Marginalization of sub-Saharan Africa

Developing countries which have the political capacity to develop an infrastructure which can take advantage of the informational economy can advance very quickly. Those which cannot are destined to languish.[99] Liberalization policies in Africa didn't attract investment or improve competitiveness, but destroyed large sectors of agricultural production for local markets and in some cases subsistence agriculture. The struggle for the control of the state became a matter of survival. Tribal and ethnic networks were the safest bet for support. The struggle to control the state was organized around ethnic cleavages leading towards genocide and banditry. This is rooted in 'the political economy of Africa's disconnection from the new, global economy'. The new global economy does not have much of a role for the African population. Primary commodities are useless or low priced, markets are too narrow, investment too risky, labour is not skilled enough, communication and telecommunication infrastructure clearly inadequate, politics too unpredictable and government bureaucracies inefficiently corrupt.[100] The percentage of world trade to and from Africa roughly halved between 1980 and 1995; foreign direct investment, growing substantially elsewhere, is not attracted to Africa.[101]

Africa is by far the least computerized region of the world, and does not have the minimum infrastructure to make use of computers. In 1991 there was one telephone line for a hundred people in Africa compared to 2.3 for all developing countries, and 37.2 for industrial countries.[102] Castells emphasizes the role of the developmental state in the rise of the Asian tiger economies. Africa has the reverse. As Colin Leys puts it: 'few theorists of any of these persuasions [Marxists, dependency theorists] expected the postcolonial state of all ideological stripes to be corrupt, rapacious, insufficient, and unstable, as they have almost all been.'[103]

The Asian tiger economies and Japan

In dramatic contrast to the fate of sub-Saharan Africa, Castells provides a fascinating analysis of the rapid growth experienced in post-war Japan, the role of the state in four of the leading tiger economies of the Pacific – Singapore, South Korea, Taiwan and Hong Kong, and the prospects for continued rapid growth in China. He argues that there has been an important role for what he identifies as the developmental state. He also argues that the tiger economies experienced a crisis in the late 1990s in part because they needed to make the move from societies under the aegis of the developmental state to fully networked advanced economies.[104]

Castells and Marxism

Enough of Castells' account of informational capitalism has been given to demonstrate that it could form the basis of a modernized version of historical materialism. It starts from significant changes in the means of production which in turn have profoundly affected the working of the capitalist mode. Considerable work would be needed to analyse whether all the linkages along the way are satisfactory, and, as suggested above, Castells arguably operates with an unduly flexible concept of network. He does, however, manage to explain major and significant features of the development of capitalism over the past 40 years on a global basis. Not surprisingly, several difficult questions remain. The changes which Castells discusses have been accelerated in Britain and the United States by neoliberal politics, notably pursued by Reagan, Thatcher and Bush Junior and Senior, but also pursued in a diluted form by Clinton and Blair. Are these political figures simply going with the flow, or are they significantly accelerating it? To what extent can states and other actors mitigate the anti-egalitarian features of informational capitalism? To what extent can they resist the tendency of their economies to export jobs to China, India and other countries offering advanced facilities and cheap labour?

What sort of socialist politics can be pursued in a globalizing world of informational capitalism? Traditional Communist politics, meaning political strategy is intended to introduce an economy and system of government similar to that in the former Soviet Union, looks particularly unattractive. To go through all the pain and bloodshed involved in revolution, likely intervention, and isolation in order to produce a system which cannot keep up with informational capitalism and which is likely to collapse does not make any sense. Similarly, strategies based on social democracy but which put the accent on changes within a nation state and which aim to secure a substantial degree of isolation from the global economy such as the Alternative Economic Strategy advocated by the Labour left in the 1980s do not look at all promising. There are plainly benefits from, for example, trade with China or the export of technologically advanced products such as pharmaceuticals which would be jeopardized by such an approach. Moreover, as Castells points out, people who make their living through working in the advanced countries are becoming increasingly divided between skilled and unskilled labour. These divisions amongst working people are fairly slight compared to the gap between low pay or welfare benefits in the advanced countries and rates of low-skilled pay in countries such as China and India. Thus it is certainly a scandal that the chief executive of Wal-Mart is paid 871 times as much per hour as the $9.68 average hourly pay of US Wal-Mart employees, and even more of a scandal that he gets about 50,000 times as much per hour as garment workers in China and Bangladesh working for Wal-Mart subcontractors on $0.17 per hour. However, this still leaves a gap between the notoriously underpaid US Wal-Mart employees and the Chinese garment workers such that the Wal-Mart workers are paid about 57 times as much as the Chinese workers.[105] Even if one focuses on minimum wage Wal-Mart employees and assumes that these are particularly unlucky Chinese workers who could be paid double what they are getting if they moved to a better employer there is still a massive gap.

If we can talk about a global proletariat it is plainly a very divided one. Some sort of worldwide Trotskyist revolution looks just as unlikely as its Stalinist rival. Actions to produce rough equality between workers in the Third World and those in advanced countries are likely to be resisted by the latter. However, there is at least a degree of common interest on a range of issues: reasonable working conditions including both hours and health and safety, at least a minimum level of welfare state provisions, corporate responsibility and transparency, being able to join an independent trade union, some degree of protection for the environment and the avoidance of global warming. The interests of working people worldwide are not served by imperialist adventures such as the current American and British occupation of Iraq. If Chinese and Indian growth rates continue to be close to double digits, while those in the advanced countries are more modest, the gap between wages should lessen over time. In the meanwhile, there is scope for trade union and political lobbying to try to bring about minimum standards.[106] There is also a role for non-governmental organizations such as those involved in the campaign to Make Poverty History.[107] Some of what are generally seen as anti-globalization protesters have objectives which are fully compatible with a socialist agenda. None of this is as inspiring as the revolution predicted and strived for by Marx, but it does suggest that socialism is not entirely dead. There is some scope for socialist initiatives which are going with the grain of history. We shall return to Castells when discussing contemporary authors in the Marxist tradition who offer an analysis of crime.

2
Marxism and the Definition of Crime

Which of the various definitions of crime is most appropriate for an attempted Marxist analysis? Are there some forms of crime which Marxism *ought* to be able to explain and others where it has no special relevance? This chapter starts by considering Paul Hirst's claim that crime is not a Marxist category and shows that this leads him to simply pick out passages from Marx where crime (undefined) is discussed. It is argued that crime is such a major feature of capitalist societies that any decent social theory ought to be able to say something about it. Simply identifying crime with the existing criminal justice system is, however, too limiting. However, there are good reasons for not fully accepting the symbolic interactionist and labelling perspective in which it is an arbitrary matter as to what is criminalized and what is not. This leads on to a brief consideration of the Tappan–Sutherland debate largely siding with Sutherland but agreeing with Slapper and Tombs that an attempt at a Marxist criminology must restrict itself to bourgeois legal categories or obvious extensions thereof. This is followed by a discussion of the case for working with a concept of social harm instead of crime, as proposed recently by Tombs et al., and some brief remarks on the Schwendingers' attempt to define crime as a violation of human rights. This is followed by a discussion of Nils Christie's contention that much of criminal law would be better replaced by community values and care. It is argued that there is a case for a more conventional conception of crime. Within this it is argued that there should be a broad five-fold distinction between types of crime, suggesting that the contribution that Marxism can make to explaining each of them is likely to be very different.

Paul Hirst on crime

This section takes as its starting point a rather pedantic book chapter written by Paul Hirst in 1975 as part of a collection entitled *Critical Criminology*.[1] Because of its pedantry the chapter gives a very clear account of the problems of conceptualizing crime within a Marxist framework. At the time Hirst was a dogmatic Althusserian. His argument was that radical criminology or radical theories of deviance were not 'compatible with the object of study and conceptual structure of Marxism'.[2] He sees radical deviancy theory as an attempt at a critique of the way in which the criminal is 'the victim of processes of labelling and punishment which serve the interests and represent the values of the establishment', and says that it aims 'to question the nature of laws and values as the property of that establishment'. It is thus effectively a critique of orthodox criminology.[3] Hirst's first step is to argue for a division of Marx's works on the lines of that proposed by Althusser in *For Marx*.[4] The effect of this is that attempts at a critique of criminology based on the writings of the young Marx are seen by Hirst as not Marxist.

He then goes through a series of possibilities for making sense of crime in Marxist terms. The lumpenproletariat present an obvious possibility, given that they are either criminals or a likely recruiting ground for criminals. Hirst quotes passages from Marx and Engels which show that the lumpenproletariat are the enemy of the workers' movement and tend to be recruited to fight against the proletariat.[5] Another possibility is the forms of struggle undertaken by people turned into vagabonds by enclosures and the like. Depending on circumstances they may engage in forms of Luddism or become bandits. The aim of the workers' movement should be to develop these primitive forms of struggle into more advanced forms carried out by trade unions and a workers' political party.[6] The state itself may carry out crimes by attempting to criminalize the activities of socialists. Marx and Engels' position was that whilst it might be necessary in some circumstances to engage in illegal struggles the basic aim should be to develop, preserve and use to the maximum political and legal freedoms.[7]

Hirst moves on to analyse the famous passage in which Marx satirizes bourgeois apologists who want to argue that the labours of respectable people are productive by showing that similar arguments demonstrate that criminals are highly productive and that their labours lead on to many further economically important activities.[8] Hirst insists that productive labour produces surplus value (and that criminals, the monarchy, the clergy etc. are thus unproductive labourers) and then moves on to analyse some further forms of crime, making use of this distinction. Extortion and theft under capitalism are parasitic on the economic activities of other social classes, whereas under feudalism, where the ruling class is not directly engaged in organizing production, the activities of theft and ruling are very similar. Under capitalism, private property is not theft. Theft presupposes private property as a condition of existence. Under developed communism theft becomes an inconvenience because the system guarantees 'to each according to his need'.[9]

Hirst then moves on to look at illegal services, arguing that they are unproductive when carried out for subsistence but productive when carried out for a capitalist to make money out of them. The category of illegal services is a wide one, and probably needs to be broken down if it is to be helpful. I also agree with the critique by Hirst and others in *Marx's 'Capital' and Capitalism Today* that the distinction between productive and unproductive labour is unclear and unhelpful.[10] He finally looks at outlaw capitalism, meaning illegal capitalist enterprises, arguing that their labourers do not share the protection that is available to legal labour, and the same problem applies to outlaw capitalists themselves. He concludes with a comment which at this historical juncture has become gloriously anachronistic and optimistic:

> In general criminal enterprises are absent from the central forms of capitalist production, from large-scale industry, and large commercial and financial enterprises. Criminal enterprises are economically marginal compared with the productive power of modern industry.[11]

Crime and capitalism today

Hirst's comment may have been untrue when he wrote it, but it is certainly untrue today. The trade in illegal drugs fluctuates, and seems to have gone down slightly in the last two years. In 2005 the United Nations estimated the global retail value of illegal drugs sold amount to about US$ 321.6 billion . This was higher than the GDP of 88% of countries.[12] Another recent estimate puts the illegal drugs trade at about 6% of world trade. The United States' war on drugs has cost over $500 billion over the last decade or so.[13] Another major illegal activity is people trafficking. Estimates of the scale of this activity vary, but a reasonable judgement would probably be that of Thoraya Ahmed Obaid,

Executive Director, UNFPA, the United Nations Population Fund, that the value of the global trade in people trafficking is $8–12 billion annually.[14] It is thus about the same size as the global export trade in wholesale chocolate products.[15] In the United Kingdom, tobacco and drink smuggling is estimated to cost the government about £3 billion annually.[16] Turning to corporate crime, the Savings and Loan scandals got under way in the United States in 1980, soon after Hirst wrote. They are the largest theft in history and will cost the American taxpayer some $1.4 trillion by the time they are fully resolved. They could not have occurred outside the G-7 countries: there is not enough money to steal elsewhere. The deregulation of business pioneered under President Reagan has blossomed into a series of massive scandals at the highest reaches of business life in the United States of which the Enron scandal is only the most famous.[17] There is at least an argument that President Bush is a war criminal responsible for over 10,000 deaths in Iraq and motivated by industrial interests, particularly those of the oil industry (and, of course, that Tony Blair is his accomplice).[18] A substantial work of analysis and untangling would be needed to work out to what extent criminality is 'marginal' to the American or British economy, but it seems unlikely to be anything less than a big and important margin. As Castells points out, in some respects crime has come to be significantly entangled with the global capitalist economy, perhaps most notably in the contribution that money laundered from the drugs trade contributes to the huge amounts of money which can now be transmitted rapidly around the globe, and in the dubious origins of major Russian enterprises which were hastily denationalized in suspect circumstances.[19]

Crime is not just economically important; it is also a major political issue. It forms the main part of the work of the Home Office, one of the three leading offices of government in Britain, and occupies a similar position elsewhere. It is a major theme of the mass media: one would expect a typical news broadcast to include discussion of crime at some point. Similarly, it forms a major part of television drama, and the workings of the police and criminal justice system are an important theme in documentaries. One does not have to be a Durkheimian to accept that some decisions about crime are an important indication of the way that a society identifies itself.[20] Thus the legalization of abortion and of consenting homosexuality in 1967 are widely seen as a move to greater tolerance; current legal changes to facilitate the prosecution of rape and domestic violence are part of moves to recognize women as fully equal citizens. In South Africa the ending of the apartheid laws was a major part of fundamental changes in relations between the races; in Catholic countries the legalization of divorce and abortion is part of the erosion of the standing of the Catholic Church etc. Thus even if crime is not a central category of analysis for Marx and Engels there is a good case for saying that Marxism ought to be able to tell us some interesting things about crime if it is to be a worthwhile social theory.

Anyone attempting to see how well Marxist theories fare in analysing crime is bound, I think, to follow some of Hirst's approach in identifying passages where Marxists talk about crime and seeing what they say about it. However, Hirst simply picks on likely looking passages without attempting to give any sort of account of what he conceives of as crime. As he says, crime is not a central category of orthodox Marxism, nor was it a central theme in the writings of Marx and Engels. It is therefore not surprising that they do not produce any systematic or extended writings on crime. In turn, Hirst's chapter leaves us with no way of judging how well (or badly) the conception of crime in Marx and Engels matches up with other conceptions.

Defining crime using the law and the criminal justice system

One way of approaching things would be to accept that crime is defined by the law and the criminal justice system, and to treat these definitions as central. As we shall see, although there are some reasons for respecting this definition there are also powerful reasons for refusing to swallow it wholesale. The *Oxford English Dictionary* takes roughly this approach, identifying crime as: 'An act punishable by law, as being forbidden by statute or injurious to public welfare', but it then extends the definition in an interesting way: 'An evil or injurious act; an offence, a sin; *esp.* of a grave character'. The first half of the dictionary definition corresponds to Tappan's famous account: 'Only those are criminals who have been adjudicated as such by the courts. Crime is an intentional act in violation of the criminal law (statutory and case law), committed without defence or excuse and penalised by the state as a felony or misdemeanour.'[21]

Tappan's definition fits quite neatly with an approach where the definition of crime is dominated by the interests of the Home Office in England and its equivalents elsewhere. Thus crime would be measured by statistics of numbers of people complaining of particular crimes at police stations tracked through to detection, prosecution and sentencing. Even the Home Office, however, acknowledges that this is too limited, and in its British Crime Surveys reports on the extent to which people say they have been victims of crime when asked by an interviewer.[22] It is widely acknowledged, however, the surveys will understate domestic and sexual violence, partly because the victims may not identify what is happening to them as crimes, and partly because the perpetrator may be sitting next to them on the sofa at the time of the interview.[23] They will also understate victimless offences connected with drugs and prostitution. The Home Office acknowledges these problems. Others are more intractable. The Home Office does not ask direct questions about any of the following. Many people have suffered pension or endowment mortgage mis-selling, and would certainly regard it as an evil or injurious act, but it is not a crime. It is easily possible to be a victim of pollution, but not to currently be aware of being such a victim. Causing the pollution may be a breach of regulations rather than a crime. Consumers are frequently victims of misleading advertising, which may be anything from failing to understand the joke about Lynx deodorants through to a criminal offence. Many Iraqis are victims of Tony Blair's war crimes, but it will not show up in Home Office surveys because the Home Office does not ask the question and its surveys do not extend to Iraq.

Symbolic interactionism

There are, plainly, a whole series of problems in simply accepting official definitions of crime. One approach to them which has been popular in radical criminology is symbolic interactionism and labelling theory. Interactionism came to prominence in the 1960s. This is perhaps no coincidence as its founders were 'at home in the world of hip, Norman Mailer, drug addicts, jazz musicians, cab drivers, prostitutes, night people, drifters, grifters and skidders',[24] and rather relished being seen as such. What a symbolic interactionist must do is to stick very closely to the experiences and meanings of the worlds in which particular groups of deviants live, using participant observation which involves seeing and understanding behaviour. The aim is to move from shared meanings to the specific meanings generated amongst groups of prostitutes, drug takers etc. In particular, following the ideas of George Herbert Mead, it involves seeing how the 'me' of deviants develops thanks to the activities of their 'I'; the deviant can come to terms with his or her deviance and its acceptability.[25] Symbolic interactionism is not simply labelling theory, but labelling theory plays a large role in it.

Let us follow this through in terms of Howard Becker's classic *Outsiders*.[26] His starting point is that people become outsiders by breaking rules, but that *'social groups create deviance by making the rules whose infraction creates deviance,* and by applying those rules to particular people and labelling them as outsiders'.[27] This opens a very considerable can of worms. It further inflames the above worries about official statistics: not all offenders are apprehended; not all those apprehended are fully labelled; the process of getting labels to stick is quite complex. For example, at the police stage the police in question might be overwhelmed with paperwork and disinclined to worry about minor breaches, or under pressure to get convictions, or just at the end of the shift or looking for overtime. Similar comments would apply for magistrates, judges, prisons etc. The attitude of the person who has broken the rules will vary. She may agree with the rule and regard her penalty as legitimate, as may be the case quite often with motoring offences. He may decide to come to terms with being labelled as a drug smuggler. At the opposite end of the scale the deviant may regard his prosecution as a breach of his human rights as in the response of sadomasochists to the Spanner case. The rulebreaker may want to argue he is sick. How much a rulebreaker becomes an outsider thus varies considerably according to a range of circumstances.

Although symbolic interactionists start from a very different set of assumptions from Marxists some aspects of their theories could probably be grafted onto Marxism. They basically see the process of making rules as a matter of power, which looks as though it may fit readily with a Marxist framework. However, they are quite happy to acknowledge all sorts of power, for example the power of older people over younger people, and not at all systematic about their approach. They acknowledge the possibility of changing laws and rules through lobbying, demonstrations etc., which would fit perfectly well with a Marxist approach. They make a further point which could also be incorporated into a Marxist approach: the forces of law and order themselves may have an input into the process of making laws. Thus Tony Blair's proposal to march vandals to cashpoints for instant fines was vetoed by the police themselves as impractical. However, Becker himself gives an interesting case study of the way in which the Federal Bureau of Narcotics campaigned in the 1930s to have marijuana made illegal, lobbying members of Congress and planting stories in the press about a young man in Florida who murdered his family with an axe whilst under the influence.[28]

An approach of this sort is popular amongst radical criminologists, and it leads on to an argument that crime is simply a matter of labelling. This approach is taken, for example, by Muncie.[29] The argument runs that it is an arbitrary matter what labels are stuck on crime. Thus murder, the most serious individual crime, can be classified as legitimate, acceptable in duels or even commendable if you are a member of the army in time of war. One author who took this line was Richard Quinney. His definition runs: 'Crime is a definition of human conduct that is created by authorised agents in a politically organised society.'[30] He takes this quite literally:

But the most significant consequence of a criminal conception is the creation of crime. Without the concept of crime, crime would not exist as a phenomenon. It follows that the more concern that surrounds the concept of crime, the greater is the probability that criminal definitions will be formulated and applied. The concept of crime must be reified in order to justify its existence.[31] Murder is thus simply a matter of defining certain actions as murder.[32] This arguably works well for victimless crimes: if marijuana smoking was not defined as a crime there would be nothing much to worry about. However, it is difficult to accept that the activities of Harold Shipman were a problem only because the politically powerful defined them as murder.

Symbolic interactionism is thus superficial. It works best for victimless crimes such as marijuana smoking. Its limitations can be realized if one thinks briefly about a radical decriminalization strategy. There may well be benefits to the decriminalization of drugs and prostitution. There is a strong argument that the harms inflicted by these activities are mainly the harms of prohibition rather than the harms intrinsic to the activities. For example, clean, legalized heroin would have to be sold with a warning label that it may cause drowsiness or constipation, but it seems as though many of the other harms associated with heroin are actually caused by its illegal status rather than by its intrinsic properties.[33] After all, homosexuality between consenting adults was illegal in England prior to 1967; yet, we now have openly gay Cabinet Ministers and worry about their political views rather than their sexual proclivities.

Following on from this success we could take the Cairo approach to traffic laws. As my Egyptian relative explained: 'the only rule is – there are no rules!'. We could follow an extreme neoliberal approach to commercial regulation, making Reagan and Thatcher look like advocates of the nanny state. The next step would be to decriminalize robbery and all forms of interpersonal violence, with or without weapons. This last step would surely leave most people feeling very worried that we were heading for something on the lines of a Hobbesian war of all against all. We would surely start thinking about clubbing together with other people to set up something akin to the current police force, courts and criminal justice system. The obvious examples of persistent failure to criminalize interpersonal violence in real societies all apply to limited instances. Thus domestic violence and marital rape have been slow to be criminalized, but violence and rape against strangers have been treated seriously. Killing has been regarded as a very serious offence, and the exceptions are at the margins. Thus killing in war may be legitimate, but wars demarcate the boundaries of societies; states kill their own people, but normally in strictly demarcated circumstances which distinguish executions from other killings; minorities of one kind or another sometimes become 'fair game'; killing people who are in the course of carrying out a crime is sometimes seen as legitimate; sometimes people are held to have deliberately volunteered for activities where they may get killed, such as duelling or extreme sports.

An extended definition of crime?

As we have seen, crime is not a Marxist concept. There are strong reasons for not sticking to a definition in terms of the workings of the criminal justice system. Perhaps there is a good case for trying to include in our definition 'injurious acts' which are not strictly speaking crimes. This takes us to the debate between Sutherland and Tappan and its subsequent ramifications.[34] Sutherland is famous for having initiated the discussion of white-collar crime as a regular and reasonably substantial topic in criminology. He defined it as 'a crime committed by a person of respectability and high social status in the course of his occupation'.[35] Such crime, he said, was often undetected; was often unprosecuted if detected, and was often not convicted if prosecuted. Thus in seeking for the scope of such crime criminal statistics are not very helpful. A further problem is that these crimes are frequently not dealt with by the criminal courts but by administrative bodies which impose punitive sanctions. Sutherland insists that despite this we are really looking at crimes and not just technical violations: the acts concerned 'are distributed along a continuum in which the *male in se* are at one extreme and the *mala prohibita* at the other'.[36]

Thus the common image of a typical crime and typical criminality was inaccurate. Crime is widespread throughout society. In turn this meant that simply discussing the pathology of lower-class individuals was inadequate. Sutherland maintained that his own differential association theory was adequate for explaining white-collar crime. It also meant that the scope of criminology needed to include a wider range of conduct and political processes that decided whether abuses of power by the wealthy were less well known because they manage to manipulate public consciousness using the media; and the courts collude with them.[37] Pretty obviously anyone writing from a Marxist perspective is likely to be instinctively sympathetic to Sutherland's ideas.

Tappan's definition of crime which was rehearsed above was a riposte to Sutherland. As we saw above, there are whole series of reasons for regarding Tappan's definition as unduly narrow. Here we revert to the definition in its original context, which is basically the issue of corporate crime. Tappan's argument continues by pointing out that there are lots of business practices which some people consider immoral, for example, making exaggerated claims in advertising, breaking trust with employees in order to keep wages down, perhaps being found guilty by a labour relations board of an unfair practice, or undercutting fellow merchants in violation of an agreement. Tappan has three main points. If you extend the label 'crime' beyond those who have been formally processed as criminals you enter the sphere of moralizing; it is no longer clear what the limits of your enterprise are. Regulatory offences are inherently different from criminal offences. Much of what Sutherland is condemning is actually 'within the framework of normal business practice'.[38]

Marxists would also be sympathetic to most of Sutherland's riposte to Tappan. He says that many tribunals use rules of proof and evidence similar to those of criminal courts. Criminal intent and presumption of innocence is not required for all offences, for example those of strict liability (Slapper and Tombs, who broadly support Sutherland's arguments in their book on corporate crime, extend this by commenting that the concept of *mens rea* is an anthropomorphic anachronism).[39] Sutherland's basic argument is that the distinction between criminal and other offences is contingent. Non-criminal offences generally have a logical basis in common law and are adaptations of it. This is true of antitrust regulations; false advertising regulations; labour relations regulations and copyrights and patent laws (these are laws but they are civil laws). Sutherland further comments that some of the reasons that white-collar crime is dealt with by regulations rather than by criminal law is because legislators and judges share material and/or ideological influences with business people.[40]

Slapper and Tombs, who are working to some extent in Sutherland's tradition, stress that their focus is on corporate crime, in other words crime carried out in a framework of limited liability corporations, and furthering their aims, rather than white-collar crime more generally.[41]

This seems to be an obvious point of focus for a Marxist account of crime, although it has to be acknowledged that corporate and white-collar crime more generally are often linked. For example, a corporation may encourage individuals to engage in crime in order to meet production targets. If one looks at scandals such as the Enron scandal there seems to be elements of both corporate crime in which the corporation defrauds other firms or customers and individual crime in which, for example, higher-ranking employees defraud junior employees. For Slapper and Tombs the illegality could be administrative, civil or criminal. However, they insist that they are not just engaged in moralizing; they insist on some form of legal infraction. In Marxist terms they are discussing bourgeois legal categories and demonstrating that capitalist corporations by and large do not and cannot routinely adhere to them.[42] This last point is very important and will be discussed at greater length in Chapter 10.

Should social harm be the focus rather than crime?

More recently Tombs and Hillyard have argued that the main focus of people interested in criminology should be social harm rather than crime.[43] They accept the idea that the definition of crime is arbitrary:

> But in reality there is nothing intrinsic to any particular event or incident which makes it a crime. Crimes and criminals are fictive events and characters in the sense that they have to be constructed before they can exist. In short, crime has no ontological reality; it is a 'myth' of everyday life…. For example, rape, credit card fraud, the use or sale of certain illegal drugs, and the (consensual) nailing of a foreskin to a tree, are all defined as crime. As such, they should entail punishment. However, these situations can and do occur in very different circumstances and for widely differing reasons.[44]

In terms of the worries already discussed there is a problem that some of these acts disappear as crimes if we simply legalize them, but rape and fraud have definite victims. Hillyard and Tombs accept this. Their point is that many acts defined as crimes are relatively harmless, whilst other acts which are legal cause serious harm. Starting with examples taken from their list, without the intervention of the law the use and sale of some illegal drugs would be regarded by many as merely a form of recreation. The key issue in consensual foreskin nailing, an activity which occurred in the Spanner case in which consenting sadomasochists were deemed to have broken the law, would be possible damage to the tree. Even crimes with victims frequently do little harm: burglary from a garage may simply result in an insurance claim and a new lawnmower. Issues of workplace safety are generally dealt with by administrative rather than criminal law, but the consequences of workplace accidents can be horrific. There are over 1 million workplace accidents in Britain every year, but criminal prosecutions cover only about 1,000 of them, and very many extremely serious accidents are simply not investigated by anyone outside the firm where they occur.[45] A fundamental feature of most crimes is that the person who commits them must have a guilty mind. In the case of corporations and states it is very difficult to pin responsibility on particular individuals.[46] But there is certainly an argument that an executive who cuts corners where safety is concerned and knows that someone is liable to get injured is just as reprehensible as someone who intentionally causes harm to another person.[47] Pinning responsibility on any one person, however, is notoriously difficult. The focus, therefore, should be on the degree of harm created not on the legal status of the act.

Hillyard and Tombs argue that the concept of social harm encourages criticism of the status quo whereas the concept of crime tends to bolster it. The study of crime tends to focus on street crime, the 'dangerous' activities of the poor, and to deflect attention from white-collar and corporate crime. It focuses on individuals, thus deflecting attention from the harm caused by social structures such as poverty or growing inequality. It bolsters the crime control industry, which is now a powerful force in its own right. The 'crime problem' is exploited by politicians.[48]

The concept of social harm is an interesting idea worthy of further elaboration and debate. However, there are several reasons for sticking to the extended version of crime as advocated by Sutherland for the purposes of attempting a Marxist analysis. The concept of social harm does not feature in standard Marxist concepts, so linking Marxism to a concept of social harm would probably be no easier than linking Marxism to a concept of crime. Crime is an activity of humans, but social harm can surely be caused by the natural world: earthquakes, volcanoes, storms, drought, floods etc. A lot of human activities (and, indeed, natural events) cause good to some people and harm to others. Building a motorway may help many people get around faster but damage the environment of people living near it. Rain which fills reservoirs and waters crops can also cause flooding for some people. Both these examples are simplistic: the motorway is also causing global warming; perhaps the victims of flooding live in houses which should not have been built on a flood plain. Often the benefit of human activity will go to members of one class and the harm to another. A proper analysis of social harm thus involves some kind of felicific calculus, applied for preference on a global scale, backed up with theories about how society works. This would be very useful, but requires an account of distributive justice and a range of social sciences which attain a high degree of certainty. I am also assuming that it would be possible to find some way of equating the various forms of harm listed by Hillyard and Tombs: physical harm, financial/economic harm, emotional and psychological harm, sexual harm,[49] but some people might wish to argue that no amount of financial compensation could make up for a particular form of sexual harm, for example. In other words the concept of social harm leads rapidly to an extremely wide-ranging and difficult set of problems from which its proponents might well never emerge. Hillyard and Tombs also want to retain the option of criminalizing particular activities,[50] so we now have two difficult concepts to cope with instead of one.

Beyond this, the concept of crime arguably has some role to play in any society. Faced with particular pressures and temptations, some individuals give in for various reasons and others do not. This can be illustrated in the context of another article in the same collection by Danny Dorling: 'Prime Suspect: Murder in Britain'.[51] In a fascinating article he argues that British murder is typically carried out by young men in poor areas, and that the victims are mainly other men. He ties an increased rate of murder in poor areas to the devastation wrought from 1981 onwards by Mrs Thatcher, arguing that most of the murders they commit involve fights with knives or bottles and to some extent are down to luck rather than to extensive premeditation. We should therefore look to Mrs Thatcher and the political process that brought her to power as the major suspect rather than worry very much about individual responsibility.[52] This is a politically very interesting argument. However, amongst the young men in poor areas of Britain some will have devoted themselves to getting an education, others to getting parties opposed to the Conservatives elected, others to relatively quiet and harmless activities. Getting drunk and stabbing people is a hobby over which there is an element of choice. This is one reason why the murder rate in Britain is low, even in the poorest areas, compared to many other societies. Some degree of incentive is surely needed to encourage conduct which benefits other people and discourages conduct which does them harm. A civilized society makes as little recourse to prison and repressive measures as possible, but some sanctions need to be available. The authors of *Criminal Obsessions* point out that the criminal justice system is not effective in dealing with domestic violence.[53] However, feminists working against domestic violence invariably insist that perpetrators need to take responsibility for their actions, and would not welcome a major role for explanations which blame social conditions.

Crime as a violation of human rights

In a classic article 'Defenders of Order or Guardians of Human Rights?'[54] Herman and Juliet Schwendinger argue that the best humanistic way to define crime is in terms of human rights.[55] They pursue this argument with vigour:

> If the terms imperialism, racism, sexism and poverty are abbreviated signs for theories of social relationships or social systems which cause the systematic abrogation of basic rights, then imperialism, racism, sexism and poverty can be called crimes according to the logic of our argument.[56]

In some ways this is an attractive approach. It lines up most things decent people are opposed to and denounces them. However, it opens up too many difficult problems to be adopted as the foundation of a Marxist approach to crime. To start with, the extended legal approach advocated above and elaborated in more detail below offers the prospect of tightly defining particular acts or omissions as criminal offences which could be prosecuted. It is very difficult to define imperialism, racism, sexism and poverty precisely, still less to identify them in the real world in a way that would command widespread assent. By poverty do they mean absolute or relative poverty? Is pornography a form of sexism which objectifies women or a form of human expression which some women are beginning to produce? George Bush Senior and Junior would claim that their respective wars in Iraq were in defence of human rights, and deny that they were imperialistic incursions. Marxism is not an approach to society which starts from human rights, and it is relatively difficult to defend human rights within a Marxist framework. The analysis of the evils identified by the Schwendingers is best pursued in the framework of normative political theory rather than criminology.[57]

Nils Christie on reducing the role of criminal law

The veteran criminologist Nils Christie pursues a theme which complements the idea of replacing crime by social harm. He notes that in face-to-face societies or in families, acts which would be considered crimes in the wider society are dealt with by humane persuasion. Thus children who are fighting each other or who steal money from the mother's purse are dealt with kindly because everyone remembers how they have done many good things that counterbalance the current misdeed.[58] He gives another example of a local community where, because of difficulties caused by a bankrupt property developer, everyone gets to know each other. The community is next to a small park where one Sunday morning Peter arrives. He sings, talks and entertains a group of children whilst drinking beer, but then gets drunk, retreats into the bushes and exposes himself. Elsewhere this might be treated as a serious case for the police, but because everyone knows that this is Anna's son who is a bit limited mentally but basically harmless he is simply taken back to Anna.[59] Christie himself comments that this approach has limitations. For example, it might well be more appropriate to involve the police in a case of domestic violence.[60] An obvious limitation is that it is not realistic to assume that modern societies will have enough face-to-face contact to deal with most crime problems in this way. If Peter is basically decent but with some peculiarities, and makes his living by driving lorries across Europe, or if he strays from one area to another of London, it can hardly be expected that people will know him. The nearest that such large and mobile societies can hope to come to Christie's ideal is to soften the edges of the criminal justice system, giving Peter a favourable probation report or involving him in restorative justice. A further difficulty is that this involves dealing with Peter as someone who does not deserve the full force of the law because he is mentally challenged and harmless. What happens if he is not mentally challenged but wants to engage in practices that the face-to-face community finds deplorable? What if it is an Islamic face-to-face community which does not approve of homosexuality, or of its daughters marrying the wrong people? One of the standard critiques of anarchist communities which replace criminal law by face-to-face pressures is that they can be oppressive for harmless individuals who fall foul of the community's conventions. There are real advantages to more anonymous societies where harmless people who do not fit can form their own little communities. British examples would be the concentrations of gay men in Brighton or in the Canal Street area of Manchester; in the south of the United States, New Orleans functioned this way for many people. Presumably it is possible for individuals who fall foul of face-to-face communities to sometimes persuade the community that it should change its values, but it is probably easier for groups of people to argue for legal changes in larger societies. It should be stressed that this is one small part of Christie's ideas. His general view that civilized societies try to minimize their prison populations by a variety of means is wholly admirable.[61]

Marxism and the classification of crime

Is it possible, then, to develop a specifically Marxist analysis of crime? Having discarded the idea that crimes are entirely arbitrary the most promising approach is to abandon the assumption in much writing on criminological theory that all crimes can be explained in the same way. Marxism can then be seen as more applicable to some types of crime than others. A classification on the lines proposed might run as follows. The most central crimes which are unlikely to alter in a major way are those necessary to any orderly society: killing other members of the society without good reason (good reason would be identified on the lines suggested in the previous paragraph); violence against other members of the society, again, without good reason; taking other people's possessions without good reason. These crimes are what John Hagan calls consensus crimes.[62] Obviously all kinds of changes can happen around the margins of these central crimes and in the way in which they are treated, but they are unlikely to simply disappear.[63] On first sight Marxism ought to be able to explain, or partially explain, these crimes where they have an acquisitive basis. Where they are founded on individual jealousy or desire to dominate Marxism seems unlikely to supply a full explanation.

A second group of crimes which Marxists would be particularly keen to identify are those essential to the functioning of the mode of production. Thus capitalism will not work without the buying and selling of labour power, the enforcement of contracts required for buying and selling, and a market. Beyond this, all kinds of other crimes relate to the stage of development of capitalism and to its relations to other modes of production in the society. Thus in early capitalism there was a great emphasis on the punishment of idleness, directed particularly at people displaced from precapitalist modes of production who were unwilling to accept a capitalist pattern of labour.[64] Later on a legal framework is needed for joint stock companies so as to regulate the relations between shareholders, directors and outsiders who make contracts with the company. And beyond this there are offences which clearly relate to the mode of production, but which depend on the state of the class struggle, or to strategies developed by part of the ruling class. Thus the role of trade unions may be more or less restricted, provisions may be made to enforce international trading agreements such as those made in the framework of the European Union or the World Trade Organization, or insider trading may be illegal as in the United Kingdom and the United States or legal as in Japan. There is likely to be some degree of flexibility also between civil laws, administrative laws and criminal laws. The law of copyright has mainly historically been enforced as part of the civil law, but the possibilities of the widespread copying of music has led to pressures for criminal sanctions.[65] The relations between an individual and his or her insurance company are also normally the province of the civil law. Individuals are prone to inflate their insurance claims for obvious reasons, insurers naturally want to keep claims low, and there is often a degree of uncertainty as to exactly what losses were experienced. By and large both insurers and insured will prefer to strike bargains within the framework of the civil law, but there is a role for allegations of fraud in either direction at the extreme margins.[66] There is a surprisingly low level of prosecution for tax evasion in the United Kingdom, but the tax law is generally enforced by threatening individuals with prosecution or maximum penalties and then striking some form of bargain with them. Something similar is supposed to apply to breaches of health and safety legislation, but the work of Tombs and others shows that this system is not very effective.

The same sort of analysis of core and peripheral crimes could be carried out on other modes of production. Thus a feudal society needs to have laws which tie serfs to the land, forbidding them to leave and the feudal lord to evict them. It also needs laws restricting the sale of estates if land is not to become simply a commodity as under capitalism. All sorts of additional laws may not be essential but are likely because they facilitate the running of a feudal society. There are likely to be laws restricting the growth of capitalism in the towns, enforcing the status of lords and serfs, enshrining the ideological justifications of the system etc. And then additional laws such as the notorious *jus primae noctis* are not essential to the system but are based on it. Similar comments can be made about slavery. For slavery to exist it has to be possible for some categories of people to be the property of other people. Thus in Brazil, for example, assemblies of slaves tended to be illegal, particularly for the pursuit of capoeira (a mixture of martial arts and dancing) or Candomblé

(African religion). An abolitionist movement developed in Brazil, and was proud to get the Law of the Free Womb passed in 1871, declaring that all children of slaves born after its passage were free. Children born before that date who had one free parent and one slave parent followed the status of their mother. None of these laws follow logically from the status of slavery, but all are quite likely in a slave society nervous about a revolt on the lines of that in Haiti but also moving towards abolition.

Beyond these two broad categories a third and very important class of crimes is based on the enforcement of religious and moral ideas. These crimes are much more arbitrary and much more amenable to the symbolic interactionist perspective. Perhaps the most extreme enforcement of such ideas in the modern world was the regime of the Taliban, whose fundamentalist account of Islam restricted women to the home unless dressed in a burka and accompanied by a male relative. They also banned cinema, television, video, music other than religious music, portrait photography, pork, alcohol, homosexuality, adultery and fornication, thus leaving few of the leisure pursuits of modern society. It seems reasonable to hope for a Marxist explanation of why a fundamentalist group such as the Taliban should become dominant in Afghanistan, but perhaps not the full details of what they prohibited.

Even in a basically secular society such as our own the enforcement of moral ideas remains a contentious and uncomfortable area. There is a conflict between a desire to protect the vulnerable and to enhance personal freedom. We have debates over euthanasia, abortion, cloning, the age of sexual consent, sadomasochism, prostitution[67] and recreational drugs. It is not clear that Marxism has anything distinctive to say about what constitutes a person or the boundaries between childhood and adulthood, and thus about the core of several of these issues. Marxism may make some contribution to the analysis of areas where there are major economic interests such as prostitution or the drugs trade, although the economic interests involved are an important part of the story but not the whole story.

A fourth area of crime needs to be noted: what might be called derivative or secondary offences put on the statute book because they are easier to prosecute than the offence which is really intended. Thus possession of an offensive weapon is illegal not because such possession does any harm in itself but because someone is more likely to commit serious offences when attending a football match carrying a hunting knife and an AK-47 than without these accessories. Membership of an illegal organization such as the IRA is perfectly harmless in itself, but has been consistently linked to shootings, explosions etc. The boundaries between primary and derivative offences are not, of course, totally rigid. Providing funding or a safe house could be seen as on the margins. Marxist explanations of such offences could be expected to be as good or bad as the explanation attached to the more fundamental offence. A fifth and final area can also lead to bizarre offences of the kind relished by symbolic interactionists but should be amenable to Marxist explanation, at least at a fundamental level. This is to do with maintaining the authority of the state. Thus pretending to be a police officer or a soldier or the monarch in the course of his or her duties, or failing to respect such officials is liable to be an offence because holding such people in widespread contempt undermines the state. This in turn can lead to the criminalization of wearing a uniform which looks like that of a police officer or, in China, wearing yellow which was a colour reserved for members of the imperial court.

Conclusion

Marxism does not include the concept of crime within its conceptual framework. However, crime is so extensive and important within capitalist societies that Marxism ought to be able to explain some forms of it, notably most varieties of acquisitive crime, corporate crime and state crime. It should also have useful things to say about some other sorts of crime where it would not be expected to supply a full explanation. Although some thinking about social harm or face-to-face communities as a possible replacement for a concept of crime is interesting, there are good reasons for attempting a Marxist explanation of crime as it is generally understood, but extended to incorporate wrongs which are currently dealt with by administrative means or simply left unchecked.

Part II
The Critique

3
The Classics – Criminology Encounters *Das Kapital*

> According to the theory of Marx 'every system of production (e.g. the feudal, the capitalistic etc.) has the crimes it deserves'.[1]

This chapter focuses on two classic books which are interesting as attempts to apply the theories of Marx's *Capital* to criminology and criminal justice.

The first of these is Willem Bonger's *Criminality and Economic Conditions*.[2] Bonger was the tenth and last child of a middle-class Protestant family living in Amsterdam, born in 1876. He became involved with the socialist movement as a law student at the University of Amsterdam.[3] *Criminality and Economic Conditions* was published in 1905 and comprised his PhD thesis. It was translated into English in 1916. From 1905 to 1922 Bonger was the director of an insurance association but retained an interest in criminology and sociology. From 1922 until his death he was professor of Sociology and Criminology in the University of Amsterdam, bringing out various publications but particularly *Introduction to Criminology* in 1933 (translated into English in 1936) and *Race and Crime*[4] in 1939. He was well known as a socialist and as an opponent of Nazism, and committed suicide when the Germans invaded Holland on 10 May 1940.[5] His work is immensely scholarly, displaying an impressive familiarity with criminological writing not merely in Dutch but also in German, French and English. The discussion which follows will largely be based on *Criminality and Economic Conditions*.

The first half of the book is taken up with an extensive review of previous attempts at producing a theory of crime, but mainly comprises lengthy quotations rather than discussion. The second half starts with the definition of crime:

> [a] crime is an act committed within a group of persons forming a social unit; that it prejudices the interests of all, or of those of the group who are powerful; that, for this reason, the author of the crime is punished by the group (or a part of the group) as such or by specially ordained instruments, and this by a penalty more severe than moral disapprobation.[6]

This definition is carefully thought out. Outside the social unit acts that might otherwise be crimes are better thought of as acts of war. A crime is not biologically abnormal: Bonger is scathing about Lombroso's view of crime as atavistic.[7] Bonger recognizes at least some of the complexities of crime and moral disapprobation. Immoral acts are 'harmful to the interests of a group of persons united by the same interests',[8] but because the social structure is changing continually ideas about what is immoral also change. Some penal law represents the interests of the ruling class, such as a law making strikes illegal, there is a very little that represents the interests of the dominated classes, but most laws are directed against acts which are prejudicial to both the ruling and the subordinate class.[9] In modern countries almost all crimes are also felt to be immoral by the great majority; some acts are so obviously hostile to the interests of virtually any society that they are almost universally prohibited, for example theft.[10] Bonger associates crime with egoism. Historically egoism appears to be on the wane, but Bonger argues that under capitalism it is as powerful as ever but exploitation based on poverty has replaced direct extortion by violence.[11] However, Bonger agrees with Kautsky that a key reason for human survival is association.[12] Within primitive societies a form of communism prevailed based on their difficult struggle against nature for existence, and the social instinct was very strong.[13] Social instincts diminish and egoism grows in societies where the productivity of labour brings a surplus.[14]

From this Bonger moves on to discuss the aetiology of crime. He says there are three problems:

> First. Whence does the criminal thought in man arise?
> Second. What forces are there in man which can prevent the execution of this criminal thought, and what is their origin?
> Third. What is the occasion for the commission of criminal acts?[15]

Capitalistic exchange aims to make a profit, and thus involves attempting to fleece others in the process of buying and selling.[16] The press in capitalist society is run by proprietors who want to make money; it therefore represents the interests of those who pay for advertisements or articles rather than enlightening the public. It satisfies a morbid interest in crime, thereby encouraging crimes of imitation.[17] Besides carrying on a struggle against suppliers and consumers with a view to maximizing profit the bourgeoisie also come to see their workers as fit only to satisfy their desires. This in turn undermines the social feelings of the proletariat. Their egoistic tendencies are exacerbated by long hours of labour and poor, crowded housing.[18] The children of workers start work when they are very young, and are therefore forced to think only of their own interests. Their paid labour renders them independent at an age when they need guidance, hence the enormous amount of juvenile crime in England.[19] This way of life fosters illiteracy, which correlates with crime.[20] Because they do not go to school children of the proletariat are 'deprived of moral ideas', are ignorant and therefore give way to the impulse of the moment; greater interest in art or science would render them less susceptible to evil thoughts.[21] Bonger moves on to consider the conditions of the lower proletariat (lumpenproletariat?), who do not manage to sell their labour and in consequence lead a life of chronic poverty, their intellectual faculties 'blunted to such a point that there remains of the man only the brute'.[22] It is therefore not surprising that the poor supply a great proportion of the convicts.[23]

Bonger makes some fairly inconclusive comments about crime and marriage, but makes a couple of interesting incidental points. The criminality of women is much less than that of men, he says;[24] and he associates women having to suffer domestic violence with economic and legal dependence.[25] Women's criminality approaches that of men most closely in countries where their general social and economic position is closest.[26] He sees prostitution as degrading for both sexes and a significant source of crime.[27]

Bonger is happy to link criminality with education. The children of the bourgeoisie are better educated than those of the proletariat, but the education makes them egoistic. Their morality is based purely on prudential considerations.[28] The poorest classes 'furnish the greatest number of juvenile criminals'. The proletariat lack enough money to pay for adequate education; there is an absence of pedagogical ideas; the father is away for most of the day working, and frequently the same is true for the mother, so that there is no question of education properly speaking.[29] In the lower proletariat there is a total lack of care and surveillance and at least some children are actually brought up to crime.[30] Elsewhere he talks of 'the overwhelming importance of environment during youth, for the genesis of criminality'.[31]

Militarism in peacetime debases men who join the army through excessive discipline which leads men's moral qualities to deteriorate;[32] war arouses violence in the army and in the population generally.[33]

Bonger argues that crimes need to be divided into four different categories in order to find a satisfactory explanation of them. The first of these is crimes with an economic motive, recognizing that some thefts are carried out for reasons of revenge and is therefore not strictly speaking economic etc.[34] The second category is sexual crimes and the fourth political crimes. The third category is heterogeneous and mainly motivated by vengeance. Such crimes include malicious mischief, assaults, homicide etc. However, he places infanticide committed for fear of shame and perjury committed for fear of falling into the hands of justice in the same category. He says this is the largest group of crimes.[35]

The most promising group of crimes for an explanation in terms of economic conditions is obviously economic crimes, but they need to be subdivided. Vagrancy and begging arise under capitalism because some workers always cannot sell their labour; there are many more of these at times of crisis and in the winter.[36] People who fall into the 'blackest poverty' are faced with the choice of begging, theft and suicide.[37] Some people turn into professional beggars, for which they are doubtless to be blamed but the blame must also be 'attached to a state of society in which honest labour is so poorly paid that begging is often more lucrative'.[38]

Bonger moves on to consider thefts. A society with a high degree of division of labour could not exist without the strict prohibition of theft. Bonger starts from thefts committed from poverty, pointing out that in capitalist society there are people who are faced with a choice between theft and starvation, perhaps also the starvation of their dependants.[39] As capitalism develops theft tends to be motivated more by cupidity, a desire to enjoy the luxuries already enjoyed by the rich. Cupidity increases as social inequality advances, which it does under capitalism.[40] A society which encourages egoism in the economic domain also encourages theft, frequently carried out by people who have very little on well-to-do persons who do not suffer much.[41] The advance of capitalist society leads to a decline in robbery (i.e. theft with violence) as brigandage recedes thanks to improved means of travel, non-violent economic crime becomes easier with increased wealth, and violence becomes more exclusively the concern of the state.[42] Robbery is particularly encouraged by the brutalized environment in which poor children grow up.[43] '[C]olonial wars often resemble a colossal robbery.'[44]

Bonger's final group of economic crimes are those committed by the bourgeoisie, for example fraudulent bankruptcy or the adulteration of food. Some of these are based on a sudden decline in business leading to a criminal act out of desperation. These crimes are of an 'entirely social nature'. They could not arise in, for example, a village community.[45] Members of the bourgeoisie have usually been well brought up and have learned the importance of honesty, but have also learned the paramount importance of making money, which is prone to outweigh moral principles.[46] Other bourgeois crimes are based on cupidity, which capitalism strongly inculcates amongst the bourgeoisie. They thus engage in acts which are difficult to detect such as the adulteration of food.[47] A third category of bourgeois criminals are exclusively tied to the capitalist mode of production. These are people who engage in massive frauds or stock-market swindles, crimes which are both encouraged by and only possible within capitalism.[48] The treatment of these bourgeois crimes clearly demonstrates the class character of the penal law. There are relatively few such crimes on the statute book, and punishments are relatively light.[49]

Sexual crimes would seem to have less connection with the mode of production, but Bonger argues that there is nonetheless a relationship. To start with, the social forms of sexual life, meaning marriage and prostitution, are determined by the mode of production.[50] He starts by considering adultery, which appears to have been a – rarely prosecuted – crime in Holland at the time he was writing. Marriages of convenience tend to lead to adultery, and are most common amongst the bourgeoisie; however, the intellectual bourgeoisie tend more to marry for love and are less prone to adultery. The frivolous and trifling life of the idle rich also tends to lead to adultery, whereas the petty bourgeoisie have more substantial social reasons for getting married and are less prone to adultery. Marriages concluded for purely physical reasons also tend to lead to adultery, which is more common in the proletariat for this reason. Sexual instincts, predispositions to polygamy and the immediate environment vary from one person to another and explain why some members of the proletariat commit adultery whilst others do not etc.[51]

What about rape and indecent assault? Better nourishment renders the sexual instincts stronger. Rape is mainly committed by men who are not married because of their lack of economic resources. It is also rarely committed by persons who have more than a primary education and is most commonly committed by the lower proletariat whose education and upbringing is virtually devoid of moral restraints.[52] Similar explanations basically work for paedophilia as well.[53] This account would now – obviously – be seen as seriously flawed. It omits the relatively frequent occurrence of rape within marriage and the lack of any clear distinction on class lines in surveys which attempt to identify perpetrators. Paedophilia would also appear to be spread across social classes.

Bonger then moves on to consider crimes based on vengeance and points out that the fundamental principle of the capitalist mode of production is competition, which involves doing injury to others and excites widespread desires for vengeance.[54] A major category of vengeance is based on male sexual jealousy and the belief that the man has rights over his wife. If women had greater economic independence there would be less basis for this belief. This explanation works even better for revenge taken by women who are seduced and then abandoned.[55]

Economic explanations also work for murder and assault based on revenge. These are much more common amongst people who are poor and illiterate. Feelings of revenge are less common amongst people who are more civilized, and an aversion to violence grows.[56] This can be seen if one correlates votes for the socialists with crimes of violence: as working people become more interested in cultural life and the running of society, they develop feelings of solidarity and crimes of violence diminish.[57] The decrease of violence due to increased civilization unfortunately confronts a countervailing factor: increased alcoholism, although civilized people are less violent when drunk.[58]

Infanticide has a ready economic explanation, being caused by poverty and the severe condemnation of female dishonour.[59]

The final category of crimes is political crimes. These will occur when 'the oppressed class, having become more powerful, breaks the political power of the ruling class and seizes it for itself'. This will lead to substantial political crimes if the ruling class tries to hang on to power until the last minute. An example of this is likely to happen in Russia. Political criminals of this sort are likely to be remembered as heroes. Individual members of the oppressed class may also attempt to assassinate a member of the government. This is probably futile but is understandable. There are also political crimes which are analogous to ordinary crimes in which, for example, an individual kills the monarch and hopes to install himself in power.[60] In a democratic country there is very little justification for political crimes committed by social democrats. It may be necessary for the German social democrats to turn to political crimes if the government tries to overthrow universal suffrage.[61]

What about pathological criminals? There is a substantial element of heredity. In our society someone who is diseased but rich can procreate but well and strong individuals who are poor lack the means to do so. Militarism leads to the deaths of strong individuals allowing the weak to procreate. 'The ignorance of the harmful effects for humanity of the reproduction of degenerates is one of the principal reasons why degeneracy is so frequently present.... The weak and the diseased to continue to reproduce themselves to the detriment of all society.'[62] Poverty, insufficient food, particularly for nursing mothers and the young, unsanitary dwellings, long duration and intensity of work, particularly in dangerous conditions and the work of women and children all contribute to degeneracy. Degeneracy is a major source of crime.[63]

In contrast, a communist society would eliminate poverty:

> Thus one great part of economic criminality (as also one part of infanticide) would be rendered impossible, and one of the greatest demoralising forces of our present society would be eliminated. And then, in this way those social phenomena so productive of crime, prostitution and alcoholism, would lose one of their principal factors. Child labour and overdriving will no longer take place, and bad housing, the source of much physical and moral evil would no longer exist.
>
> With material poverty there would disappear also that intellectual poverty which weighs so heavily upon the proletariat.[64]

Crimes of vengeance and sexual crimes will also largely disappear. The economic and social preponderance of man will cease, as will the harmful effects thereof. The community will see to it that all children are well educated and well looked after, thus eliminating a major source of crime.[65]

Socialist society will remove the causes of egoism which now exist and awaken a strong feeling of altruism. The crimes committed by pathological individuals will remain, but 'this will come rather within the sphere of the physician than of the judge'.[66]

Comments on Bonger

Bonger presents a twenty-first-century reader with a fascinating mixture of thoughtful and illuminating insights and ideas which we would now regard as outdated.

In many respects his definition of crime is superior to that of more contemporary Marxists, who have been seduced by extreme relativism in the form of symbolic interactionism. His idea that there is a substantial area of crime which is widely condemned by differing classes and differing social systems agrees very well with the arguments of the first chapter of this book. His comment that in modern societies crimes are generally also subject to moral condemnation would need to be qualified because we have a greater plurality of moral beliefs, and the range of technical offences has expanded. Thus there is lively debate about abortion, euthanasia, drugs, pornography, prostitution and animal rights, and many European countries have substantial minorities, particularly of Muslims, who are attracted to sharia laws.[67] There are therefore quite a range of existing offences which many people would wish to see abandoned and conversely a range of currently legal activities which many would criminalize. By 'technical offences' I mean very detailed legislation which is probably intended to follow general principles which would command widespread assent but where the detail is not intuitively obvious to many people. Examples might be exactly what one is allowed to do with a mobile phone whilst driving (the general idea of concentrating on the road would be accepted);[68] the principles involved in Best Available Technology Not Entailing Excessive Costs where industrial pollution is concerned (the general idea of avoiding pollution would be accepted);[69] the exact details of what counts as insider trading (the general idea of not defrauding people is uncontroversial); the exact details of taxation laws (there is obviously argument about which categories of people should pay how much tax for which activities, but even once the general principles are agreed the detail is mind-boggling).

Much of Bonger's theorizing depends upon the distinction between egoism and altruism. Because capitalism is based on competition between capitalists, competition between workers for work, and class antagonism, it encourages egoism. In contrast, either primitive communism or post-capitalist communism encourages altruism. In a very general sense this is obviously true, but Bonger places too much weight on this straightforward distinction. Consider a capitalist who manufactures tools which are sold for people who want to do DIY (Do it yourself). He is forced to compete with other tool manufacturers, that is, forced into egoism. He has not done it himself, but he knows of capitalists who engage in illegal price-fixing in order to make life easier. They behave towards their fellow capitalists in an altruistic, or at least not belligerent way. However, collectively they are keeping up their prices at the expense of consumers who are deprived of the benefit of capitalist competition. Our tool manufacturer is a good husband and father. He provides for his wife and children and makes time for a share of domestic work and childcare. Is this behaviour egoistic because it concerns just his own family, or altruistic because he could get away with doing much less? He is also the unpaid secretary of an association of tool manufacturers which helps set standards and which promotes DIY activity. Is this egoistic because it promotes his interest or altruistic because he could get away with not doing it? The association facilitates some charitable activities in which volunteers use tools it provides to repair and improve housing occupied by impoverished pensioners (altruism or a particularly cynical form of egoism?). He protests about excessive red tape in employment laws (egoistic unless the laws are genuinely totally unnecessary), but does his best to comply with them (altruistic? Prudential?). Eventually he finds his business badly undercut by a rival and pays the local Mafia to assassinate him (egoistic and criminal).

The final activity above is undeniably egoistic and criminal. What about looking after his family? If people live in private families then taking care of his family might be seen as a duty, altruistic where he puts himself out, and legitimately egoistic in relation to the wider society in the sense that looking after one's family reasonably well is seen as desirable and not particularly damaging to other people. There would almost certainly be a socialist version of many of our capitalist's activities. In the discussion of socialist society in Part II of this book, it will be argued that socialism would not be purely limited to altruistic activities.

It is also not clear that crime is a purely egoistic activity. Bonger himself acknowledges this where many political crimes are concerned and when he considers theft intended to feed one's starving family. In this context it is worth thinking about the techniques of neutralization which Matza identified amongst juvenile delinquents drifting in and out of delinquency, but which are plainly much more widely applicable.[70] The first technique, denial of responsibility, is the most compatible with Bonger's approach. Sophisticated criminals could argue that capitalism has encouraged their egoism, which has spilled over into criminal behaviour. The second, denial of injury ('nobody got hurt'), is specifically used by Bonger in the discussion mentioned above of modest thefts from wealthy people by those who possess very little. It is already used widely in the discussion of victimless crimes: those who carry them out are arguably not causing any harm. It could also be used with some justification by poor people engaged in modest thefts which are covered by insurance or where the victim is a large corporation. None of this would demonstrate that crime is altruistic, but it throws doubt on the idea that it is always damagingly egoistic. The third technique, denial of victim ('they had it coming') overlaps to some extent with the second, but could be used to argue that some crimes committed on other criminals or on corporations or individuals who make their money in an unethical way are less damagingly egoistic than they would be if carried out on innocent victims. The fourth technique, condemnation of the condemners ('what right do they have to criticise me?') could be used on a class basis to attack the credentials of judges and prosecutors. This would also mitigate accusations of egoism even if it failed to demonstrate altruism. The fifth technique is an appeal to higher loyalties ('I did it for someone else'). Even if the someone else is another criminal the form of this technique is altruistic. How much we are looking at genuine and substantive altruism would need to be debated on lines analogous to those used above in discussion of the hypothetical capitalist above.

It might be possible to take this discussion of crime and altruism further, but enough has been said to suggest that Bonger's central distinction is unworkable. Probably it is not at all workable, certainly it is unworkable without much further development.

Let us now turn to Bonger's approach to classes. Some of his discussion of the proletariat and lumpenproletariat makes a modern reader profoundly grateful for the benefits of the welfare state. Relatively little crime in modern Europe is committed by people facing the alternative of starvation, although much may have its origins in a grey existence on benefits without very much prospects. However, Bonger's comments that capitalism inculcates a desire to consume without necessarily providing the means to do so, and therefore fosters crime have remained pertinent. Indeed, the emphasis on the consumption of images – Nike trainers rather than just shoes, the latest product of the electronics industry even if the previous one was quite satisfactory etc. – so that theft is very much based on induced desires, gives his ideas new life.

What about his idea that there is a lack of morality because of poor housing and education? It is pretty clear that our version of overcrowding is much preferable to his. We normally expect people to have a bed each, running water, a bathroom and an indoor toilet, none of which could be taken for granted by the poorer people Bonger discusses. Leaving aside the exact meaning of 'morality' in this context, few would argue that poor housing is a major source of immorality in modern Britain, and the same would probably be generally true of at least

Western Europe. When Bonger talks of lack of education he is pretty clearly meaning lack of *any* sort of education. Free, universal, compulsory education at least for the primary years was the norm in Europe and the United States at the time he was writing, although it was introduced late in Holland (1901). However, because it had been introduced in the previous 20 or 30 years in several countries there would have been a legacy of people who had never been to school. We may now have worries about the standard of education, or about what sort of moral ideas are appropriate in school education, or the percentage of school leavers who we should encourage to go to university, but the idea that the children of workers and poor altogether lack education is not valid. These issues are more valid for Third World countries today.

Bonger does not present a systematic picture of the bourgeoisie, and therefore his treatment of their criminality is limited as compared with modern writing developed since Edwin Sutherland's *White Collar Crime*. Although he does not explicitly say this, his picture seems to be of individual entrepreneurs who are brought up with good basic ideas of right and wrong, but who are pressured or tempted into fraud or adulterating food. He does not work with a concept of corporations, and hence also lacks a distinction between corporate and individual white-collar crime. Along with this there is no discussion of the distinction (or lack of it) between crime and breaches of administrative regulations. The contemporary concern that a corporation might export its murkier operations to Third World countries is also lacking, probably because there was much less pressure in this direction in his day. However, Bonger's view of the press would need to be extended to television, and might benefit from some additional nuances, but works surprisingly well a hundred years later.

Bonger's idea of subdividing crimes in order to see to what extent they can be explained by economic conditions is broadly in line with what is proposed earlier in this book, although his actual divisions are different. Many of his explanations are interesting. Thankfully in the advanced countries crimes based on gross poverty have receded. Infanticide still occurs, but less stringent sexual morals and better welfare support have made it more of an individual tragedy. Similarly, revenge taken by women who are promised marriage, seduced and abandoned is less necessary, given greater equality, contraception and almost universal sex before marriage. One feature that makes Bonger appear old-fashioned is his trust of official statistics. He frequently bases arguments on international statistical comparisons with virtually no discussion of the way in which the figures from different countries are compiled. Statistics based on surveys were extremely rare when he was writing. The arguments he produces having accepted the statistics are always cogent and ingenious, but many of them are rendered dubious by lack of inquiry into their foundations.

Finally, we come to his contention that crime would become rare and would become more of a medical matter under socialism. This will be taken up again in the final chapter.

Georg Rusche and Otto Kircheimer, *Punishment and Social Structure*[71]

Despite notionally being a product of the Frankfurt School with a preface from Max Horkheimer, the analysis in Rusche and Kircheimer's classic is almost exclusively based on political economy, with a recognition of ideas on penal policy as a somewhat autonomous force which interacts with economic conditions. They may thus be seen as extending to the criminal justice system of Bonger's analysis of crime causation. Their central idea is that 'Every system of production tends to discover punishments which correspond to its productive relationships.'[72]

However, a major form in which the determination of penal policy by economic conditions is said to occur in their work is the scarcity or surplus of labour.[73] More available labour power equals worse conditions for working people equals a need for punishments to be harsher. Here are some examples. In Europe in the fifteenth century the numbers 'of downtrodden, unemployed and propertyless rose everywhere',[74] hence 'The creation of a law effective in combating offences against property was one of the chief preoccupations of the rising urban bourgeoisie.'[75] and '(t)he poorer the masses became, the harsher the punishments in order to deter them from crime.'[76] In England these conditions led to an extraordinary rise in death sentences, with 72,000 thieves hanged under Henry VIII, or vagabonds strung up in rows under Elizabeth I, 300 and 400 at a time.[77] This led to a decrease in the value of human life and an increase in spectacular physical punishments.[78] These punishments acted as a way of controlling the population; enabled people to cope with an atmosphere of oppression by laying the blame for anything that went wrong on witches or Jews; and fed a demand for sensation, hence leading to ever more spectacular punishments.[79] Note that these last comments depart from economic determinism: a lust for sensation and cruelty, fear of witches, and anti-Semitism – doubtless all have economic dimensions but are not primarily economic phenomena.

Rusche and Kircheimer, make no real attempt to explain what they are doing theoretically. Rusche and Kircheimer do not consider white-collar crime, but it could be fitted quite well into their 'least eligibility' economic analysis. Prison would always be substantially worse than life as a member of the bourgeoisie. Sentences for typically bourgeois offences would therefore not need to be lengthy in order to act as a significant deterrent.

In contrast, from the end of the sixteenth century under Mercantilism there was a profound change in methods of punishment: the possibility of exploiting the labour of prisoners received increasing attention, looking at galley slavery, or deportation and penal servitude at hard labour.[80] This change was brought on by severe shortages of labour, and led to imprisonment becoming much more humane, but only because the labour of prisoners could be used to make a profit.[81] Houses of correction were set up. They were primarily manufactories, turning out commodities at a particularly low cost because of their cheap labour. It is probable that they were paying concerns. That was clearly the intention of their founders.[82] This was the early form of the modern prison. The inmates tended to be kept according to how useful they were for manufacturing rather than sentenced for a determinate period.[83]

In the early eighteenth century transportation became a regular sentence in order to provide servants for the colonial plantations. 'The only difference between deported convicts and slaves was that the former were under constraint for a limited period of time after which they were freed.'[84] Transportation became less of a threat by the early 1800s. Conditions for workers under the early factory system, with a surplus of labour, were so bad that it was difficult to make punishment worse than daily life. Conditions in Australia were much better, so transportation became a benefit not a punishment.[85]

The deterioration of living conditions for workers in the first three decades of the nineteenth century was so bad that between 1805 and 1833 the number of convictions in London increased by 540%. Workers were left with the choice of starving, stealing or suicide.[86] The miserable standard of life outside meant that prison conditions had to sink well below the official minimum to maintain the principle of less eligibility. At this time forms of punishment such as the treadmill or solitary confinement were introduced in order to maintain prison as a deterrent.[87] Rusche and Kirkheimer mention the Quaker origins of the system of solitary confinement, but do not follow up this ideological origin. Houses of correction fell into disuse at this time because free labour was so cheap and factories so efficient.[88]

In the United States at this period labour was scarce. Prison as manufacturing remained as a profitable option. There solitary confinement was soon replaced by the Auburn system, which involved solitary confinement at night and collective labour in workshops during the day. There rehabilitation appeared to be easy because the country offered good wages to those willing to labour and convicts could easily find work.[89]

In the second half, and particularly in the final quarter of the nineteenth century, the conditions of workers improved considerably in Europe. This provided the basis for 'humanitarian' reforms to the criminal justice system, notably a greater use of fines, which workers were now earning enough to pay, and the use of probation as an alternative to prison.[90] Limits to how much could be paid to prisoners for their work were set because representatives of free labour argued that paying them would mean placing such work on more or less the same level as free labour.[91] In the First World War there was a massive demand for labour and prisons became major sources of manufacturing.[92]

As has already been noted, Rusche and Kircheimer do not stick entirely to economic explanations. Within properly economic explanations they achieve more variety than might at first be imagined. They do not simply stick to their initial idea that punishment, notably prison, needs to be worse than labour – or idleness – outside prison. They also use the idea of innovation. Thus the discovery that prison could be used as a source of profit by making use of the labour of prisoners led to a greater use of imprisonment than would have happened otherwise. Economic conditions in parts of an empire may vary, and this will have an effect on the possibilities of using transportation as a punishment.

Not all of Rusche and Kirkheimer's analysis is strictly economic. They argue that one reason for the popularity of Beccaria's ideas, particularly in France, was that arbitrary punishments for domestic servants were prone to lead to political unrest.[93] Beccaria's ideas were supported by the bourgeoisie because they offered them greater freedom; they were less keen on Beccaria's enlightenment when their own interests were threatened.[94] However, the implementation of Beccaria's humane reforms was interrupted at the end of the eighteenth century because of the rise of the factory system and the consequent economic unattractiveness of the houses of correction.[95] They also have some reflections on, for example, the independence of the judiciary, which they argue functions to conceal the law-making powers of the judges.[96]

In summary, Rusche and Kirkheimer generally stick very closely to an attempt to show that punishment is determined by economic conditions, although they offer at some times other possibilities from a Marxist framework, such as the idea that the law may be directed towards the preservation of the state. Their work has given rise to quite a substantial literature.[97] Much of this tries to correlate data on punishment, particularly on imprisonment, and data on economic conditions. Although this is attractive as a general idea it seems very difficult to pin down statistically. Two articles can be used as examples of the problems.

Bernard Laffargue and Thierry Godefroy attempt an ambitious correlation between unemployment and imprisonment in France from 1920 to 1985.[98] Their basic postulate is that street crime is mainly committed by a fraction of the working class which falls into the sub-proletariat at times of economic recession. 'This leads to an increase in prison populations, regardless of variations in recorded crime.'[99] Although the overall statistical consequences of this theory are straightforward, they comment that the process is modified by various factors: the Second World War and the rise in imprisonment because of illegal acts related to the Algerian war; welfare policies which may 'prevent least favourable workers from falling into the sub-proletariat'; attitudes of the public – difficult economic times harden attitudes towards delinquency; attitudes and policies within the criminal justice system may have an effect, be they the general move in the twentieth century away from imprisonment and towards fines, probation and community service, police attitudes and practices, judges who see the rise in recorded crime as a threat to society and therefore pass harsher sentences; budgetary constraints or the French habit of declaring prison amnesties when a new president comes into office.[100] Although the article uses sophisticated statistical techniques in examining carefully chosen data one is left with the overall impression that the central issue at stake is less these correlations than a judicious examination of factors which are not immediately economic.

A similar impression is generated by the second article, in which Raymond Michalowski and Susan Carlson identify four different social structures of accumulation in the United States from 1933 to 1992. They argue that it is then possible to achieve fairly good correlations between unemployment and imprisonment using highly sophisticated statistical techniques. However, a social structure of accumulation includes not simply economic variables but political factors and government interventions:

The strength and direction of the U–I [unemployment–imprisonment] relationship depend on the particular constellation of social characteristics that give unemployment its qualitative social meaning within any SSA [Social Structure of Accumulation]. Thus, factors such as the quality of available jobs, whether unemployment is frictional or structural, and the extent of government intervention through job programs or public assistance interact in ways that influence whether increased unemployment will be perceived as causing increased crime and necessitating greater social control through imprisonment.[101]

Thus, again, the validity of the analysis depends heavily on the proper identification of qualitative factors.

In general, Rusche and Kircheimer's approach is vulnerable to a series of fairly standard criticisms.[102] First and foremost, Rusche and Kircheimer claim that prison mops up the reserve army of labour, but actually it could only possibly mop up a small part of it. This comment is valid as a general summary of the situation in Europe historically. It may however be worth modifying their claim and asking whether it would be *possible* for prison to do this, and then to consider the United States today. According to the CIA website the US workforce is currently just over 150 million, and the rate of unemployment just below 5%, meaning that 7.5 million people are unemployed.[103] A large number of these will be simply between jobs and not in any sense part of the reserve army. Some 2.2 million people are currently in prison in the United States.[104] The idea that prison is playing a significant role in mopping up the reserve army of labour is thus not totally silly. For what it is worth, Charles Murray, a right-wing social critic, was arguing that the dramatic rise in imprisonment in the United States was part of the reason why the 'underclass' had not really disappeared during the Clinton presidency.[105] Prison is, of course, also generating many kinds of employment, some of which will go to people who would otherwise be in the reserve army of labour. However, there is every reason to think that the criticism is valid in general. This also links to another criticism, which is that different capitalist societies have widely varying forms of punishment and length of sentence, and that these do not correlate in any precise way with labour market conditions. It is easy to illustrate this by looking at the number of people in prison per hundred thousand of population in different countries.

The United States is currently the world leader when it comes to imprisonment with some 750 prisoners per hundred thousand of population.[106] This is wildly different from most other capitalist countries. Some examples are Canada 107, England and Wales 148, the Scandinavian countries with figures close to 70, France 85, Germany 93, Spain 147, Australia 125, New Zealand 183 and Japan 61. There is surely no need to try to correlate these figures with unemployment or inequality or poverty – something else must be at work. A glance at some regional variations looks more promising. Thus there was a high level of imprisonment in the Soviet Union, and the successor states tend to have higher levels as well: Russia 628, Belarus 426, Estonia 333, Latvia 292, Lithuania 235, Kazakhstan 348 and Uzbekistan 184. It might be thought that communist states have high levels of imprisonment, but there is quite a wide variation amongst communist and former communist states. Apart from those quoted, Cuba comes out high with 531, Vietnam 116, Cambodia 58 and China 119, and the component parts of former Yugoslavia between 62 and 117. It might make more sense to look at Cuba in the context of the Caribbean, where rates of imprisonment are typically high. Although Cuba's rate is the highest, many other islands have rates well over 300. It seems to make more sense to say, following David Garland, that countries develop particular cultures of control, leading to a greater or lesser degree of imprisonment.[107] Indeed, in the former states of the Soviet Union, such a culture would appear to have survived the transition to capitalism, and, where the Baltic states are concerned, membership of the European Union.

According to Garland, nineteenth-century prisons were generally a massive financial expenditure and could rarely cover even their day-to-day costs. Fines, corporal punishment and executions were much cheaper.[108]

It is plain that a huge amount of additional analysis is needed before the wide variations in forms and lengths of punishment and size of the prison population can be plausibly explained. Obvious things to consider might be the role of crime and punishment in the ideology of a particular society, whether crime is a salient political issue, the possible role of the prohibition of victimless activities such as drug-taking in expanding the prison estate, and whether features of the criminal justice system such as mandatory sentences, the efforts of prison reformers or the return of paroled prisoners to jail for trivial breaches of probation conditions are at work. It may well be possible to fit at least some of these explanations into an overall Marxist account of the society and the role of criminal justice within it, but clearly economic analysis on its own is not sufficient.

4
Radical US Criminology

Social and Intellectual Background

Radical American criminology became a major force following the turbulent decade of the 1960s. The relative complacency of the most affluent and powerful country in the world was jolted by a series of shocks. It was challenged by the war in Vietnam, in which a nation of peasants was moving towards inflicting military defeat on the South Vietnamese and the United States. The war had a profoundly radicalizing effect on young Americans. Young men were liable for the draft, which presented them with an agonizing personal moral choice: either fight for the army of an imperial power which was propping up the corrupt and dubiously democratic regime in South Vietnam; or face obloquy and imprisonment, or exile, or engage in various dubious methods of evading the call to duty. Black Americans had achieved most of what they sought in the American South through non-violent protest, but were now attacking informal segregation in the north and west by force of arms in the case of the Black Panthers or simply by rioting. The material contentment of the 1950s was challenged by hippies in the 1960s. Universities played a significant role in these developments. Their students became radicalized or dropped out, and many of the younger faculty provided intellectual support.

Not surprisingly the decade saw the development of radical criminology along with radical or critical versions of other social sciences. Two lines of thought which were already established within the discipline offered some radical potential. The first was Merton's strain theory, originating in an article written in the 1930s, but becoming more widely taken up in the 1950s, which became very influential.[1] Crudely it argued that the culture of American society places enormous emphasis on material success but without a strong countervailing emphasis on legitimate means. The economic structure of American society, however, whilst offering legitimate opportunities to some, generates significant inequalities. Most people are not going to attain success. Merton sketched various ways in which people might come to terms with this discrepancy, one of which he termed 'innovation', meaning turning to crime in order to acquire money. Merton's views were taken up by several academics in the 1950s and 1960s, most prominently by Cloward and Ohlin.[2] These ideas were taken up to some extent by the US government, particularly in Lyndon Johnson's War on Poverty. Richard Cloward was, indeed, able to try putting the ideas directly into practice in the Mobilization for Youth programme, which was intended to reduce crime in a depressed area of Manhattan by expanding opportunities for education and employment. They were not a spectacular success, and crime rates increased dramatically during these liberal reforms in the 1960s and early 1970s. Although it is possible to argue that the War on Poverty was too little too late and was subverted by the war in Vietnam, inflation and the arrival of Richard Nixon as president, Merton's theory does not seem to have worked very well.[3]

Merton's theory was couched in terms of American culture, which could then be compared with the culture of other capitalist societies. However, his description of American culture makes it clear that it is the most extreme capitalist culture in the world. It is only a short step from broadly accepting Merton's ideas to the notion that capitalism is a major cause of crime. His ideas also point towards vigorous social intervention in the interests of increased equality. Whilst this is far short of socialist or Marxist ideas, it is certainly locating the cure for crime at the level of society more generally rather than the individual criminal or the criminal act. Indeed, it is interesting that Messner and Rosenfeld, writing in the 1990s from a position favouring Merton, criticize the War on Poverty on the grounds that even if it had succeeded and produced a more meritocratic society there would still have been winners and losers and considerable inequality, so that much of the impetus to achieve material success through crime would remain. Messner and Rosenfeld argue that the logic of strain theory points towards social reorganization by which they mean policies to revitalize families, schools and the political system, thus enhancing their capacities for social control and reducing cultural pressures for crime. They want greater social support for marriage and the family, noting, for example, that family and emergency leave was only signed into law in the United States in 1993. This was unpaid leave in contrast to

12 weeks of paid leave in Japan and greater amounts in other countries up to Sweden's 37 weeks of paid leave.[4] American employers typically do not help either. Schools should be able to devote themselves to formal education rather than placing a very strong emphasis on fitting children for economic success.[5] Young adults who have dropped out of school should be encouraged to join a national service Corps, which would provide them with a social anchor and would have an accent on crime control.[6] A greater share of national wealth should be distributed on the basis of non-economic criteria to provide support for families, schools and other aspects of the polity. Messner and Rosenfeld note that there is quite a strong correlation between decommodification of aspects of the economy and homicide rates. Thus the United States has little decommodification and a very high homicide rate, whereas the Scandinavian countries have considerably more decommodification and much lower homicide rates.[7] They thus use Merton's theories to argue for a social democratic conclusion. So far as I am aware they are unusual in taking the argument as far as this, but their line of thought illustrates the potential for movement from strain theory to advocating socialism.

The second established line of thought with radical potential has already been described in the section on the definition of crime above. Symbolic interactionism, particularly as advocated by Howard Becker's book *Outsiders*, which first appeared in 1963, sees crime as a matter of labelling. Those in power typically have the ability to label people who are powerless. This could work in many different ways, for example older people are typically more powerful than younger people, but the theory is certainly capable of being grafted on to a Marxist approach which sees the criminal justice system as created by or skewed towards the interests of the ruling class. If Merton provided the inspiration for a more general social critique, symbolic interactionism provided a justification and technique for criticizing existing laws and provisions.

Richard Quinney[8]

Richard Quinney has been through a complicated theoretical trajectory. He started as an exponent of the labelling approach, but with the addition of an explicit idealism, in works such as *Crime and Justice in Society, The Problem of Crime,*[9] and *The Social Reality of Crime.*[10] In the mid-1970s he went through a Marxist phase, which is what interests us here, but by 1980 he was moving in the direction of existentialism and Buddhism. His Marxist phase is exemplified in *Critique of Legal Order,*[11]

Criminal Justice in America: A Critical Understanding[12] and *Class, State and Crime.*[13]

Critique of Legal Order is a book with a strangely thin set of theories. Quinney starts by sketching four different philosophical approaches to the legal order – positivism, social constructionism, phenomenology and a critical philosophy – and identifying himself with the fourth of these, a creative form of Marxism which is devoted to ending alienation and fostering the authentic human being.[14] He outlines his own theory by indicating that he accepts six propositions: American society is based on an advanced capitalist economy; the state is organized to serve the capitalist ruling class (which he largely demonstrates, following Miliband, in terms of the social origins of state personnel rather than in terms of the necessary functions of the capitalist state)[15]; criminal law is an instrument of the state and ruling class (and civil liberties 'are not a safeguard of human rights .... [They are] parcelled out to us at the discretion of the authority we wish to dissent from'[16]); crime control has as its purpose establishing domestic order; the contradictions of advanced capitalism require the continued oppression of the subordinate classes; only a socialist society will solve the crime problem.[17] 'Criminology', he says, 'has served a single purpose: legitimation of the existing social order'.[18] Whether one considers Bonger, Rusche and Kircheimer, or the work of Howard Becker, this seems too sweeping.

In the rest of the book he has relatively little to say about Marxism, his main concern in this direction being to demonstrate that various commissions set up to examine the crime problem in the United States were dominated by representatives of the capitalist class,[19] and produced recommendations in the interest of the class. He also has strikingly little to say about crime or the criminal justice system, except that the criminal justice system is directed to repressing attempts at revolution or social change in the United States, and that there is a move by the capitalists and their representatives to apply social and natural science to make the criminal justice system work better.[20] Law, he says, 'is a tool of the ruling class'.[21] As Sheldon comments in the introduction, this is simplistic, ignoring both cross-class interests (e.g. the law prohibiting rape) and any notion of conflicting interests within the ruling class.[22] The mass media reinforce the ideology of crime as a threat to the American way of life and controlling it as the only legitimate reality.[23] It is not surprising that they do this because they are capitalist enterprises in their own right and heavily dependent upon capitalist advertisers.[24]

One would expect Quinney to have something to say about street crime or, indeed, corporate crime, what causes them, the way they are currently tackled, what would happen to them under socialism and so forth, but discussion of these questions is virtually non-existent in his text. The only examples of crime and criminals which interest him are actions directed towards the overthrow of capitalism.[25] He is – not surprisingly – successful in finding representatives of capitalist interests on the various government commissions that he considers, and the government sponsorship of legislation and research projects devoted to tackling riots, student unrest, demonstrations and other features of the social upheavals that characterized the late 1960s. Many of the official reports which he castigates as devoted to propping up the existing, exploitative order demonstrate a level of care for the oppressed considerably greater than would be expected from equivalent bodies subsequently: '[S]ociety must seek to prevent crime before it happens by ensuring all Americans a stake in the benefits and responsibilities of American life'[26]; 'The wholesale strengthening of community treatment of offenders and much greater commitment of resources to their rehabilitation are the main lines where action is needed...'[27]

Quinney has rather more to say about socialist society. It is founded on true human nature, which is not satisfied with acquisition and consumption alone.[28] A socialist society would be equal – in material benefits, in decision-making and in encouraging everyone's full potential, particularly via non-alienated work.[29] There would be a strong emphasis on democracy.[30] Law would be replaced by custom, presided over by neighbourhood committees which would work with offenders in the community.[31] There are some attractive ideas here but it is difficult to know what they would look like in daily practice.

Frank Pearce: *Crimes Of The Powerful*

Frank Pearce has spent his working life in Britain and Canada, and *Crimes of the Powerful*[32] was published in Britain, but the intellectual content of the book belongs in the United States. His book starts with a discussion of labelling theory and symbolic interactionism, because they focus attention on the role of society in causing deviance rather than on the individual deviant.[33] He feels the need to defend US radicalism against the criticisms of Edwin Lemert, one of the founders of labelling theory.[34] He points out that Lemert is a pluralist, and as a critique of Lemert Pearce introduces the ideas of radical pluralism, namely that some groups such as the poor, blacks, drug users, women, youth and homosexuals lack power and are always the losers in the social world.[35] Symbolic interactionism could be used to study all kinds of deviance, including upper-class crimes, but in practice is used by Lemert to study the poor and unproductive.[36]

He moves on to argue that Marxism provides a scientific theory to explain the state and the economy, taking as its starting point the Preface to *A Contribution to Critique of Political Economy*.[37] Moving on to the analysis of the state and crime within a Marxist framework he uses Marx's analysis of the rise of Louis Napoleon Bonaparte to argue that capitalist democracy is provisional, and that the ruling class is not necessarily the group that does the actual business of day-to-day government.[38] It will be recalled from the section on the definition of crime above that Paul Hirst agrees with the link drawn by Marx and Engels between the lumpenproletariat and crime. Pearce is critical of Hirst. He stresses that it is difficult for monopoly capital to cope with even limited democracy, which means that ideology is an important support. Part of this involves stigmatization of forms of crime and deviance which have potential to undermine necessary supports of capitalism such as the family and work ethic. In addition, the doctrine of the rule of law enables the law to be presented as an expression of people's will, when actually the majority of laws work in favour of the capitalists.[39] This enables the police to be presented as a friendly and neutral body to fight crime, when in fact they also function as a Repressive State Apparatus to help maintain and reproduce the capitalist mode of production. This means it is possible on occasion for the police to investigate the criminal activities of the ruling class such as offences against factory safety regulations or corruption, but such unusual actions largely function as a safety valve.[40]

Pearce's image of socialism is of a society where anti-capitalist forms of deviance would be allowed free rein: '[h]omosexuality calls into question the naturalness of family institutions; drug usage and its attendant "expressive" culture can undermine the division of social time into work and earned leisure.'[41] He quotes Taylor, Walton and Young to the effect that 'Under real Socialism diversity would be freed from the forces of all but communal restraint', and continues 'an economically, socially, sexually and racially liberated socialist society would have practical democracy operating within work, education and all other institutions.... Certain kinds of deviant activity have within themselves a positive potential for social change'.[42] This leads him to reflect that some of the values of the lumpenproletariat might make them revolutionary allies.

In the next section of his book Pearce moves on to consider the crimes of the powerful. He starts by pointing out that although the Republicans campaigned in 1968 on the issue of crime, and particularly violent crime, violent crime constituted only 13% of 'index crimes' in the Uniform Crime Report for 1965. Burglary was the most lucrative of the index crimes, involving the theft of $284 million. In contrast in 1967 organized crime made an estimated $7 billion from gambling.[43] In 1957 the richest 1% of the American people defrauded the tax system of $9 billion. Illegal excess profits by corporations are also enormous, making them 'the most efficient and largest examples of organised crime in America'.[44] It thus makes sense from a bourgeois point of view to focus on lower-class criminals. They can be presented as individually inadequate failures; this deflects attention from the system's failure to provide for their employment and education; and criminalizing them makes it difficult for them to develop revolutionary ideas and organization.[45]

Pearce next considers legislation governing US corporations. His overall analysis is that the larger corporations generally support regulation in order to acquire a more predictable environment and to disadvantage smaller corporations. In pursuit of a more predictable and profitable environment they are happy to engage in extensive illegal price-fixing. The prosecution of corporations is rare, and its function is not to regulate business activity but to portray the economic structure as generally advantageous and the state as neutral.[46] Turning to relations with labour he argues that 'corporatist presuppositions are fundamental': if the unions are weak firms try to make all employees join a company union; if the unions are strong attempts are made to form joint organizations on a national level to achieve capitalist goals.[47] Even American foreign policy is geared to corporate objectives, which can extend to undermining legitimate governments.[48]

In the third part of his book Pearce considers the relationship between American society and organized crime. One theme of this is that laws passed ostensibly to combat organized crime have mainly been used against those who are politically dangerous.[49] He argues that recent concentration on the role of the Mafia is actually a digression. Organized crime is not surprising in a society dominated by the market where there is a large demand for illegal commodities such as alcohol, prostitutes, drugs and gambling. The emphasis on the Mafia shifts the blame to a foreign country and culture and away from the racketeering connections of politicians such as Johnson and Nixon.[50] Pearce sees organized crime as the instrument of capital. One illustration of this is the role of Al Capone in Chicago: allowed to function freely until he interfered with the interests of corporate capital.[51] Another is the role of organized crime in union busting.[52]

Pearce's book remains a significant achievement. It opens up areas which have since been explored in much more depth and detail, analysing corporate and state crime and the social function of organized crime. His engagement with Marxism is also quite sophisticated. There are, however, some issues in his analysis which will need to be taken up later. One is the role of the idea of the reproduction conditions of the capitalist system, a form of analysis very popular in the 1970s. Some of the reproduction conditions of capitalism would also be required for a socialist system, although they would doubtless need to be transformed. There needs, for example, to be some way of reproducing people who are able to function as workers or capitalists or members of a socialist polity. The conventional family of two adults and children is one way of doing this, but other alternatives such as gay and lesbian communes are doubtless possible. There is no particular reason why homosexuality points towards socialism: modern Britain with civil partnerships, gay adoption, anti-discrimination legislation and particularly hospitable areas such as Brighton or the Canal Street area of Manchester seems to have achieved quite a good framework for reconciling homosexuality and a capitalist economy. Pearce links his advocacy of anti-capitalist values with a view of the lumpenproletariat as possible potential allies, another issue which will be taken up later.

A second area where a passage of time has shown some problems is in the assumption that corporatism is the obvious way to run a capitalist economy. Ronald Reagan in the United States and Mrs Thatcher in Britain implemented a new right programme with a strong emphasis on attacking monopolies generally and on strengthening competition. Trade unions were seen as an obstacle to the free working of the market and were attacked rather than incorporated. A new pattern has developed in which particular operations or whole companies are transferred to countries overseas where labour is very much cheaper, perhaps leaving a core of highly skilled employees in Britain or the United States.

William Chambliss

William Chambliss was initially interested in the concept of legal realism, the study of law in action as opposed to abstract legal theory, but gradually evolved through studies from this perspective towards the acceptance of a Marxist perspective by 1974. This is most clearly seen in an article where he lays down the basics of a Marxist political economy of crime.[53] The article starts by laying down some basic features of Marxist theory, and then says that crime is the result of the contradictions of capitalism. The first of these is the stimulation of a desire for the consumption of the system's products. Workers are kept at their dull and meaningless tasks by the threat that their jobs could be taken by the reserve army of labour. There is an inevitable conflict in a society divided between a capitalist ruling class and a subservient class that works for wages. The capitalist class criminalizes the behaviour of the working class in the class struggle; the criminal law is a set of rules laid down in the interests of the ruling class. The laws are violated with impunity by members of the ruling class.[54]

He goes on to comment that prohibition in the United States was brought about by a downwardly mobile segment of the middle class; other laws stem from the efforts of groups such as the American Civil Liberties Union or the National Association for the Advancement of Coloured People.[55]

Most of the rest of the article comprises a comparison of Ibadan, Nigeria and Seattle, Washington. Chambliss demonstrates that

> In both Nigeria and the United States, many laws can be, and are, systematically violated with impunity by those who control the political or economic resources of the society. Particularly relevant are those laws that restrict such things as bribery, racketeering (especially gambling), prostitution, drug distribution and selling, usury and a whole range of criminal offences committed by businessmen in the course of their businesses (white-collar crimes).[56]

A much fuller account of his observations of Seattle may be found below. His conclusion is that everyone commits crime. 'Crime is a matter of who can pin the label on whom, and underlying this sociopolitical process is the structure of social relations determined by the political economy.' The label does not get pinned on the ruling class as much because of the discretion of law-enforcement agencies, bias in the legal system, bribery, coercion and use of political influence.

Although the article includes several interesting ideas which could contribute to a Marxist criminology, it also contains several problems. Is crime simply a matter of labelling, or are there consensus crimes? If laws are simply made in the interests of the ruling class why do lobbies for prohibition, civil liberties and African Americans ever succeed? Why does he include the interesting comment that in Ibadan the Hausa area and in Seattle the Japanese-American area are officially low-crime areas but actually contain much more criminal behaviour than appears in the official statistics – interesting, but requiring some kind of additional explanation if it is to be compatible with a Marxist framework? Is extensive bribery and racketeering simply helpful for a capitalist economy or does it create problems for at least some categories of capitalists?

On the take

Chambliss's work is characterized by a strong empirical dimension. Perhaps the best example of this is his splendid *On the Take: From Petty Crooks to Presidents*.[57] This is a study of illegal business in Seattle. Chambliss claims that

> Crime is not a byproduct of an otherwise effectively working political economy: it is a main product of that political economy. Crime is in fact a cornerstone on which the political and economic relations of democratic-capitalist societies are constructed.[58]

He estimates that the business of organized crime is grossing between $40 and $100 billion annually in the United States (circa 1978), and comments that it is a mainstay of the electoral process.[59] Although the book contains occasional mentions of the profits of crime with victims, such as burglary, the major emphasis is very strongly on victimless crime, notably drugs, gambling, prostitution and loan-sharking. The basic point is that there is a continuing demand for these services, which is supplied by 'a coalition of politicians, law-enforcement people, businessmen, union leaders and ... racketeers'.[60] Chambliss is describing the coalition as it existed in Seattle, but something similar may be found in all American cities. Much of the book comprises a fascinating account of Chambliss doing his research by engaging in conversations with people who conducted illegal activities in Seattle. Because the businesses were illegal but subject to a continuing demand they offered an opportunity for the police to supplement their income by taking bribes from those running them. Money from the crime network percolated up the police hierarchy and provided support for politicians; various professionals such as lawyers, bankers and real estate agents also serviced members of the crime network.[61] Chambliss supplies an organizational chart of civic worthies including financiers, attorneys, assorted businessmen in various entertainment businesses, politicians and members of the police, who presided over racketeers who in turn presided over gamblers, pimps, prostitutes, drug distributors, usurers and bookmakers. Entertainingly this is headed 'Seattle's Crime Network'.[62] Later in the book Chambliss describes how the network came apart, in large part because of a change of senior officeholders amongst state prosecutors. However, because of the ongoing demand for illegal services, a modified crime network was rapidly reconstituted.[63] Chambliss looks at the wider picture and argues that there is also a national crime network on broadly similar lines to the one in Seattle.[64] This network provides a major source of revenue for the Democratic party; a coalition between labour unions and organized crime supplies political contributions which helped to balance the lower legitimate business contributions received by the Democrats compared to the Republicans.[65] Of course, this situation exists only because of the very large sums of money necessary to conduct political campaigns in the United States. Given this background, ironically, egalitarian politicians tend to depend on crime networks more than those representing the wealthy.[66] Chambliss claims that there are similar crime networks throughout Europe, including Scandinavia and the communist countries of Eastern Europe. In order to reduce the amount of crime it would be necessary to decriminalize the illegal activities on which they are founded.[67] *On The Take* wears its theory very lightly, but is certainly compatible with some version of Marxism in that it demonstrates the role of organized crime in the democratic processes of capitalist societies.

Power, Politics and Crime[68]

Power, Politics and Crime is a much later book by Chambliss and contains several theoretical ideas which anyone attempting a Marxist analysis of crime needs to consider. Chambliss starts by charting a massive increase in expenditure on crime control over the 25 years to 2001, with virtually all other areas of government expenditure cut back, over a period when the crime rate has been declining. The federal budget for crime control tripled between 1995 and 1999. In 1994 the Violent Crime Control and Law Enforcement Act authorized the expenditure of nearly $24 billion to enable state and municipal governments to hire 100,000 new police officers.[69] Chambliss's big point is that various players in the criminal justice system, aided and abetted by politicians and the media, have managed to cook the books, leading Americans to believe that crime is much worse than it was 50 years ago when in fact the position is much the same.[70] Going along with this the prison population has risen particularly dramatically from 320,000 in 1980 to nearly 2,000,000 in 2000. The number of people under the control of the criminal justice system increased from 2,000,000 in 1980 to more than 6,000,000 in 2000. Over the same period the number of people employed in the criminal justice system increased by nearly 50%. A major explanation for the rise is the war on drugs, with 60% of inmates in federal prison sentenced for drug offences. About 30% of federal prisoners appear to be addicts not involved in other crimes.[71]

The political dimension of this, Chambliss argues, stems from the Republican 'southern strategy' for gaining control of the southern states from the Democrats by appealing to voter's fears of social unrest and violent crime, initially used by Nixon in 1968 and subsequently by the Republicans nationwide.[72] They have been aided in this enterprise by the Federal Department of Justice, and notably by the FBI. The FBI are responsible for preparing the annual Uniform Crime Reports, based on citizens reporting crimes to the police and crimes that police officers observe. Chambliss argues that the FBI produced news releases which highlight the most alarming statistics. One technique is the use of a crime clock, showing the frequency of particular crimes. Thus in 1998 the clock showed a murder every 27 minutes, forcible rape every 6 minutes and burglary every 13 seconds. The United States is very big, so even taking these numbers at their face value the rates are not as serious as they look. However, the crimes are counted in a misleading way. For example, if a police officer finds a dead body and believes the person was murdered the event is recorded as a murder, and remains as a murder even if the coroner decides it was not. In this way the United States has 20,000 murders every year but fewer than 13,000 convictions for murder and non-negligent manslaughter. Other countries count only convictions. A similar tactic is applied to other crimes, so that if three men are involved in one carjacking, three carjackings are counted; if one man attacks five others in a bar the incident counts as five aggravated assaults.[73] The proportion of murders committed by strangers was reported to have increased substantially between 1965 and 1992, but this is another FBI scam: they counted couples living together as strangers, and the number of couples living together but not married has increased substantially in recent years.[74] Similar manipulations, this time by criminologists, led to predictions of a wave of violent crime committed by teenagers.[75]

The reporting of the results of the annual National Criminal Victimization Survey has also been manipulated by the Department of Justice. In their report of the 1998 figures they start with the statement that people aged 12 or older experienced a total of 31.3 million crimes. Chambliss comments that this looks very alarming but further investigation shows that 85% of the population were not the victim of any type of crime; three quarters of victims were victims of property crime, only 14% of which involved the theft of over $250; 40% of victims do not report to the police because the item was recovered or they could not prove that it was stolen. The 8.1 million crimes of violence look alarming, but over 70% of these were attempts or threats of violence, not completed violence, and most seem to have been trivial. For example, an attempted assault without a weapon not resulting in injury accounts for nearly half of all violent crimes.[76]

The figures are manipulated in the opposite direction as well. The 1990s saw dramatic falls in violent crime in most major cities in the United States, led by New York's zero tolerance policies. Part of what was happening, however, seems to have been that homicides were being redesignated as suicides and accidental deaths.[77] The Uniform Crime Reports also reflected this decline in violent crime. However, there were numerous reports of the police manipulating data, and a careful investigation in Baltimore showed that serious crime had gone up by 3.5% rather than down by 14%.[78] The practice of plea-bargaining also allows for the manipulation of figures: in order to start from a strong bargaining position it is in the interest of the police and prosecutors to maximize the possible charges. These maximum charges can then find their way into the crime statistics.[79] Or not, if the desired direction is down.

Chambliss moves on to look at crime in the ghetto. The ghetto is the home of the urban underclass, particularly of poor African Americans. Chambliss argues that much of the high rate of crime is a self-fulfilling prophecy. One police tactic involves an undercover agent asking to purchase drugs from someone who initially does not have any but knows where to buy them. He or she goes to fetch them and is then arrested as a drug dealer.[80] The intensive use of tactics of this sort turns a rather lower use of drugs by blacks into a much higher rate of sentencing and incarceration, which in turn leads to many young black men being in prison rather than starting family life.[81] A rational society would decriminalize drugs and treat addiction as a health problem; it would also take drunk driving, a crime primarily committed by whites, more seriously.[82]

Chambliss then moves on to describe a study of two groups of juvenile delinquents, which has the same theme that the police find more crime amongst working-class youth than middle class because the community has an image of the former as tending to be delinquent, whereas arrests of the latter leads to unpleasant encounters with highly paid lawyers in court. His overall view is that the activities of the middle class delinquents were more dangerous and socially damaging.[83]

Chambliss's overall conclusion is that the US criminal justice system has got out of control, and is using resources that would be better devoted elsewhere. At the federal level there has been a major shift of expenditure from higher education to corrections. At state, county and municipal government levels more money is being spent on criminal justice than on primary and secondary education.[84] The War on Drugs is particularly responsible for this: its budget increased from $1 billion in 1981 to more than $20 billion in 2000. Meanwhile cities are cutting their other public expenditure, notably spending on education.[85] At the federal level Aid for Families with Dependent Children was being slashed so that a mother with two children and no outside employment would have received $7,836 in 1982 but $4,101 in 1999.[86]

Chambliss comments that it is particularly irrational to imprison so many people for possession of drugs. The average cost of imprisonment is about $22,000 a year, whereas outpatient drug treatment costs $3,500. Why is this 'irrational, inhumane, costly and ineffective' policy pursued? The answer, says Chambliss is

> The existing system is a consequence of publicising and exploiting crime to further politics, bureaucratic organisational demands and media popularity. It is also a mechanism for controlling and repressing a large percentage of the US population that is unemployed and for the foreseeable future unemployable. The fact that this unemployable population is predominantly African-American also both reinforces and expresses the ubiquitous racist ideology of US culture ... . [It] also hides far more serious harm being done by those in power.[87]

The hidden crimes that Chambliss has in mind are crimes of corporations that 'kill, maim and cause serious illnesses to hundreds of thousands of Americans every year', with scarcely a mention in the media and no recording in the national crime reporting system. The crimes of law-enforcement officials,[88] politicians[89] and the state[90] are also largely hidden and unpunished.[91] Chambliss's account of corporate crime is broadly similar to that of Reiman below. He starts by quoting an estimate of street crime at $4 billion a year and an estimate of corporate crime at over $200 billion a year, both taken from congressional committees.[92] The charge sheet includes deaths of employees, money laundering, the savings and loan frauds, routine pollution, price-fixing, massive medical fraud etc.[93] Chambliss calls for measures to reverse these wrongs which are also very similar to those proposed by Reiman: political leadership more like that of Lyndon Johnson, advocating more jobs and better education for the poor as a solution to crime. Other measures would be the decriminalization of drugs with the money saved going to drug clinics and education, an independent agency to gather data and make reports on levels of crime, law-enforcement agencies which aim for social justice, rewarding officers who resolve disputes without making arrests.[94]

Jeffrey Reiman: *The Rich Get Richer and the Poor Get Prison*[95]

This classic text was originally published in 1979, but has run through at least seven editions. It is beautifully argued by a philosopher, and is pretty clearly pursuing a Marxist agenda, but, as might be expected in a book which aims to influence American students of criminology, this is introduced gradually and without much fanfare.

Reiman develops what he called the Pyrrhic Defeat theory of crime and punishment: 'the goal of our criminal justice system is not to eliminate crime or to achieve justice, *but to project to the American public a visible image of the threat of crime as a threat from the poor*'.[96] In order to achieve this goal the system must maintain a sizeable population of poor criminals, which means that it must fail to eliminate the crimes that poor people commit. From this perspective the fall in the rate of crime since the mid-1990s is something of a puzzle, but Reiman maintains that the difference is only marginal, fails to touch the social causes of crime, and involves massive financial and social costs.[97] The fall is due to factors such as a period of stabilization in the drug trade and a fall in the number of young men in the population.[98] Instead he places the emphasis on the continuing very high level of crime, and very high cost of combating it. Thus, in 1965 some $4 billion was being spent annually on the US criminal justice system to deal with 4,710,000 reported crimes. By 1992, this had risen to $94 billion, a rise of 500% allowing for inflation. Over the same period, reported crime rose to 13,867,143.[99] He argues that the system is well designed to maintain a criminal class. Features which help in this respect include: laws which create victimless crimes such as those against drug use, prostitution or gambling, which also generate secondary crimes committed in order to pay for drugs; imprisonment is applied unequally, so that prisoners experience their confinement as arbitrary and unjust and become more antisocial in consequence; prison is humiliating and brutalizing, thus encouraging prisoners to engage in aggressive violence; prisoners are not provided with marketable skills, and their records discourage employers from hiring them, thus encouraging recidivism; their pariah status is reinforced by depriving them of the right to vote and returning them to prison for trivial parole breaches.[100]

Reiman comments that the criminal justice system is not entirely useless. Some features of parts of the system are more constructive, and he is not opposed to imprisoning people for murder or armed robbery. The system is thoroughly distorted rather than entirely perverse. The American criminal justice system is like a carnival mirror which shows a distorted image of the dangers that threaten us. It tells us that the typical criminal is a young black urban male.[101] The system functions to deflect 'the discontent and potential hostility of Middle America away from the classes above them and toward the classes below them';[102] in particular, attention is directed away from occupational injury or disease, unnecessary surgery, shoddy medical services, dangerous chemicals and avoidable poverty.[103]

Reiman says that the Pyrrhic defeat theory is an amalgam of ideas from Durkheim, Kai Erikson, Richard Quinney and Marx. He contrasts it with more traditional Marxist approaches, because it emphasizes the ideological function of the criminal justice system instead of its repressive function. Indeed, the ideological function succeeds *because* the repressive functions largely fail.[104] This failure 'does not merely shore up general feelings of social solidarity; it allows those feelings to be attached to a social order characterized by striking disparities of wealth, power and privilege, and considerable injustice'.[105] In the final chapter of the book Reiman reinforces the message that the United States is a profoundly unequal society with such dramatic disparities of wealth and prospects in life that it must require an ideology to maintain it in place.[106] It does this by concentrating on individual wrongdoers rather than on institutions, and by putting forward the criminal law as a politically neutral set of ground rules for social living.[107]

Reiman's view of the criminal justice system is that it acts like a distorting carnival mirror – it presents us with a distorted view of crime rather than a totally false one. Much of the harm perpetrated by the well-to-do is not defined as crime; and to the extent that such harm is defined as crime it is not vigorously prosecuted. However

> economic pressures work with particular harshness onto the poor because of their condition of extreme need and their relative lack of access to opportunities for lawful economic advancement vastly intensify for them the pressures towards crime that exist at all levels of our society.[108]

This leads poor people to commit a higher proportion of the crimes that people fear than their numbers in the population.[109] Thus Reiman subscribes to a version of Merton's strain theory.

Reiman supports his Pyrrhic defeat theory by arguing that it would be easy to reduce crime in the United States if the political will were there. He rapidly dismisses some possible explanations of the high rate of crime in the United States and the failure to reduce it. The problem is not that the US criminal justice system is insufficiently harsh: it has a much higher rate of incarceration than any other country in the world, and has retained the death penalty unlike most civilized countries.[110] High rates of crime are not simply a consequence of urbanization, or modern life. There is a marked lack of correlation between nations and between cities within the United States where these two dimensions are concerned.[111] The crime rate correlates somewhat with the number of young people in the population but far too little to attribute crime to the proportion of young people.[112] Legislators seem willing to press on with increasing the numbers of police and prisons despite acknowledging that this is failing to have much impact on crime. They are unwilling to fund research on the effectiveness of anti-crime measures.[113]

There are some obvious measures that would reduce crime. The foremost of these would be a reduction in unemployment, particularly, youth unemployment. This particularly affects black people, and their substantially higher rate of incarceration further damages their economic prospects.[114] Another would be a reduction in the number of guns in circulation in the United States. Two estimates from the early 1990s would suggest that there are about 200 million guns in civilian hands; nearly a half of US households have at least 1 gun. According to the FBI in 1993 32% of violent crimes were committed with firearms; in 1992 85% of murders of persons aged 15 to 19 were attributable to guns; other estimates suggest that if crimes currently committed with guns were committed with knives instead there would be 80% fewer fatalities.[115] An easy way to make a huge reduction in the amount of crime would be to legalize drugs and deal with the consequences of addiction as a health issue, on the model of current policy with tobacco and alcohol. There would be no need for drug smuggling and no corruption of officials bribed by drug smugglers.[116]

Reiman moves on to discuss the crimes of the powerful. His point is that 'the label "crime" is not used in America to name all or the worst of the actions that cause misery and suffering to Americans. It is primarily reserved for the dangerous actions of the poor'.[117] The image of the typical criminal is a young, tough, lower-class male.[118] The typical harm that he does is a one-on-one crime; he causes physical injury or loss of something valuable. The media reinforce this image of crime as a one-on-one event, but interestingly both news reporting and fictional shows deal with crimes of violence more frequently than they occur by a factor of 12, and the criminals they show are older and wealthier than those who appear in the FBI's Uniform Crime Reports. The impression given is thus that the criminal justice system pursues rich and poor alike, and that crime is not solely caused by poverty.[119]

Far more harm, however, is done by the rich and the powerful. The harm frequently happens to groups of people, and is a consequence of the pursuit of profit, for example by a neglect of safety features in a mine. The mine owner would genuinely prefer no harm to occur. For this reason the corporate murder of – in the example Reiman gives – ten miners is not thought of as a crime and the most that happens is a criminal indictment for breach of safety regulations.[120] After all, the miners have chosen a relatively dangerous occupation and thus in some sense consented to the dangers. Ryman answers a series of four objections to the charge that the mine owner is a criminal.

First, the executive who cuts corners with safety regulations does not aim to harm his victims, unlike the mugger. However, answers Reiman, whether actions are done purposely, knowingly, recklessly or negligently they are all intentional and thus to some extent culpable. The greater the risk taken by the executive and the larger the number of workers, the greater the likelihood that one or more workers will be killed, so that the gap between the executive and the typical criminal shrinks. The actions of the executive are more calculated than those of someone in the midst of a heated argument, and show a greater indifference to human life. If the executive covered up evidence of risk he is even more culpable.[121] Crimes carried out by individuals are probably more terrifying than corporate crimes, which is certainly a factor, but most people would probably prefer to be terrified and not injured rather than injured and not terrified.[122] The executive is basically engaged in a legitimate activity, but if the risks are great enough he is still committing a crime.[123] There may be some degree of choice for workers between jobs, but they are compelled to work by economic necessity and may well not be in a position to know about the risks of any particular job.[124]

Reiman goes on to consider some examples of crimes of the rich and powerful. He takes as his baseline the Uniform Crime reports for 1995 which show roughly 21,000 murders and non-negligent manslaughters, 1 million assaults leading to severe bodily injury, and $15 billion of property crime. In comparison he starts with the risks of working. A very conservative estimate of deaths from occupational disease is 25,000 per annum. A similarly conservative estimate of job-related serious illnesses in the United States is 250,000 per annum. The result of this is that four workers die as a result of their occupation for every three victims of murder and non-negligent manslaughter. To get a true comparison with street crime it is necessary to halve the above estimates, because the labour force is about half of the population. Death and disability from work-related injuries also needs to be added in. It can now be seen that work kills 34,100 workers each year whereas crime kills 10,500 of them, and work physically harms 3,450,000 workers in contrast to 500,000 harmed by crime.[125] In contrast to the size of the criminal justice system, the Occupational Safety and Health Administration is tiny compared to the task it faces and tends to be subject to government cuts.[126]

Reiman goes on to look at various dangers associated with health care, where he argues that some 20,000 Americans die unnecessarily each year as a consequence of improper emergency care; and between 12,000 and 16,000 people die each year as a consequence of unnecessary surgery; up to 10,000 people are killed each year by antibiotic medicines. In addition, unnecessary surgery and medication cost between $20 and $24 billion annually, thus significantly outstripping the costs of crime as recorded in the Uniform Crime Reports.[127]

Moving on to avoidable chemical hazards from pollution (at least 10,000 deaths per annum), cigarette smoking (400,000 deaths per annum, bolstered by political contributions by the tobacco companies and deliberate concealment of the hazards of smoking) and food additives (harder to quantify, but considerable evidence of the dangers, plus also dangers from pesticide residues), Reiman concludes that Americans suffer 'a chemical war that makes the crime wave look like a football scrimmage'.[128]

Finally Reiman discusses poverty, which he links with worse health and lowered life expectancy, and which accelerated under Reagan, the older Bush and Clinton. Because blacks are generally poorer this also has a racial dimension.[129]

Reiman moves on to look at imprisonment. He concludes that

> *For the same criminal behaviour,* poor people are more likely to be arrested; if arrested, they are more likely to be charged; if charged, more likely to be convicted; if convicted more likely to be sentenced to prison; and if sentenced, more likely to be given longer prison terms than members of the middle and upper classes.[130]

He notes that blacks are more likely to be in prison than white people, but concludes that most of the explanation for this is that they suffer from poverty rather than from racism.[131] Reiman concedes that the poor commit a larger proportion of crimes against persons and property than do the middle and upper classes. His point in this respect is that the crimes of the middle and upper classes are more dangerous and extensive than those recorded by the FBI.[132] Even remaining with crimes that get recorded, 91% of Americans have violated laws at some point that could have subjected them to a term of imprisonment; middle- and upper-class individuals, however, rarely get arrested. Much of what is being referred to here is juvenile delinquency with middle-class delinquents being treated more gently.[133]

Turning to white-collar crime Reiman estimates tax evasion as about $400 billion for 1994, and more standard white-collar crime such as bribery, computer crime, consumer fraud, credit card and cheque fraud, embezzlement, insurance fraud, theft and frauds of securities and cellular phone fraud at $208 billion for 1994, more than 13 times the total amount stolen in all the thefts in the FBI Uniform Crime Reports for that year.[134] These do not, however, normally lead to prison. A more typical measure is the use of non-criminal sanctions. The US Securities and Exchange Commission has a fairly tough reputation, but of every 100 suspects they investigated up to the mid-1980s, at least, only 11 were selected for criminal treatment and only 3 of these get sentenced to prison; 88% never have to contend with the criminal justice system at all. Comparing embezzlement with property crime, Reiman notes that in 1995 there was one property crime arrest for every $7,000 stolen and one embezzlement arrest for every $742,000 'misappropriated'.[135]

The court process is also uneven. Poorer defendants tend to be held in jail whilst awaiting trial, which makes preparing their defence more difficult. Their legal representation is appointed by the court and has relatively little time to devote to their defence. White-collar defendants tend to be at liberty before their trial and to have expensive legal representation; corporate defendants have an army of legal expertise which makes prosecutors less inclined to take them on. A very high percentage of poorer defendants are convicted following plea-bargaining. In contrast, about half of defendants who can afford a private attorney are found not guilty.[136] When it comes to sentences, white-collar criminals tend to suffer fines and probation rather than prison, and if imprisoned tend to serve shorter sentences than those found guilty of street crimes. The notorious Savings and Loan frauds of the late 1980s, where they led to prison at all, led between 1988 and 1992 to an average sentence of 36 months. This may look relatively harsh compared to an average sentence of 26 months for a first-time property crime offender, but the average loss per property offence was $1,251 compared to the average loss in a Savings and Loan case of $500,000.[137]

This comparison is brought up to date in an Internet essay by Geoffrey Reiman and Paul Leighton. This compares the agreement under which Andrew Fastow, the Chief Financial Officer of the Enron Corporation, accepted a sentence of 10 years imprisonment in a plea bargain for his part in the fraud with the 50-year minimum sentence (two life sentences with a minimum term of 25 years each) imposed on Leandro Andrade, caught stealing nine children's videos in two episodes of shoplifting under California's notorious 'three strikes and you're out' laws. Andrade's sentences were upheld by the US Supreme Court. This may look as though American justice is starting to catch up with corporate criminals, but it needs to be remembered that Fastow was a central player in an enormous fraud which left employees without pension provisions, corrupted accountants, bankers and stockbrokers, and ruined numerous investors. He was initially charged with 109 felony counts.[138] As if to reinforce the point of the essay Fastow's actual sentence imposed in 2006 was of 6 1/2 years because he had been so cooperative. Likewise, the sentence of 25 years on Bernie Ebbers, the CEO and chief player in the World.com fraud, might appear harsh but the fraud had massive ramifications for shareholders, pension funds, employees etc., and seems likely to have involved the theft of about $1 billion rather than the mere hundred million dollars on which the sentence was based.[139]

In his conclusion Reiman calls for a wide-ranging set of changes linked to his critique: an end to poverty; a matching of the treatment of 'all harm-producing acts in proportion to the actual harm they produce', which particularly means finding ways to penalize corporate crime with a strong accent on holding individuals in charge of corporations to account; linked to the idea of matching penalties to harm, the decriminalization of victimless crimes, and in particular the legalization of illegal drugs and treatment of addiction as a medical problem; the development of correctional programmes which offer ex-offenders a decent chance of succeeding as law-abiding citizens; stringent gun controls; a reining back of plea-bargaining; the ending of harsh minimum sentences; a reduction of discretion in the criminal justice system and development of procedures to hold its officials accountable to the public; a right to equal counsel for all, and a more just distribution of wealth and income.[140] Sadly these measures currently appear utopian, but they would surely feature as significant parts of a move towards a socialist United States.

In an appendix Reiman provides a good summary of the basics of Marx's version of the labour theory of value and theory of ideology. He argues that criminal law and criminal justice in capitalist societies can be read as an idealized version of the concept of equality in exchange.[141] He then finally argues that Marxism leads to the conclusion that capitalism is unjust because of alienation, exploitation and maldistribution of wealth. The alienation charge is based on the point that under capitalism 'each person's well-being is in conflict with that of others' – class against class, worker against worker and capitalist against capitalist. He argues that exploitation and maldistribution may be seen as part of the same phenomenon, to be cured by the replacement of private ownership of the means of production with social ownership by everybody. Reverting to criminal justice, those normally labelled as criminals can be seen as victims of a prior crime who are trying to improve their situation. Relatively privileged individuals, or those whose crimes bear little relation to their class position such as some rapists may be seen as more culpable than the general run of criminals. The Marxist critique of criminal justice is linked to a moral condemnation of distributive justice under capitalism.[142]

In 1998 Reiman was invited to reflect on the twentieth anniversary of the first publication of his book.[143] He notes that the economic bias in the criminal justice system which he described remains, although some of the mechanisms have altered. For example, bias in sentencing tends to be the work of prosecutors behind closed doors rather than judges in open court; and the police are less racist but laws such as the notorious distinction between crack and powder cocaine still have a racist effect. More dramatically the level of concern about the bias of the system has very much diminished both at the elite level and amongst scholars. Reiman questions why this should be, and concludes that the formal legal equality between workers and capitalists renders the systematic social bias in favour of the latter invisible except at times of crisis such as the depression of the 1930s or the upsurge of the 1960s.

Discussion of Chambliss and Reiman

Chambliss and Reiman have sufficient in common for it to be sensible to comment on them together. They provide a superb critique of more conventional approaches to crime, one which is certainly susceptible to a Marxist interpretation, although it is probably also compatible with the sort of socially concerned liberalism that supports affirmative action. Chambliss's critique of official statistics, which is largely absent from the other authors discussed so far, is perfectly compatible with Marxist interpretations and is very important for any commentator in this area to bear in mind. To review it properly would require an extensive discussion of the use of crime statistics, which would take us too far afield from Marxist criminology. It is undoubtedly true that politicians and the press emphasize any growth in crime and particularly violent crime, with a view to furthering a political agenda. However, the role of official bodies in preparing and publicizing crime statistics is a very complex issue. The general approach arguing that corporate crime is more serious than street crime is also fully applicable to other countries such as Britain, and certainly needs to feature as part of a Marxist criminology. Chambliss and Reiman are quite right to castigate the massive expansion of corrections and particularly imprisonment in the United States in recent years. At this point however it is necessary to think about the peculiarities of the United States; imprisonment levels in Britain, although they have risen considerably in recent years, are still very substantially lower than those in the United States, and the more civilized Western European states have still lower levels of imprisonment.

It is clear that there are a variety of ways of running a capitalist state. Some of these may enable capitalism to develop faster than others, but all of them seem capable of lasting for quite long periods of time without triggering massive crises of the capitalist system. A larger or smaller nationalized sector, a larger or smaller welfare state, differing approaches to trade unions, rather different family patterns, substantial ethnic divisions amongst workers or not are all possibilities compatible with the medium-term survival of capitalism. The current bloated US criminal justice system would appear to be one of these variations. It obviously performs various functions for the American capitalist system, making profits for private corporations, mopping up black and white unemployment, helping to maintain racial divisions and a politics based on radicalized fears of crime. It is however, also possible to run reasonably stable capitalist systems with a low rate of imprisonment and with higher spending on education on the model, for example, of the Scandinavian countries. Whether it would be possible to move from one to the other over time is a complicated, difficult and fascinating conundrum, but we should beware of the idea that capitalism is necessarily run in one way or the other.

Christian Parenti: *Lockdown America: Police and Prisons in the Age of Crisis*[144]

As the title suggests, the focus of Parenti's book is on the US criminal justice system, and specifically on its massive expansion in recent years.

Much of the book comprises a relatively detailed description of the expanded apparatus of the state, but it is set against an overall explanation within a broadly Marxist framework. His basic argument is summarized in the Preface:

> Beginning in the late 60s US capitalism hit a dual social and economic crisis, and it was in response to this crisis that the criminal justice buildup of today began ...
>
> Initially this buildup was in response to racial upheaval and political rebellion. The second part was/is more a response to the vicious economic restructuring of the Reagan era. This restructuring was itself a right-wing strategy for addressing the economic crisis which first appeared in the mid- and late-60s. To restore sagging business profits, the welfare of working people had to be sacrificed. Thus the second phase of the criminal justice crackdown has become, intentionally or otherwise, a way to manage rising inequality and surplus populations. Throughout this process of economic restructuring the poor have suffered, particularly poor people of colour. Thus it is poor people of colour who make up the bulk of American prisoners.[145]

The political crisis of the late 1960s to which Parenti refers is essentially the same as the one described at the beginning of this chapter: the combined effects of losing the war in Vietnam, the urban riots, the sexual and psychedelic antics of middle-class youth, to which Parenti adds various liberal justice reforms which tilted the balance somewhat towards defendants.[146] He argues that various reforms made by Lyndon Johnson laid the groundwork for subsequent expansion of the criminal justice system, but the rhetoric which would support it was developed by Southern Republicans.[147] This rhetoric claimed that the war on poverty was leading to criminal violence. The criminal violence was identified with urban blacks.[148] In this way anxieties about crime were used as a cover for racist politics. Richard Nixon used this tactic to get elected as president in 1968, but was then faced with the problem that most of the criminal justice system worked at a local level. He managed to resolve this by emphasizing the war on drugs, which was a federal issue.[149] A significant federal body used to transfer funds to more local policing was the Law Enforcement Assistance Administration, initially set up by Lyndon Johnson.[150] The funds were particularly devoted to police training and improved equipment including computers, radios and helicopters.[151]

Beyond the political crisis there was also an economic crisis. American capitalism had dominated the world in the years immediately following the Second World War but by 1960 European and Japanese productivity had recovered considerably and was very competitive with the United States, particularly because US labour costs were roughly 3 times as high as in Europe and 10 times as high as Japan.[152] The American working class had become powerful thanks to the favourable conditions following the war. Strikes and individual indiscipline were rife by the early 1970s.[153] Not surprisingly rates of profit suffered, going from an average after-tax profit of nearly 10% in 1965 to less than 6% in the second half of the 1970s. This problem was exacerbated by the passage of numerous health and safety and environmental laws, complete with bodies to administer them.[154] In this climate the ideas of the New Right became increasingly popular, particularly in Republican circles. When President Reagan took office interest rates increased rapidly and by 1981 the United States suffered a severe recession; by 1982 10 million people were unemployed, and average wages fell by 8% and remained depressed for the next five years.[155] At the same time there was an assault on the welfare state with an overall reduction of 24%, while taxes for the richest 1% were reduced.[156] Alongside these measures American manufacturers increasingly exported jobs to places with dramatically lower wages: Mexico, South Korea, Taiwan or Singapore. Between 1980 and 1985 2.3 million jobs disappeared in this way, leaving the industrial base of many cities devastated, with particularly bad effects on African Americans.[157] The resultant class and racial polarization, homelessness and destruction of public education and public health constituted a social crisis which was used to justify a new criminal justice crackdown.[158]

Just as Nixon had used the federal responsibility for drugs as a mechanism for more general federal criminal justice intervention, so also Reagan declared war on drugs. He doubled the funding of the FBI, gave a 30% increase to the US Bureau of Prisons and increased the budget of the Drug Enforcement Administration.[159] From 1984 new legislation permitted federal, state and local agencies to seize assets in drug cases. These seizures increased dramatically, so that in 1987 alone over $1 billion was seized, most of it, apparently, from small dealers.[160] The war on African Americans really started with the passage of the Anti-Drug Abuse Act of 1986, which included the notorious five-year mandatory minimum sentence for possession of 500 g of cocaine or 5 g of crack.[161] Narcotics arrests went from 800,000 in 1985 to 1.4 million in 1989, particularly helped by a new focus on users as opposed to dealers.[162] It was hoped that with the election of Bill Clinton in 1992 the war on crime would be replaced by a war on poverty, but instead he promoted the Violent Crime Control and Law Enforcement Act of 1994, intended to help the States hire 100,000 new police officers, and which also provided $7.9 billion in grants for state prison building.[163]

The police, of course, are a major aspect of the war on crime. Parenti discusses zero tolerance policing in New York, pointing out that although misdemeanour arrests increased in New York by 73% between 1994 and 1997, and overall crime dropped by 43%, the policy had very much the quality of a war on the poor and homeless, and involved a 62% jump in complaints of police brutality.[164] Similar patterns have emerged in other cities that have imitated New York's zero tolerance policies.[165] A typical pattern has been for the poor and homeless to be moved out of city centres, which are then available for offices and middle-class living.[166]

Increased police funding has gone along with increased militarization, in particular the growth and increasing use of SWAT teams. Their use, argues Parenti, has tended to expand well beyond any remotely appropriate circumstances. He describes how in Fresno, California, the team effectively goes hunting for black and latino youth who have associations with gangs, often of a minimal sort, or who have in some minor way violated parole conditions. This is carried out seven days a week employing armoured vehicles, sub-machine guns, automatic rifles, attack dogs and helicopters. This is extreme, but similar actions take place across the United States, reinforced with video footage on real-life television policing shows. Parenti comments that this seems to be a reversal of Foucault's idea that power has shifted away from spectacular public punishments to affirm the power of the state and towards softer forms of control in which discipline acts upon human consciousness and subjectivity. SWAT operations are more like a reversion to public executions.[167] The tendency to militarization has also extended to the Immigration and Naturalization Service, whose sweeps in pursuit of undocumented immigrants helps to keep their labour cheap and non-unionized.[168]

Parenti charts the massive rise in imprisonment, chiefly stemming from the 1980s onwards. His explanations for the rise are interesting. He sees it partly as a way of augmenting the power of the police, reinforcing their capacity to terrorize. It is also a way of mopping up huge numbers of poor African-American and Latino people, but is also a by-product of the electoral strategies of right-wing politicians.[169] In addition, in California at least, there was a strategy by the prison authorities in which inmate violence was encouraged with a view to extracting more money from the state budget, which succeeded so well that by 1994 the prison service was on a budget of $4 billion a year, more than California was spending on higher education.[170] Parenti also provides a careful discussion of the relationship between prisons and capitalist profit-making, to which we shall return.[171]

The same right-wing rhetoric which has fuelled the expansion of prisons has also worsened conditions for prisoners, deprived them of any real chance of improving their conditions through litigation, and removed the possibility of higher education from most US prison systems.[172] The guards have been happy to encourage rape and gang warfare in order to keep prisoners divided and docile.[173]

Parenti's book offers compelling journalistic descriptions of the bloated US criminal justice system but his section on what might be done about it is very short. Essentially he recommends much less policing and incarceration, pointing out that two-thirds of people entering prison are sentenced for non-violent offences and therefore pose no major threat to public safety. Like other US radicals he favours the decriminalization of drugs and sex work and a reduction in the supply of firearms. He notes that activists and pressure groups are beginning to campaign against police violence, excessive imprisonment and prison abuse and hopes this will flower into a better way forward.[174]

Parenti provides graphic and compelling descriptions of the expansion of the US criminal justice system. His book was published in 1999, and therefore does not include the boost given to the system by the events of 9/11 and the subsequent emphasis on homeland security. His explanations appear to have a Marxist background, but with a strong emphasis on contingent features of the United States as opposed to necessary features of capitalism in general. For example, his strong emphasis on the exploitation of racial divisions would not be applicable in a society where these did not exist to some extent already. This makes quite good sense. To take an extreme contrast, the Scandinavian countries have experienced the same pressures of global competition and possibilities of capitalist outsourcing as the United States but have responded in completely different ways. For this reason their current rates of imprisonment average about a tenth of that of the United States. This raises the issue of whether it would be possible to run a capitalist system in the United States with a much lower level of imprisonment.

Another paradox which is implicit in Parenti's book is that there is serious unemployment amongst young urban blacks because industries have moved to countries where labour is cheaper than the United States.

In consequence they have turned to drug dealing and gang warfare, offering an excuse for paramilitary policing and unprecedented levels of imprisonment. This same American economy attracts large numbers of immigrants, particularly from the south, to work in agriculture, service industries and unpleasant jobs such as meat processing. We need an explanation in terms either of culture or of the notoriously limited US welfare state to explain why more urban blacks do not take jobs that currently go to latinos.

Henry and Milovanovic's Constitutive Criminology[175]

Up to this point the texts discussed have either been explicitly linked with Marxism or have been amenable to interpretation as part of a Marxist body of work. Although they occasionally make reference to Marxist influence, the constitutive criminology of Henry and Milovanovic decisively breaks with Marxism at numerous points. It is mentioned here because it presents a sensible location for briefly indicating some reasons for preferring Marxist modernism to the fashionable postmodernism. Also, constitutive criminology is presented as a far more radical doctrine than anything modernist such as Marxism, making it desirable to point out some of its more obvious failings.

The two books which are the starting point of constitutive criminology are Stuart Henry and Dragan Milovanovic's *Constitutive Criminology: Beyond Postmodernism*[176] and their edited collection *Constitutive Criminology at Work: Applications to Crime and Justice.*[177] These are backed up and further explicated by extensive writings.[178] Most postmodernism engages in the deconstruction of existing discourses. Postmodernists find it harder to construct positive theoretical frameworks. Henry and Milovanovic attempt just that.

Henry and Milovanovic's account of postmodernism is fairly standard. There are no privileged knowledges: everyone or anyone is an expert. Postmodernism celebrates diversity, plurality and the subjugated. It does this so much that it includes authors who deny that they are postmodernists. Postmodernism had its roots in post-structuralist French thought in the late 1960s and 1970s. Its starting point is a disillusion with the modernist thought, notably Marxism, but also with liberal theories of progress. Postmodernism links to a shift from manufacturing of goods and services for their usefulness to the manufacturing of goods and services valuable only for their image. This could be described as a shift to a 'consumer society', an 'informational society' or a 'risk society'. The chief way in which modernism is attacked is through 'deconstruction' of 'texts'. All discourse of any kind is a text, as are all phenomena and events. Thus discourse can be written, spoken or can be a film or television image or indeed, a dream. Deconstruction tears a text apart and reveals its contradictions and assumptions. Various earlier ideas anticipated some of postmodernism, notably Freud's ideas as interpreted by Lacan, symbolic interactionism and Matza's theory of neutralization and drift. As we have seen, postmodernism involves discourse analysis. Discourse analysis sees people as formed by and through their use of language. People do not occupy 'roles', they occupy 'discursive subject positions'.[179]

There is a fairly standard and widespread riposte to postmodernism, some main features of which are as follows. There *are* arguably some quite widespread patterns of oppression, for example capitalism, patriarchy, which have quite well-established explanations, even if there are problems and anomalies. It denies grand theory except for its own grand theories. Given the overwhelming number of dubious theories employed, it is a bit hard to know where to start in producing a critique. Postmodernists play fast and loose with scientific theory. Heisenberg's indeterminacy principle properly applies to subatomic phenomena, and society is not subatomic. Postmodernism is a reaction to the failure of the left in France in 1968 and in Britain from 1979. A very lengthy book would be needed to give a thorough account of these criticisms, which are in any case available elsewhere.[180]

Postmodernists emphasize some features of the modern world which lead to claims that we are now living in 'postmodernity'. This is one major reason for their advocacy of what might be called the postmodernist theory of knowledge involving the death of grand theory and the equal status of a multiplicity of approaches to truth. There is a two-fold critical riposte to these claims. The first line of argument is that the division between postmodernity and modernity is not at all sharp. There may, for example, be more emphasis today on the consumption of images than in past. However, 'postmodern' societies still manufacture steel, aluminium etc. using large quantities of gas, electricity and coal. Looking back to 'modern' societies, they were not exclusively concerned with usefulness. The consumption of products linked to image was discussed at least as far back as Thorstein Veblen's *The Theory of the Leisure Class*[181] and noted in the pop sociology of Vance Packard.[182] Recognizing a greater shift to the consumption of images does not in itself require a new theory of knowledge. The same comment is made in the context of criminal justice by Penna and Yar.[183] They point out that Hallsworth's identification of a 'postmodern penality' involves the conflation of statements from politicians and selected aspects of the criminal justice system of some countries mixed with a new epistemology to produce an entity which has very limited and dubious claims to reality.

The unthinking conflation of modernist and postmodernist elements is also found in the work of the constitutive criminologists. Having set out their postmodernist credentials and criticized the foundations of modernism, one would expect the central concepts used by the constitutive criminologists to be found within a postmodern analysis. However, the constitutive criminologists depend on aspects of modernism in order to identify variables to put in their equations and to identify the marginalized, oppressed etc. To take just one example, Milovanovic states that the 'control parameter' in the bifurcation diagram that chaos theory offers us to understand – 'the dynamic movement toward the creation of new master signifiers and replacement discourses' – is 'the emerging postmodern society characterised by alienation, the intrusion of the hyperreal, and capital logic (the commodification process and the law of equivalence)'.[184] 'Alienation' and 'capital logic' are both concepts derived from Marxism, part of the modernist social science that the new paradigm overthrows; and the three concepts listed would require considerable work before they could appear in any sensible way on a diagram with a numerical basis.[185]

Sometimes Henry and Milovanovic mention Marxism as one of the origins of constitutive criminology, or of its component theories, for example[186]

...it draws on complexity theory,[187] structural coupling,[188] strategic essentialism,[189] relational sets,[190] critical race theory and intersections,[191] autopoietic systems,[192] dialectical materialism,[193] and topology theory.[194]

In practice, however, the two main theoretical foundations of constitutive criminology are a particular interpretation of Lacan, and chaos theory. I have explained these briefly elsewhere.[195] Neither concept is really compatible with Marxism.

The use made of Lacan is in practice similar to Freire's concept of conscientization. The central idea here is that instead of presenting the peasant (in Freire) or the oppressed person or group (in Milovanovic) with a bank of knowledge the educator engages in a dialogue in which the knowledge and desires of the oppressed are articulated. In Marxism the basic claim is that revolutionaries develop and criticize existing knowledge so that it can be used by the working class or leading elements of it. *Capital*, for example, constitutes a substantial bank of knowledge. The idea is that it is tested against reality both in terms of explorations of features of the real world and through the experiences of revolutionaries attempting to bring about change. It is not, therefore, a matter of intellectuals from outside the working class simply inculcating existing knowledge into workers, but neither is it just a matter of the workers themselves elaborating their own ideas.

The more specifically Lacanian aspect of this process is that the aim is to articulate the desire of the oppressed. There are considerable problems about this. If the oppressed are prisoners of the criminal justice system they may have desires which are unjustly oppressive to others (e.g. paedophiles, members of right-wing militias, Muslim radicals who want to make Europe and the United States part of the caliphate). They may have desires which are legitimate in principle but too demanding of resources when the needs of others are taken into account. For example, sufferers from multiple sclerosis legitimately want money to be spent on research and on immediate help for their condition, but the rival claims of people in Africa suffering from AIDS or at risk of malaria need to be borne in mind. To balance such competing claims a theory of distributive justice is needed, but the constitutive criminologists elevate the claims of local, sectional systems of justice instead.

The second major underlying theory is chaos theory. Chaos theory works with fractal geometries in which there are, for example, 3.7 dimensions. The constitutive criminologists do not give an explanation of how many dimensions there are in society, but it generally seems to operate in three dimensions. Chaos theorists are interested in situations where a very small initial difference becomes massively magnified following repeated iteration.[196] The stock example is of a butterfly waving its wings in the Brazilian rainforest and causing a hurricane in Florida three weeks later. Constitutive criminologists adopt three main outcomes from chaos theory: undecidability or uncertainty, the idea that one individual can make a difference and the analysis of far from equilibrium conditions.

Sufficiently radical undecidability renders social science and basic ethical principles useless. We normally condemn acts of random violence and commend acts of charity because the former cause harm and the latter benefits. However, it is not difficult to think of occasions when the opposite applies. If someone had happened to hit one of the tube bombers on 7/7 over the head with a baseball bat for no good reason whatsoever there would have been a considerable social benefit.

However, we base social science and morality on probabilities rather than extreme unlikelihoods.

The examples which the constitutive criminologists give of one person making a difference are of one person helping a young boy to avoid becoming a juvenile delinquent, or of someone going on a demonstration which makes a difference. These are familiar examples, but the kind of random dramatic effect triggered off by the Brazilian butterfly is much less predictable. The nearest analogue I can think of is of Gary Hart who allegedly fell asleep at the wheel of his car and instead of waking up on the rumble strip at the edge of the road caused the Selby train crash with the loss of 11 lives and millions of pounds. Such events are so unpredictable that nothing very much can be done with them.

In chaos theory far from equilibrium conditions arise when perhaps four initial conditions are altered in such a way that the system as a whole changes dramatically. The social example of this which is offered is of the United States in the 1960s, faced with a war in Vietnam, rioting blacks and demonstrating students. This led to withdrawal from Vietnam, the war on poverty and affirmative action. However, it is not difficult to think of other societies faced with extreme stress where the outcome was some form of right-wing dictatorship. Obvious examples would be the Weimar Republic leading up to Hitler or the failed revolution in June 1848 in France leading to the rise of Louis Napoleon Bonaparte III.

The constitutive criminologists praise various practical interventions, but apart from trying to produce far from equilibrium conditions – which is highly unpredictable and potentially disastrous – their suggestions are part of the established repertoire of radicals in a liberal society. They favour prison abolitionism with some mentions of restorative justice but without very much explanation as to how it would work out in practice. They praise self-help groups for victims and ex-prisoners. They favour intervening in the media. They are keen on social judo in which the power of oppressors is turned against them, which is a more interesting idea but probably only applicable in some special instances.

Conclusion on constitutive criminology

What has been presented here is only a sketch of the voluminous writings of Milovanovic and associates, and the critique of their theories is similarly limited. However, enough has been presented to show that their approach is quite different from Marxism in spite of their occasional references and use of Marxist concepts. It should also, hopefully, be clear that the practical outcome of constitutive criminology is generally very limited. The only exception to this is their espousal of far from equilibrium conditions, which has the potential to lead to dramatic but entirely unpredictable change.

5
British Critical Criminology

Introduction

Just as American radical criminology developed against the background of the late 1960s and early 1970s, so also did its British counterpart. Some of the major political and social changes since that time are shared with the United States, whilst others are not.

One really dramatic change is the position of socialism itself. Britain was seen as a country where socialism, involving the collective ownership of the means of production was to some extent on the political agenda. After all, some 25% of the British economy was publicly owned thanks to the nationalization programme of the Attlee Labour government from 1945 onwards. In the 1970s British socialists in the main did not regard the Soviet Union or China as a socialist paradise on earth. There was, obviously, much debate about exactly what criticisms were appropriate and about how the Soviet economy should be characterized. However, the human rights abuses involved in the gulag, the relative lack of freedom of criticism, the lack of genuine democracy and substantial economic inequalities would form part of most people's picture of the problems to be considered. Nonetheless, the Soviet system was widely seen as a demonstration that a planned economy could be made to work. In international terms, moreover, the Soviet system had been doing rather well. In 1975 the United States finally acknowledged defeat in Vietnam. The domino theory worked in that Cambodia and Laos became communist countries. At about the same time the fall of the Portuguese dictatorship nearly led to a communist society in Western Europe, and led to what were seen as communist victories in Angola, Mozambique and Guinea-Bissau. Memories of the glorious near miss in France in May 1968 were still strong. Many in the West felt they lacked a good understanding of the Cultural Revolution in China, but found the idea that young people could overthrow bureaucracies and make major changes in their society inspiring.

In Britain – and this forms part of the background to critical criminology to which we shall return – there was a set of problems linked to the difficulties of running a capitalist economy with a powerful trade union movement. Over the 1960s and 1970s the unions were able to win a series of inflationary wage settlements, and various attempts at a wages policy failed. Critical criminology was developed at a time when socialist politics to the left of Labour (as it then was) were more realistic than socialist politics to the left of Labour (as it now is).

The reverses suffered by traditional socialism in various guises since that time hardly need spelling out. Internationally the Soviet Union has ended, as has the planned economy in its various component parts both there and in Eastern Europe. China remains an officially communist country but has been fostering capitalism since 1978 with annual growth rates close to 10%. Vietnam and Laos have also experimented with a capitalist sector. Cuba has had to encourage tourism in order to survive following the collapse of its trading arrangements with the eastern bloc. In Britain the unions and the Labour Party have not recovered from their encounter with Mrs Thatcher. Union membership is down and much of the legislation contained in the five trade union Acts passed by Mrs Thatcher and her successors remains on the statute book. The Labour Party may have been rendered electable by Tony Blair but at the cost of dropping Clause 4, considerable strains with the unions, and policy changes which leave the erstwhile right-winger Roy Hattersley as a critic on the left.

At least as significant as these political defeats are a whole series of economic and social changes perhaps best summed up in the idea of globalization. Earlier, in the search for a credible, up to date version of Marxism, some of the main ideas involved in globalization were considered in an exposition of the work of Manuel Castells. What follows is a more general description. Globalization has involved a whole series of interlocking developments. The massive application of computers and microchips to production has led to much greater flexibility. It has become much easier to either automate areas of production or to outsource them to places where labour is much cheaper than in advanced capitalist societies. Along with this the workforce has had to become much more flexible. Reasonably steady employment for life is largely a thing of the past and a much larger proportion of the workforce is on temporary contracts. A large part of the newly flexible workforce comprises women whose mothers did not work outside the home to the same extent. Capital flows freely and rapidly around the world, making it difficult for individual states to place limits on its operations. Although Thatcher, Major and Blair have deliberately exposed Britain to the forces of globalization unlike, for example, France (pre-Sarkozy), the fate of nations which attempt to entirely insulate themselves from it is probably to become similar to North Korea or to Albania before the collapse of communism. Likewise there is some danger that unions which are too successful in negotiating attractive conditions for their members, or countries which provide themselves with too good a welfare state will simply trigger off a departure of capitalist enterprises for more compliant economies. Inequality has increased in Britain and the United States as a specific consequence of right-wing government policies. In addition to this, however, there has been a promotion of making profits without much thought for the social consequences, covered by the fig leaf that the benefits of capitalist growth will trickle down the social scale. Company chief executives are paid enormous packages for enhancing profitability by sacking large parts of their workforce, worsening the conditions of remaining workers and moving operations overseas. Along with this has gone an unprecedented degree of fraud perpetrated by people at the head of companies, of which the Enron scandal is only the best-known. Working people in the advanced countries and in the developing countries are faced with more powerful and aggressive capitalists then was the case in the 1970s.

There was some recognition of the possibility of multinational companies simply moving their operations to places where labour was cheaper (stressed in the 1970s particularly by left-wing advocates of Britain remaining part of the European Community). And there was certainly the recognition of the danger of a run on the pound, a balance of payments crisis and the intervention of the IMF. However, the current worry that manufacturing, data processing, call centres (much less developed in the 1970s), software development and other increasingly skilled technical labour could be moved to India, China, Indonesia, Cambodia, Malaysia etc. was much less realistic in the 1970s. Many people on the left subscribed to the Alternative Economic Strategy, which would have involved the nationalization of at least 25 leading British companies

The theoretical background has also shifted dramatically. Marxism is seen as discredited and for many has been replaced by postmodernism as a guiding theory. There is a specific discussion at the end of the previous chapter on radical American criminology of the role of postmodernism in criminological theory, particularly in the work of Henry and Milovanovic. Although it is possible to attempt to build an alliance for change between groupings in a postmodernist framework, postmodernism generally undermines 'grand theories' such as Marxism or feminism, and with them any notion that large-scale social changes would benefit large numbers of people. In the 1970s this was basically in the future. John Francois Lyotard's *The Postmodern Condition*[1] appeared in English in 1984; a couple of books by Derrida appeared in English in the 1970s, but *Of Grammatology* and a set of essays on Husserl did not spark off an immediate reaction. Foucault was known in the 1970s, but in the guise of an interesting book on *Madness and Civilisation* and another on *The Birth of the Clinic*, plus books on *The Archaeology of Knowledge*. The very influential works *Discipline and Punish* and the three-volume *History of Sexuality* appeared in English only in the late 1970s, too late to have any influence on the initial works of critical criminology. The later work of Foucault has, in my view, been particularly damaging to a Marxist perspective. Its notions that power is everywhere and power is productive allow scholars to feel that they are being very radical in demonstrating specific oppression attached to particular institutions and practices whilst failing to consider more general problems of oppression and possibilities of liberation. The link between power and knowledge undermines the idea, common to liberalism and Marxism that it is possible for the oppressed or for people who side with them to discover truths about society which will have an emancipatory effect. In brief, then, the early developers of critical criminology had less by way of misleading theories to contest.

The new criminology

The first major work of critical criminology is *The New Criminology: For a Social Theory of Deviance* by Ian Taylor, Paul Walton and Jock Young.[2] This book says surprisingly little about a new way of understanding criminology. It reads more like an unusually critical criminological theory textbook. It discusses a long series of theories from other people but has literally only a page or two about the way in which the authors think that criminology should be practised. The second half of the title gives a good indication of much of the line of argument. The authors want to insist that crime has no ontological reality but is socially defined, and that the major discipline for understanding crime should be sociology and not psychology or biology. These themes are pursued through the criticism of previous authors. Thus they object to the positivist notion that there is 'one widely held conception of reality' in which, for example, Cecil Rhodes is a philanthropist. From Stokely Carmichael's black American perspective, they point out, he was 'a murderer, a rapist, a plunderer and a thief'... 'The positivist by appealing to law or to consensus ignores the manner in which power determines these "obvious" sources of objectivity', and they agree with Richard Lictman, who argues that patterns of shared meaning are determined by the ruling class.[3] Positivism gives 'the structure of power, wealth and variety which patterns the reaction against deviancy, and sustains the authority of the existing social arrangements...the stamp of approval by "science"'.[4] A psychologist working for the Home Office is said to 'interpret hedonistic and expressive subcultures not as cultures at all but merely as aggregates of inadequate individuals who are excitable, have a low tolerance of frustration, maturity etc.'.[5] Positivism sees the majority in society as choosing the current consensus freely, whilst a minority of deviants are determined by their peculiar biology or psychology.[6] In contrast, Taylor, Walton and Young want to emphasize that a deviant may be involved in transcending or resisting existing values as a matter of free choice.[7] British analyses of urban problems by figures such as Rex and Moore, Downes and Lambert are praised for breaking away from the positivist view of deviants as pathological blemishes on an integrated whole, and allowing for the existence of a struggle over space in the city and the lack of opportunities and gratification in particular urban contexts, although they fail to develop the sociology of the overall political economy.[8] Edwin Sutherland's idea of differential association fails to stress 'human choice' and the resulting behaviour appears 'totally determined'.[9]

One theme, which emerges from the discussion of Eysenck as an important positivist, is that society is conceived of as requiring a high degree of cooperation between very large groups of people, which requires an engineering of social consent.[10] This idea, with which Taylor, Walton and Young seem to agree, is perhaps more characteristic of a modern industrial society requiring a high degree of cooperation from the working class and subject to considerable disruption from small groups of individuals than of the society we now have. Today small groups of workers have less capacity to be disruptive, partly because of more restrictive trade union legislation, but also because in many cases their jobs can be moved to other countries.

Durkheim comes out particularly well as a predecessor of critical criminology because of his insistence on social rather than ethical, psychological or economic explanation. Taylor, Walton and Young emphasize his radicalism, his striving for a meritocracy in which there is no inherited wealth, and labour is divided in such a way that social inequalities express natural inequalities.[11]

Merton is seen as engaging in a limited but sociological critique of the ideology of the American Dream. He sees the Dream as promising monetary success to everyone who works with sufficient effort. However, the rules of the game are left unclear, and it is claimed that there are equal opportunities in a society where people start from highly unequal positions. He favoured instead a properly meritocratic society in which there would be opportunities for everyone of sufficient merit and the procedural rules would be respected.[12] This may look like a substantial criticism, but the general capitalist framework which is the source of the defective American meritocracy is not discussed.[13] The strain which is the central feature of Merton's theory predicts lawbreaking by lower-class individuals but not by the well-to-do, and Merton fails to recognize the crimes of the affluent.[14] These criticisms are very much the same as those by Messner and Rosenfeld which were discussed at the beginning of the chapter on radical American criminology above.

Taylor, Walton and Young see symbolic interactionism and labelling theory as 'a remarkable advance towards a fully social theory of deviance'.[15] A crucial feature of this approach is that crime is not an ontological reality 'for an act to be regarded as deviant, a deviant label has to be conferred upon it by society'.[16] Thus, for example, the taking of life can be a patriotic duty in war or 'a normal, if regrettable, response, as in the case of *crimes passionelles* or euthanasia'. The drug LSD was legal until 'comparatively recently'. However, they comment, 'certain social meanings are only acceptable in certain social contexts'. Thus killing someone in England in 1972 would not be described as an act of patriotism because that is a social definition used largely in times of war, and England was not at war in 1972. The social meaning of acts is 'not as variable or arbitrary as many of these theorists would have them to be'. Deviants 'often endow their acts with meaning' ... 'derived from a fairly constant stock of social meanings which exist to describe physical acts'.[17] They apply this point to Lemert's distinction between primary and secondary deviation. Lemert is fully aware that people who are stigmatized because of their primary deviation are faced with a range of choices within a deviant career, but to be consistent this applies to initial infractions as well.[18] Again, in the real world rule-breaking can be taken up and dropped, even in the extreme case of imprisonment – labelling does not automatically consign an individual to a deviant career.[19] As we saw in the section on Marxism and the definition of crime, the indefinitely flexible definitions of symbolic interactionism are neither very plausible in themselves nor a suitable foundation for a Marxist account of crime.

The reader starts to expect a more positive account of the 'new criminology' in the chapter on Marx, Engels and Bonger, but even there we find more of a negative critique than of building blocks of a new approach. In contrast to their constant emphasis that deviance is frequently an oppositional choice, Engels in *The Condition of the Working Class in England in 1844* mainly sees crime, such as alcoholism as a sign of demoralization: it turns a man into an offender as certainly as heating water causes it to boil.[20] They properly understand the much-quoted 'functionalist' passage from Marx's *Economic Manuscripts of 1861–3* on 'The apologist conception of the productivity of all professions' in which criminals are depicted as productive as a polemic against functionalist analysis.[21] More positively they sympathize with Marx's view that the division of labour and, therefore, crime is not 'inevitable or normal', and that crime is an expression of 'the struggle of the isolated individual'.[22] Marx does not, however, stick to this. He also sees crime as produced with the regularity of a physical phenomenon by the conditions of bourgeois society, praising Quetelet's book and thus 'finds uneasy company with positive scientists', engaging in economic determinism rather than seeing crime as an individual reaction to economic conditions.[23] However, he does display some awareness of the role of social control in leading to deviation, commenting that the statistical decrease in crime between 1854 and 1858 'is to be exclusively attributed to some technical changes in British Jurisdiction' so that relatively arbitrary decisions by the state or the criminal justice system could lead to different outcomes.[24] But, alas, he displays feet of clay in his acceptance of the conventional view of his day that most crime originates with the 'dangerous classes', the lumpenproletariat, who are seen as unproductive and parasitical rather than rationally responding to their conditions.[25]

There are a whole series of assertions in the previous paragraph. The issue of crime as an oppositional choice; the idea of an individual reaction to economic conditions, and the concept of the lumpenproletariat will all be examined in the next part of this book. Already in the section on definitions it has been argued that consensus crimes are a feature of a variety of social systems, and the expectation of Marxism must be that it contributes to explaining why they occur under a particular system rather than portrays it as a legitimate response to oppression.

Taylor, Walton and Young are quite definite however, about the 'explicit philosophical anthropology' to be found in the *Economic and Philosophical Manuscripts,* quoting the passage

> Man is a *species-being* not only in the sense that he makes the community (his own as well as those of other things) his object both practically and theoretically, but also (and this is simply another expression of the same thing) in the sense that he treats himself as the present living species, as a *universal* and consequently free being.[26]

They see the

> bulk of Marx's later work [as] concerned with the demonstration of the ways in which the social nature of consciousness has been distorted, imprisoned or diverted by the social arrangements developed over time ... Man is struggling to be free, but cannot realise freedom ... until such time as he is free of exploitative relationships which are outmoded and unnecessary.[27]

The role of the theory of alienation as a possible explanation of crime and more generally of the capitalist system will be considered in the next part.

They give a brief description of a 'full-blown Marxist theory of deviance', which would ask with greater emphasis who makes the rules, and attempt to locate the defining agencies 'quite specifically in the relationship to the overweening structure of material production and the division of labour'. The theory would proceed with 'a notion of men which would distinguish it quite clearly from classical, positivist or interactionist "images" of man'.

> ... men's reaction to labelling by the powerful would not be seen to be simply a cultural problem – a problem of reacting to a legal status or a social stigma: it would necessarily be seen to be bound up with men's degree of consciousness of domination and subordination in a wider structure of power relationships operating in particular types of economic context.[28]

Such an approach would allow links to be made with the insights of interactionism, and it might also enable us to sustain the assertion that 'much deviance is in itself a political act'.[29] Here again we have the idea of crime as an oppositional choice, to be considered in the next part.

Taylor, Walton and Young move on to discuss the work of Willem Bonger. They note that Bonger is more seriously concerned than Marx with the causal chain linking crime with economic conditions, and that he is more concerned with the criminal activity of the bourgeoisie. They are critical of one of his major strategies which is to look for the origins of criminal thought, then to look for forces which might prevent the execution of criminal thought, then to look at the occasion for the commission of criminal acts. Criminal thought is thus crucial for Bonger. He sees its origin in the conditions of misery forced on sections of the working class under capitalism and the greed encouraged by capitalism. For Taylor, Walton and Young it is not satisfactory to see criminal thought taking over individuals. One reason for this is that it assumes that crime and non-crime are clear classes of behaviour rather than labels which get stuck on people. They are also not very happy with Bonger's antidote to criminal thought, which is moral training, which the proletariat largely lacks. Whilst they admire the way in which Bonger tries to link a variety of crimes including economic crimes, sexual crimes, political crimes, pathological crimes and crimes from vengeance to the capitalist environment, they do not like the way that these links are formed in a positivist fashion. They also admire the way that he anticipated elements of Merton's strain theory and aspects of differential association, but are less keen on his 'crudely statistical technique of verification and elaboration'.[30]

They are particularly critical of Bonger's position that the law 'while certainly the creation of a dominant class – is a genuine reflection of some universal social and moral sentiment'.[31] Thus socialism emerges in Bonger as a more orderly society. The solution to problems of criminality is 'not so much to challenge the labels and the processing of capitalist law as it used to wage a responsible and orderly political battle for the reform of a divisive social structure'.[32] He thus basically has a correctional and social democratic perspective, although on occasions he can see crimes as both egoistic and altruistic – motivated by poverty in an unjust society.[33] He thus fails generally to present deviance as a matter of 'actors exercising degrees of choice and possessing a dignity of their own'.[34] He presents 'socialism' as 'an alternative and desirable set of social institutions' which will discourage egoism and encourage corporate cooperativeness. In contrast Taylor, Walton and Young want to look at the dialectics of human action defined by the powerful in particular periods as 'criminal' and its relationship to human liberation.[35] As will have been seen from the section on the definition of crime and from the above discussion of Bonger, he comes out better from the perspective of this book than in Taylor, Walton and Young.

They move on to a consideration of the new conflict theories of Turk, Dahrendorf and Quinney, but are largely dismissive of them. Turk broadly accepts the existing order; Quinney largely accepts contemporary pluralism and Dahrendorf basically accepts the inevitability of a degree of conflict under capitalism.[36] They all, along with Marx and Bonger, basically see criminal man as pathological. An alternative view is to see men as 'purposive creators and innovators of action', and crime as individual or collective action to resolve inequalities of power.[37]

In the conclusion of the book they finally state some of the features of a fully social theory of crime. Their aim is

> A state of freedom from material necessity, and (therefore) of material incentive, a release from the constraints of forced production, and abolition of the forced division of labour, and a set of social arrangements, therefore, in which there would be no politically, economically, and socially induced need to criminalise deviance.[38]

In formal terms this requires a political economy of crime, setting deviant acts against the background of the rapidly changing circumstances of advanced industrial society; a social psychology of crime, recognizing that 'men may *consciously* choose the deviant road'; it needs to be recognized that the deviant act may not necessarily produce the intended result. The immediate origins of social reaction need to be considered: it may be thought preferable to keep odd behaviour in the family, or not worthwhile to report behaviour to the police, or not worthwhile for the police to record the behaviour. Beyond this a political economy of social reaction is needed, linking social reaction to a class society, for example in the tendency not to use the criminal law to deal with crimes of the powerful. It should be recognized that the deviant may use the reaction against him in a variety of ways which are open to choice, and that the deviant always has some awareness of the likelihood and consequences of reaction against him.[39] 'There is a crisis not just in social theory and social thought ... but in the society itself.'[40] 'The retreat from theory is over, and the politicisation of crime and criminology is imminent. Close reading of the classical social theorists reveals a basic agreement; the abolition of crime is possible under certain social arrangements.'[41] 'A criminology which is not normatively committed to the abolition of inequalities of wealth and power, and in particular of inequalities in property and life chances, is inevitably bound to fall into correctionalism.'[42] 'Crime is ever and always that behaviour seen to be problematic within the framework of those social arrangements: for crime to be abolished, then, those social arrangements themselves must also be subject to fundamental social change.' 'The task is to create a society in which the facts of human diversity, whether personal, organic or social, are not subject to the power to criminalise'.[43]

Critical Criminology

The above ideas emerge more clearly in the first two essays of the collection edited by Taylor, Walton and Young, *Critical Criminology*. In the first essay the authors approvingly quote some of the major features of the sociology of deviance that emerged from the National Deviancy Conference. Deviant action must be examined in terms of its meaningfulness to the deviant actor, taking seriously his vocabularies of motive, and not explained away as a form of pathology. Society contains alternative realities, all with their own authenticity. There was a revolt against correctionalism and a tendency to be critical of the judiciary, prison administrators, social workers and psychiatrists, all seen as agents of social control.[44] Social workers were seen as agents of control, individualizing and controlling problems of unemployment, racial tension, industrial and social discontent.[45] Orthodox criminology is an attempt to 'control the worst excesses of a punitive and repressive Conservative judicial system'.[46] Taylor, Walton and Young follow Gouldner in favouring a 'psychedelic culture' which rejects the central values of industrial society such as moneymaking, achievement, routine economic roles and the inhibition of expression. Psychedelic culture encourages each to do his own thing.[47] The criminology which goes with this orientation is anti-utilitarian and concentrates on victimless crimes. Its methodology is not scientific and empirical but intuitive. The deviant is seen as authentic and the state is seen as exacerbating his deviant characteristics.[48] Radical deviancy theory was linked to the development of radical social workers, lawyers, people classified as mentally ill, claimants, prisoners and defendants, and the development of women's liberation, gay liberation and various black power movements, an assertion of 'radical diversity'.[49]

> [Radical theory favours a] socialist conception of man [which] would insist on the unlimited nature of human potential in a *human* society, and specifically in a society in which man was freed from having to engage only in the essentially animalistic pursuit of material production in order to feed, consume and exist.[50]

Radical theory might involve exposing the double standards of ruling groups, but should not do so on the basis of a moral appeal. Instead the point is to show that rule-breaking is 'institutionalised, regular and widespread' amongst the powerful, a result of the structural position that they hold.[51] Appropriate examples would be illegal corporate profit or the much higher rate of prosecution of social security frauds than of failures to pay tax, or the massive excess profits made on some defence contracts compared to blue-collar crime. Bad publicity forced Ferranti industries to repay £4.5 million excess profit from a single defence contract in the same year that working-class criminals who robbed a train of £2.5 million in the 'Great Train Robbery' were pursued by the entire British police force, and ultimately sentences of up to 30 years were handed down to the central figures.[52] Similarly, the criminal justice system can be shown to penalize lower-class individuals rather than operate even handedly across the social scale.[53] Crime is overwhelmingly property crime, which is not surprising in 'a society predicated on the unequal right to the accumulation of property'.[54] White-collar crime against property can be shown to massively exceed offences carried out by working-class people.[55] Criminal statistics can be seen as a measure of the degree of compliance in an industrial society, of the 'extent to which the distribution of property is latently accepted or rejected among certain sections of the working population'.[56] The analysis of crime must be a social analysis.[57] This analysis must include a grasp of historical evolution, and such an analysis reveals the primacy of material conditions as the determinants of criminal and legal norms.[58] 'For Marx as for us it would appear that the central objective of a materialist criminology should be to establish the role of law in affecting production, and via production, the whole lifestyle and culture of a given society.'[59]

> A crucial task would, of course, be to explain the structural and the class differences existing within and between capitalist societies, in contributing further to our understanding of the antagonisms which result, as Marx understood, from the lack of correspondence between the development of material production and the development of social and legal relations.[60]

A radical criminology would examine the role of labour legislation in socializing labour and criminalizing those who refuse to be socialized.[61]

The second essay, by Jock Young, is entitled 'Working-Class Criminology'. After listing the major features of orthodox, 'scientific' criminology he goes on to describe the alternative:

> In the new deviancy theory the deviant is, above all, a rational, conscious actor, free of the determinants of past events and physical or psychic disturbance, and existing in a homogenous and normatively-consistent subculture.[62]

The new deviancy theory takes little interest in utilitarian crime but focuses on expressive deviancy: marijuana use rather than burglary, prostitution rather than homicide. The emphasis on non-intervention is extended to some forms of juvenile delinquency, which are held to be innocuous if left alone, and to 'homicide, rape and child-molesting' because these crimes can involve victim-precipitation.[63] Young argues that the organized Left could have contributed greatly at this point, but failed to do so. Young argues that this new deviancy theory is 'constructed out of the inverted conceptual debris of its positivist opponents' and faced a series of problems because of its limited conceptions of human nature and social order.[64]

The first of these is that there was considerable consensus over crimes against the person and at least some crimes over property, contrasting with a lack of reaction against the activities of corporations and the powerful.[65] Another problem is that the rejection of statistics in new deviancy theory excluded its adherents from important debates and from the investigation of corporate or white-collar crime, which is far more extensive than one would imagine if the law is constructed in the interests of the powerful.[66] Again, why does some behaviour appear to be irrational? Why do some men behave the way the positivists say they do?[67] Other problems are that rather than simply being rational, deviants can experience considerable psychic disturbance and bodily anxiety, and that some kind of standard of normality is needed in order to talk of lapses in rationality.[68] Why is there a continuing respect for property in 'grossly inequitable societies' rather than a widespread recourse to crime or an extensive pursuit of socialism.[69] Young does not find typical explanations such as the betrayal of left-wing leaders, the role of the mass media or that of distorted character structure plausible. Instead he argues that it is necessary to understand how bourgeois ideology contains enough distorted truth to be rationally believed, that it provides some measure of reassurance 'for the very real problems of justice and order confronting the working class', is presented with such a high degree of unanimity as to appear rational and is maintained by an effective social control apparatus.[70]

Young went on to develop left realism as an approach to crime and had obviously developed some of its central ideas by this stage. He comments: 'it is a simple fact that the majority of working class crime is intra- and not inter-class in its choice of target, area of activity and distribution'.[71] This fact, he says, provides leverage for the bourgeois ideological conception of social justice, because working-class people have a considerable stake in social justice. They want a fair return for their labour and to believe that those who cheat will be punished. In this context the criminal is 'an enormously useful scapegoat', diverting attention from the more serious activities of the powers that be.[72] The state and the consensus in society appear natural.[73] Young argues that the locus of control in societies such as ours is chiefly the work situation. The extent of conformity amongst privileged parts of the working class is hardly surprising if they can remember the experience of unemployment before the war. Harsher methods of control are directed at those outside the workplace who are seen as idle.[74]

Moving on from these criticisms to the positive concerns of socialist criminology he argues that a major task is to identify the interests of the working class, which will involve considering the approach of the Left parties to deviant behaviour.[75] Criminal statistics need to be analysed carefully as a 'blurred but useful picture of the degree of respect for property and the extent of social disorganisation and conflict'.[76] The exaggerated notions of freedom of the new deviancy theorists need to be tempered by a recognition of, for example, the role of heroin addiction as an 'insidious expression of exploitation, and an agency for passivity and defeat' in black ghettos. Mental illness can be a source of appalling unhappiness and should not simply be seen as an escape from capitalism.[77]

> The reality of crime in the streets can be the reality of human suffering and personal disaster. We have to argue, therefore, strategically, for the exercise of social control, but also to argue that such control must be exercised within the working class community and not by external policing agencies.[78]

The ultimate goal in such a struggle must be a socialist culture which is diverse and expressive – that is, a culture which takes up the progressive components in pluralism, whilst rejecting those activities which are directly the product of the brutalization of existing society (however diverse, expressive or idiosyncratic their manifestation).[79]

Critique of critical criminology

How much was critical criminology a child of its time, rendered irrelevant by the subsequent changes mentioned above? How well does it stand up as an attempt at Marxist criminology?

Critical criminology was certainly associated with some of the wilder excesses of the late 1960s. This stands out particularly strongly in the contribution to the *Critical Criminology* collection by Geoff Pearson, which promotes 'misfit sociology' based not just on symbolic interactionism but on the ideas of Laing and Cooper and Timothy Leary. For Pearson deviance as a way of fighting the system can include obscenity as a means of claiming language back from the oppressors, based on the ideas of Rubin and Marcuse and the use of drugs to liberate the mind and body, as advocated by Timothy Leary.[80] He approvingly quotes David Cooper who describes the family as a 'gas chamber': 'the most benevolent institutions of our society become our oppressors in a way that relegates the gas chambers of Auschwitz to the level of a naive fumbling attempt at massacre'.[81] Misfit sociology, he says, defends the unreasonable nature of the deviant. Personal liberation is a necessary feature of and prelude to political liberation. We get some idea of what this can involve in his approving quotation from Jeff Nuttall, the author of *Bomb Culture* on the importance of 'daring the uncountenanceable':

> it's the feeling of exhilaration following the first act which violates the previous restriction, the moment after leaving the Church, committing buggery, making love to one's own sex, when new areas of freedom open out limitlessly like vast meadows.[82]

One might think, given Jock Young's subsequent condemnation of 'left idealism' and espousal of left realism, that he has relegated much of the ideas of critical criminology to the realm of youthful excesses, but this is not so.

Two recent collections,[83] make it clear that critical criminology lives on in the work of many authors, and that left realism is seen by its leading proponent, Jock Young, as a strand *within* critical criminology, not a replacement. The account which follows is taken from Young, but it is clear others would agree with him.

The heyday of the ideas in *The New Criminology* was the National Deviancy Conferences (1968–79), of which there were ten between 1969 and 1972. Young says that there were two major influences from North American criminology in these conferences: labelling theory and subculture theory. These were put together with broadly Marxist ideas about social structure. Ideas about subcultures were put together with the work of socialist historians, thus emphasizing working-class resistance to capitalism, and particularly the resistance of working-class youth. Labelling theory was re-worked in the form of ideas about moral panics, with the idea that what lay behind moral panics was perhaps a manipulated resentment against people who challenged the work ethic. These ideas were vigorously pursued in *The New Criminology*. Young accepts that *The New Criminology* was deficient when it came to issues of gender and race, both of which were less discussed then than now. However he largely stands by the analysis in the book. He says that the very best work in the spirit of *The New Criminology* was Hall et al.'s *Policing the Crisis*, which does deal with issues of race. *Policing the Crisis* also begins to look at street crime as a serious problem for the working class, and thus to raise the issues which led to the development of Left Realism.[84]

In a subsequent article on the same theme Young emphasizes that the enemy of critical criminology was the empiricist approach of administrative criminology. The first step taken at the National Deviancy Conferences was to re-establish the link between criminology and sociology, and then to present a series of ironies which has served to turn establishment criminology on its head:

- *Self fulfilment* – that illusions and stereotypes of crime can be real in their consequences and self-fulfilling in reality.
- *Seriousness* – that crime occurred throughout the social structure and that the crimes of the powerful were more serious in their consequences than the crimes of the poorer.
- *Ontology* – that crime has no ontological reality and that the 'same' behaviour can be constructed totally differently.
- *Decentring* – a criminal justice system is a minor part of the system of social control.
- *Selectivity* – criminal law is selective and substantially unequal, although phrased in the language of equality.
- *Counter productivity* – that the prison and criminal justice system produces criminals rather than diffusing criminality.
- *Socialisation* – that the core values of competitiveness, acquisitiveness, individualism and hedonism are close to the motivations for crime.
- *Contradiction* – that the ideas which legitimate and hold the system together are the very ones which society thwarts and the frustrations generated seem to break the system apart.

- *Function* – that 'the criminal', 'the outsider', 'the other', far from destroying the fabric of society, produce stereotypes which hold the fabric together.
- *Secondary harm* – that the primary harm of a social problem is frequently of a lesser order than the secondary harm accruing from intervention to control it, the prime example of this being regulation of drug use.[85]

Young comments 'The 10 ironies I have listed would seem to me as important today as they ever were, in fact all the more so with the growth of the American gulag, the penchant for the scapegoating of the poor, the immigrant and the drug-user, and the way in which crime control has become a major currency of politics.'[86] Young then gives a lengthy list of books which are within the traditions of critical criminology, and which are quite contemporary.[87] He acknowledges, however, that there has been a major series of transformations from what he describes as modern society to late modern society, and which broadly correspond to the changes described above.

To begin an assessment of this, let us start by acknowledging briefly the seriousness of Young's comment that critical criminology was a child of its time because it did not consider gender or race at all seriously. In criminology these are particularly important omissions. If the human race all behaved like women, most criminologists would be out of a job and the criminal justice system could be wound down to a very low level. On most measures women commit only about 20% of the amount of crime committed by men, and most of the crime that they do commit is at the less serious end of the spectrum.[88] In addition, two of the crimes dealt with least satisfactorily are domestic and sexual violence. Both of these are basically crimes carried out by men on women, and they are dealt with so ineffectively by the criminal justice system in Britain as to justify the allegation that we live in a patriarchy. There are marked differences in the treatment of races by the criminal justice system, and in particular Afro-Caribbean men get an undue level of attention right through from stop and search or accusations of driving whilst black, to arrest, trial and imprisonment.[89]

Looking at other writings in the two volumes which continue the themes of critical criminology it is clear, as indicated above, that some of the work has been affected by the ideas of postmodernism and Foucault, with the effects described above.

But what, most importantly for us, of the relationship between critical criminology and Marxism?

A central theme in critical criminology is that it is based on a social theory of crime, for which the appropriate academic discipline is sociology. Marxism notoriously fails to respect academic disciplines. It would be surprising if Marxist criminology were not heavily based on political economy, but it is not apparent to me why the extensive use of sociological ideas drawn from Durkheim is a sound basis for Marxist criminology whilst some use of psychology or biology would be fatal to the enterprise. The more important issue would be how well supported the particular ideas turned out to be. My impression as a matter of fact is that most attempts to link crime to genetics, or extraversion and introversion, or maternal deprivation do not actually work very well. If someone happened to discover that a particular DNA sequence predicted a particular form of criminal behaviour with great regularity what would be the problem about fitting this into a Marxist analysis? The Marxist analysis should tell us the relationship between that particular form of criminal behaviour and, for example, social formations dominated by capitalism. The DNA analysis would tell us that particular categories of people would be expected to engage in the relevant form of criminal behaviour. The problem is more that the correlation is highly unlikely because genetic sequences have different effects in different environments, not, I think, that Marxism rules out such an approach.

A much more substantial problem concerns the definition of crime. It will be recalled that in the section on the definition of crime a five-fold division was suggested; consensus crimes which feature in most societies; crimes relating to the running of the mode of production; crimes based on moral and religious principles; derivative crimes relating to the policing of other crimes; and finally crimes relating to the authority of the state. As was indicated, this approach is more sympathetic to conventional definitions than the one taken by the critical criminologists, which is uncomfortably close to the total flexibility of the symbolic interactionists.

Having made the above criticisms it remains to register that there are extensive and valuable features of critical criminology which should certainly be incorporated into Marxist criminology. Going down Jock Young's list this would apply to every single item with minor reservations apart from the reservation about the ontological reality of crime.

Finally, as will be made clear in the next part, there are a series of reasons for reservations about the disappearance of crime under socialism or communism.

Policing the Crisis

Policing the Crisis[90] is widely seen as a high point in the development of critical criminology. It includes in one volume a whole series of themes: a Marxist framework of crisis, Gramscian ideas about hegemony, moral panics, the development of an authoritarian state, subcultures and racism. Here we have to ask how well these themes fit together, whether the analysis has become dated, and to what extent it can contribute to a coherent Marxist framework for criminological theory.

The analysis which follows falls into three sections. The first looks at the Marxist theoretical background. The second looks at moral panics. Finally, there is a discussion of the hustling black proletariat as a subculture of resistance.

The Marxist historical framework of *Policing the Crisis*

Apart from what is obviously a general Marxist background, the theoretical basis of the work, elaborated particularly in Chapter 7, is Gramsci's notion of hegemony as filtered through Althusser's essay on 'Ideology and Ideological State Apparatuses' in his *Lenin and Philosophy*.[91] The basic idea of hegemony is that the ruling class dominates not by force alone but rather by mobilizing the consent of at least a large part of the subordinated classes in the ideological sphere. Gramsci sees a role for intellectuals who side with the working class in undermining the hegemonic ideological position of the ruling class. Althusser's essay was detached from Althusser's general ideas, which were much more controversial, and used by many people on the left in Britain for a while. Some problems with it are discussed in Chapter 8 below.

The authors of *Policing the Crisis* provide a lengthy account of British history since the Second World War. Much of this would be quite widely accepted, namely that underlying the period of consensus and Butskellism which lasted from the end of the Second World War through to the beginning of the 1960s, the British economy was fundamentally weak. In particular, it had a persistent tendency to inflation driven by militant action by workers on the shop floor. Productivity tended to fall behind that of other leading capitalist states. This manifested itself in a series of balance of payments crises. Both Conservative and Labour governments contemplated the legal regulation of bargaining over pay, making strikes illegal unless there had previously been a ballot etc. The other tactic which they attempted was to impose or to negotiate national limits to pay rises.[92]

The authors assume as a background to this that capitalism in Britain needs a high degree of organization based on agreements between employers, organized labour and the government, indeed, as practised by Labour, a corporate state.[93] This in turn means that the idea of ideological state apparatuses is particularly attractive for them.

They argue that in addition to the insecurities resulting from economic instability the capitalist class in Britain was also faced with a series of cultural threats mainly linked to young people: student unrest, open acceptance of counter cultural values, drug-taking, rampant premarital sex etc.[94] On top of this they were faced with something approaching a guerrilla war in Northern Ireland, with associated incidents on the mainland:

> As the attempt by a social Democratic government to manage the state through an organised version of consensus is finally exhausted and bankrupted between 1964 and 1970, so, gradually, the class struggle comes more and more into the open, assumes a more manifest presence ... The state ... must be consolidated by the exercise of a certain kind of force – Mr Heath as 'Bonaparte'.[95]

In brief, Mr Heath came to power in 1970 with the idea of using the law in industrial relations. He rapidly passed the Industrial Relations Act, but when it came to actually imprisoning trade unionists under the Act he lost his nerve, did a U-turn, and tried to negotiate a wages agreement with the unions. The authors of *Policing the Crisis* argue that it was at around this stage when the state felt acutely threatened that a moral panic over mugging was actually engineered:

> To put it crudely, the 'moral panic' appears to us to be one of the principal forms of ideological consciousness by means of which a 'silent majority' is won over to the support of increasingly coercive measures on the part of the state, and lends its legitimacy to a 'more than usual' exercise of control.[96]
>
> [The mugging crisis] depended on at least five essential conditions: a state of anticipatory mobilisation and 'preparedness' in the control apparatuses; the sensitising of official circles and of the public through the mass media; a 'perceived danger' to social stability – such as when crime rate is read as indexing a general breakdown in

social authority and control; identification of the vulnerable 'target group' (e.g. black youth) involved in dramatic incidents ('muggings') which trigger public alarm; the setting in motion of the mechanisms by which conspiratorial demons and criminal folk devils are projected onto the public stage.[97]

A crisis of law and order would help to justify a more ready use of the police and the courts to deal with any form of dissent, perhaps including recalcitrant workers. They do not go into great detail as to what a strong state would look like, but the impression is given that it would be a democracy with hints of fascism. There is a specific reference to Marx's *18th Brumaire*. In fact what happened, of course, was that the Heath government narrowly lost the February 1974 election and was followed by a period of Labour rule up to 1979. During this period the underlying weakness of the British economy continued, the trade unions consistently rejected attempts at wages agreements and social contracts and a popular feeling developed (or was developed) that something had to be done to in industrial deadlock. The authors' version of this is

> Britain in the 1970s is a country for whose crisis there are no viable capitalist solutions left, and where, as yet, there is no political base for an alternative socialist strategy. It is a nation locked in a deadly stalemate: a state of unstoppable capitalist decline.[98]

The authors note the emergence of 'the genuinely extreme right into an independent life of its own', but they seem to see the interest of British capitalism as in management of the crisis by a social Democratic party. Noting that the Conservatives are 'the historic "block" poised to inherit the next phase of the crisis', they comment that 'it is a conjuncture many would prefer to miss'.[99] Although at first sight this looks very prescient, the book seems only to have captured Thatcher's potential for authoritarianism:

> This is where the cycle of *moral panics* issues directly into a *law and order society* ... The state has won the right, and indeed inherited duty, to move swiftly, to stand fast and hard, to listen in, discreetly survey, saturate and swamp, to charge or hold without charge, act on suspicion, muscle and shoulder, to keep society on the straight and narrow. Liberalism, that last next stop against arbitrary power, is in retreat. It is suspended. The times are exceptional. The crisis is real.

> We are inside the 'law and order' state. That is the social, the ideological content of social reaction in the 1970s. It is also the *moment of mugging.* (p. 323).

This does not seem to really grasp the point that what was coming was a *neoliberal* strong state. It would lead one to anticipate the five separate Conservative Acts intended to curb the trade unions, and perhaps the use of the police in industrial relations. However, it totally fails to antici-pate Mrs Thatcher's repudiation of the idea of the government stepping in to organize the economy. The National Economic Development Council, regional economic development councils, tripartite talks, national wages agreements, beer and sandwiches at Number 10 and the regulation of low pay through Wages Councils were all abandoned. It also fails to reckon with the genuine libertarianism which was an aspect of Thatcherism. There have been moral panics about pornography or single-parent families, but strikingly little was done about them. The overall result of Thatcher's reshaping of British society was arguably more devastating than whatever the authors of *Policing the Crisis* had in mind as the likely outcome.

Moral panics

The sudden upsurge in public concern and comment about mugging is analysed in terms of a moral panic. This concept is specifically linked in the book to the crisis in Cohen's *Folk Devils and Moral Panics*.[100] In the book Cohen is largely concerned with the process by which particular groups come to be designated as folk devils. His picture of this process essentially comes from symbolic interactionism and labelling theory, in which it is a relatively arbitrary matter who gets labelled and for what. It is a matter of who has the power to apply labels, and then whether they are accepted, resisted etc. Thus for Cohen it is societies that have moral panics. He does not seem to have any particular notion of what kind of societies. Moral panics arise when there is an apparent threat to society's values posed by some particular group. They are similar to a panic arising from a disaster in that they tend to arise suddenly; there is initial debate about how serious is the threat; a widespread, but not necessarily complete, consensus is arrived at amongst the elite groups and the media. The level of concern is excessive given any rational assessment of the level of threat.

The concept of a moral panic is thus a low-level empirical concept. It has subsequently been used by sociologists on virtually any occasion when there is public concern about anything.[101]

The concept of moral panics is thus not appropriate to be taken on board as a full-scale Marxist concept, but it does lend itself to some applications in the discussion of ideology and crises. It is in this way that it features in *Policing the Crisis*. A particular strength of the book is that the moral panic over mugging is linked not just to the general values of society but to a particular conjuncture in which a moral panic was deliberately engineered. The police played a major role in preparing the crisis, setting up a special squad to catch muggers before mugging became a significant issue.[102] The judiciary played a major role in this.[103] 'The media come... to reproduce the definitions of the powerful, without being, in a simple sense, in their pay.'[104] In particular, news about crime is almost entirely defined by the police, the Home Office and the courts.[105] There is, not surprisingly, a lengthy and detailed analysis of the press discussion of the exemplary sentences meted out to the three Handsworth muggers on 19 March 1973 (one sentence of 20 years on a 16-year-old, with 10 years each for his two companions), which argues that there was a failure of nerve by the liberal *Guardian* and goes into some detail on the press discussion of the sentences and of the role of race in Handsworth.[106] After a discussion of the role of letters pages in newspapers in building up a 'national consensus'[107] there is a fairly elaborate account of an English national ideology based around traditional conservatism, interpreted somewhat differently by different social classes, and threatened by increased affluence and more particularly by immigration and crime linked to immigrants.[108] Although aspects of this account are still recognizable, the authors suggest that it is undergoing a degree of erosion. This erosion has gone much further since the account was written. Thus voting, for example, is now explained less in terms of traditional conservatism of a part of the working class and more in terms of class and partisan dealignment.[109] Hence the dramatic Labour victory in 1997 following 17 years of Conservative government. The authors see Englishness as part of a hegemonic ideology. Plainly something fairly complicated has happened in subsequent years: a deliberate Thatcherite attempt at a 'cultural Revolution' as some Conservatives called it, which was partly successful but never fully persuasive and which has partly lived on in some of the themes of new Labour.[110]

The book deals with the mugging crisis of 1972 in very considerable detail. The basic argument is that squads of police to deal with mugging were set up in Brixton and on the London Underground well before there was a mugging crisis. British law did not recognize the crime of mugging, the equivalent offence being that of robbery.[111] Nonetheless the police managed to produce statistics about mugging, some of which seem to have been manipulated by including non-violent pickpocketing in the totals. Violent street crime was rising over the 1970s but at a slower rate than before. From 1965 to 1972 the average annual increase in 'robbery or assault with intent to rob…was only 14%' and the much-quoted figure of London muggings in the years 1968 to 1972 yields an average annual increase of 32%, which is less than that for robbery in general over the ten years from 1955 to 1965.[112] There seemed to be no rational reason to be particularly worried about mugging. Accepting all the caveats about what may lie underneath statistical generalizations, many would consider an increase on this scale would be a legitimate reason for some degree of public concern. The term was introduced to the British press by a police officer who had recently been seconded to a force in the United States. Coverage in the British press rapidly linked British muggings with the rise of mugging in North American cities, which in turn was linked to ghetto blacks. Although British muggings were by no means an exclusively black activity, a strong link tended to be made between mugging and blacks, helped along by the speeches of Enoch Powell. The idea in the book, as indicated above, is that the moral panic was engineered by the agents of capitalism in order to justify a shift to a more authoritarian framework.

A subculture of resistance? The politics of the hustling black proletariat

In the final part of *Policing the Crisis*, it is acknowledged that there is some real basis for the idea of mugging as a crime carried out by young blacks. There is then a lengthy analysis of this group as part of the lumpenproletariat. This concept will be considered in the next part, the main argument being that this concept is imprecise and best abandoned. Thus from the perspective of this book identifying a particular group as part of the lumpenproletariat is not at all helpful in working out what role they may play in a socialist strategy.

Policing the Crisis focuses on the problems of young black men who perhaps cannot find work because of discrimination, or who can only find short-term and dead-end jobs which they regard as beneath their capacity. It says that they get tempted by the possibilities of a life of hustling in the alternative economy of the black ghetto. Their resentment of racist white society may lead them to feel that mugging whites is a justifiable way of raising money. The analysis is not really fully spelt out, but there seems a suggestion that black hustlers are a model for other people because they offer an alternative lifestyle to what is on offer for those at the bottom of capitalist society, and because they have reacted more vigorously than others to the indignities of dead-end labour.

This analysis is a dubious contribution to the Marxist analysis of crime. If hustling simply refers to the provision of illegal services such as drugs, gambling and drinking, this might well be harmless or might help people from a different cultural background to feel more at home in Britain. However, using lethal weapons on rival drug dealers does not fit with any sensible conception of prefigurative politics. Similarly, whilst mugging white people may be a consequence of living in a racist society, it is surely likely to make racism worse.

Conclusion on *Policing the Crisis*

So do we conclude that *Policing the Crisis* was a heroic effort in its time, but is now largely outdated? In some ways, even disregarding the comments above about the decline of socialism and the rise of globalization and postmodernism, we live in rather different times. We have a Labour government which is presiding over a modestly successful economy, and although there are worrying aspects, such as the very high level of personal debt and inflated house prices, it would not be appropriate to say that we are in the midst of an economic crisis. There would thus not appear to be any particular need for a moral panic intended to subordinate the working class in a corporatist society with fascist aspects. However, there is certainly a worrying growth of authoritarianism linked to fears of Islamic terrorism which are all the more real because of Britain's role as a lackey of the United States. There is something of a moral panic linked to immigration/asylum seekers, which in turn links with worries about Islamic extremists.

It might also be worth attempting an analysis on these lines for the United States itself. In the United states there is arguably a moral panic based on the threat of terrorism, which justified the passage of the Patriot Act, allowing an unprecedented surveillance of dissidence of all sorts, and has also led to the imprisonment or ruin of Americans with apparent Middle Eastern connections. The war on terror allowed Bush to get away with massively regressive changes to the tax system, rewarding his capitalist friends with lucrative Iraqi contracts, degradation of the American environment and so forth. Rather than looking at corporatism, however, the current worry is the aggressive use of neoliberal globalization in which American firms sack their workers and move their operations overseas. One-sixth of American manufacturing jobs have disappeared since Bush came to office.

Left realism

Left realism was developed, mainly by British figures who had previously been critical criminologists, in the 1980s. It is still highly influential: Labour's slogan 'Tough on crime, tough on the causes of crime' has essentially been developed from left realist ideas. Although left realist writings include a critique of some central features of critical criminology, its origins lie in the political situation in Britain in the 1980s. There is a very important political background. In 1979 Mrs Thatcher won her first general election and arrived in office with a mission to make massive and permanent alterations to the running of the British state.

Major features of Thatcherism, as it came to be called, included a belief in monetarism, which in practical terms meant dealing with inflation by causing a particularly serious recession. This took effect in the early 1980s and had very damaging effects on British manufacturing. It also led to a very substantial rise in unemployment. Along with this went a strong belief in individualism and enterprise. The values of community were largely abandoned. As Mrs Thatcher put it 'There is no such thing as society, only individuals and their families'.[113] As part of the same new right philosophy, she held that trade unions had no role in running the country, and had damaging effects on the market. She thus abandoned the corporatist approach to industrial relations in which unions and bosses were regarded as equal partners in running the economy. Instead she made use of the police in a series of violent encounters with trade unionists, most notably during the miners' strike of 1984–5. Less inimical to traditional conservatism was her belief that crime was a serious problem, which could be tackled by increased spending on the police, greater use of punishment, notably imprisonment, and various measures to make crime less attractive. Mrs Thatcher's policies greatly accelerated the move in Britain from a Fordist to a post-Fordist society.[114]

The initial reaction of the left to Thatcherism was to believe that it would soon become very electorally unpopular. The initial emphasis was on writing a left-wing Labour manifesto. In fact Labour was very seriously defeated in 1983, and its manifesto of that year was famously described by Gerald Kaufman MP as 'the longest suicide note in history'. Subsequently there was an acceptance that aspects of the Thatcherite programme answered real problems and that the left's programme needed to change. This culminated in the abandonment of Labour's commitment to nationalization and to the development of New Labour.

The Thatcherite approach to crime was encouraged by American theorists such as Charles Murray and James Q. Wilson. Murray will be discussed thoroughly in the context of the lumpenproletariat in the next part. In brief, he argued that unduly generous welfare provisions in the United States and Britain had developed an underclass characterized by illegitimacy, unwillingness to work and a tendency to crime. The remedy was a dramatic reduction in welfare for unmarried mothers and a more vigorous use of imprisonment for criminals. In his very influential *Thinking About Crime*,[115] Wilson started from disillusion with the War on Poverty approach to crime because he claimed it ended in dismal failure with crime rates rocketing. Instead of seeking a general explanation for crime he advocated a more experimental approach to see what forms of immediate deterrence at the time a crime was about to be committed might be effective. He became particularly involved with the broken windows theory of zero tolerance policing which claims that minor problems of graffiti, vandalism and incivility lead criminals to believe that an area is safe for their operations.

Left realism was a response by erstwhile critical criminologists to Thatcherism, to a recognition that crime is a real problem for working-class people, and to the influence of right realist theories. For left realists the doctrines of critical criminology are seen as left idealism.[116]

Left realism starts from the recognition that street crime is a real problem, and not just a moral panic. Public opinion polls over the 1980s consistently saw crime as an issue of public concern second only to unemployment. Recorded offences increased almost five-fold between 1960 and 1980 despite an increase in welfare expenditure. During the 1980s crime continued to rise, going from 2.6 million recorded offences in 1980 to 4 million in 1990. Crime is largely an intra-class phenomenon, and the poor pay dearly for inadequate protection. Public concern about crime may, however, partly be an indication of intolerance of violence, harassment and abuse of women, racism and gay-bashing etc.[117]

Sentencing policies in the 1980s were not very consistent. There was a massive prison-building programme and funding for the police increased by 60% while police performance dropped consistently. There was thus a real question about whether all this money was being well spent. These two facts between them, argues Young, discredit positivism, with its confidence that improved conditions will reduce crime, and classicism with its confidence and that people will choose not to commit crimes if there are more effective punishments.

The 'realism' of left realism means that it accepts that crime is a real problem with damaging and disorganizing effects so that it is desirable to promote progressive reforms. It is 'left' or radical in that although it starts from conventional definitions of crime it does not take them for granted and is willing to look behind them. Also, it basically accepts the Marxist explanation of the origin of crime in capitalism, and it looks to social justice as the ultimate solution to crime even if it is not in a position to do anything about this at the moment.

The core of left realism is its idea of the square of crime. The spatial metaphor is perhaps of less help than the idea that for any crime a relationship between four different players has to be considered: the offender, the victim, the police and multi-agencies and the public. Crime rates are generated by the social relationships between each point of the square. These relationships will vary from one crime to another. For example, by buying dodgy goods at car boot sales the public create an informal economy which sustains burglaries, although burglary itself is not consented to. In contrast, in drug dealing the chain of dealers from importers to student users are all involved in consenting relationships, whilst in an assault perhaps only the offender and victim are involved and the act is purely coercive.[118]

For each crime there is a four-fold aetiology. It involves the causes of offending, the factors which make the victim vulnerable, the social conditions which affect public control and tolerance, and the social forces which propel the formal agencies such as the police. The error of previous criminological theory has been to attempt explanations based on one or two of these causal sequences. Realism puts the main emphasis on the social situation which produces the criminal behaviour, but recognizes that the bias of the criminal justice system will play a part. Realism sees relative deprivation as the major cause of crime, but stresses that this can occur throughout the social system and may take the form of young people feeling deprived of Nike trainers rather than of satisfactory footwear, that is, it can take symbolic forms. Trying to turn this into a general law without thinking about subgroups simply doesn't work: women are much less employed outside the home than men, so they 'suffer unemployment', so they ought to commit lots of crime – but, obviously, things don't work that way.[119]

Left realists take something from symbolic interactionism and insist on dealing with lived realities. Thus they did not accept the 1982 British Crime Survey as the end of the story. This survey showed that the risk of experiencing a robbery in England and Wales was once every five centuries; an assault resulting in injury once a century; a burglary once every 50 years and a family car stolen once every 60 years. But in the inner city rates are much higher, as was established by new realist surveys in Islington and Liverpool. And for poor people the impact of crime, both on households and on areas is much worse. In addition, the paradox that women are more fearful of assault whereas young men are the chief victims is dissolved when it is realized that (i) women are less tolerant of violence; (ii) young men do not like to parade their fears; (iii) women experience a very high level of harassment, and are never sure whether it will lead on to something worse; (iv) women may well be taking considerable precautions already, so that their fears are translated into precautions.[120]

Conclusions on left realism

Left realism is the tribute paid by critical criminologists to social realities, particularly the social realities of Britain in the 1980s. It recognizes that street crime is a real problem for working people, whereas critical criminology did this only sporadically. It does not revisit the definition of crime as infinitely flexible which the critical criminologists took over from symbolic interactionism, but it is obviously intended to address some of the more standard, consensus crimes such as burglary, robbery and assault, without renouncing an interest in corporate crime. In the same way the emphasis in critical criminology on decriminalizing victimless behaviour is not abrogated in left realism but it is put on the back burner. The local surveys which were inspired by the left realists should be of interest to anyone, and definitely to Marxist criminologists. They show that some common forms of victimization in Britain such as burglary and assault are very unevenly distributed geographically, being common in some inner-city areas but virtually unknown in the countryside.

The left realists were not trying to advance Marxist criminological theory, but rather to address some practical problems which had become the political domain of the right in a way compatible with socialism. In doing this they were – perhaps inadvertently – setting the agenda for problems which have arisen since 1997 under New Labour. Their strong emphasis on a democratic approach raises some problems which are classic liberal dilemmas but which would also arise in a genuinely democratic socialist society. A particularly prominent one is the question of acceptable behaviour in public spaces. Opinion polls and consultations suggest that people are frequently less concerned about crime than about antisocial behaviour, for example dropping litter, spraying graffiti, teenagers hanging around in large groups and looking threatening but not doing anything drastic, drunkenness, shouted insults, street prostitution etc. This behaviour is on the borderlines of being victimless. It depends to some extent on one's attitude to particular forms of behaviour, level of tolerance of young people, views about the aesthetics of graffiti etc. New Labour have tried various measures against antisocial behaviour, notably forms of curfew for young people and the use of ASBOs. Home Office ministers present these measures as a vigorous and at least somewhat effective pursuit of a democratic agenda. It is also possible to see them as criminalizing relatively harmless behaviour, or a mechanism for imposing jail sentences on people guilty of minor crimes such as soliciting. Similar sorts of dilemma apply to planning issues. Treatment in the community is probably the best way forward for many offenders, but residents tend to object to living next door to a rehabilitation centre for drug addicts or paedophiles. There can also be problems in deciding whether residents' groups or councillors are genuinely representative of a community.

Ian Taylor: *Crime in Context*

We now move on to two recent British attempts to analyse contemporary realities and the role of crime within them using Marxist concepts. In *Crime in Context*[121] Taylor tries to give an account of market societies based on political economy. He does not want to be seen as oversimplifying, and ends up arguably overcomplicating. He emphasizes that modern society is post-Fordist and that we now experience global capitalism.[122] He cites the exposition of Fordism offered by Stuart Hall and Martin Jacques.[123] 'Fordism' is the industrial and social set-up which characterized capitalist societies at least from about Second World War to around 1975. Economically it is founded on mass, factory based production. Consumption tended to fit mass production ('any colour you want so long as it's black'); the economy responded tolerably well to Keynesian demand manipulation. Stable lifetime employment was available for most men; with little unemployment the welfare state could provide a social safety net from cradle to grave. Although Hall and Jacques gave an extensive account of post-Fordist production, in which the application of computers allows for much more individualized consumption, and for production geared to the needs of small, specific groups of consumers, the main focus in Ian Taylor is on the collapse of Fordist employment. Industrial areas in the advanced countries experience high unemployment as the demand for steel or bulk chemicals goes down.[124] A series of social changes go along with this move to post-Fordism, which are summarized in Table 5.1.

Table 5.1 Fordism and post-Fordism[125]

Feature	Fordism	Post-Fordism
Work and gender	Masculinist	More feminine
Work organization	Production line	Decentred: small enterprises
Objectives	Production	Marketing
Induction to work	Informal or apprenticeships	Qualifications
Unions?	Corporate agreements	Individual agreements
Career	Lifetime	Short-term contracts; some sweatshops
Domestic	Matriarchy	More diverse; 2 career households; unemployed households
Leisure	Male dominated spectator sport	Individualist; fitness industry

Taylor then lists nine transitions which followed the end of Fordism. These are 'overdetermined by' the end of Fordism, that is it affects them but they have some autonomy. They are a substantial rise in unemployment, particularly affecting young people; increased poverty, especially child poverty, and inequality, with top incomes rising disproportionately; increased insecurity with everyone worrying more about becoming unemployed. The rise of a global economy dominated by one superpower leads to a crisis of the nation state; states are less able to provide security for their populations; going along with this there is a rise of ethnic mobilization in some states. In the United Kingdom another feature is the crisis of confidence in policing: under Mrs Thatcher spending on the police rose very substantially but crime had risen except very recently.[126] Racial tensions were increasing; there were also fears of immigration; in the United States the racial divide grew worse with rising fears of blacks amongst the white population. The ghettos became sink places; young black males were incarcerated at an unprecedented rate. Post-Fordism tends to be linked with postmodernism, and is certainly associated with a crisis in culture and the growth of postmodernist uncertainties. A crisis of masculinity develops, with males under challenge from feminism and post-Fordist insecurities; this is linked to the excluded males being physically violent and dominating public spaces. Family life is transformed. There is a rise of single-parent families with attendant fears about the control of children, and a rise of working women in two-parent families, with similar fears.

The dominant ideology is the *market;* the shopping mall tends to replace the town hall as the centre of urban life; entrepreneurs such as Richard Branson become popular heroes; some of those who fail in the market economy create an alternative market based on crime and drugs.[127]

Taylor's nine aspects undoubtedly reflect significant features of Britain in the early 1990s. They are, however, very ill digested. It is not clear, to me, at least, how much they are a consequence of post-Fordism as such, or of globalization, or of Mrs Thatcher's particular policies. To what extent did the same features apply to other countries in Europe or to Japan? As I write in 2008 Britain remains part of a global economy, and post-Fordism has not retreated. However, the generally less aggressive approach of John Major followed by ten years of New Labour has ameliorated some of the worst features noted by Taylor. Unemployment has fallen, and with it child poverty; substantial immigration from Eastern Europe has helped to fill jobs that British people are reluctant to take on, and has led to a civilized debate about possibly over-stretched local resources rather than demagogy about an alien wedge; even the rise of Islamic terrorism has been met relatively phlegmatically. The night-time economy is certainly booming. However, it requires considerable theoretical argument to conclude that it is simply based on the crisis of masculinity suffered by excluded males, the intolerable stresses of market society and young adults out of control. It could also be seen as a more relaxed way of growing up than previous generations enjoyed, where instead of settling down in their early twentiess to marriage and child rearing, people have a more extended time to enjoy drink, drugs, sex and rock and roll.

Marxism has traditionally included the idea that there is relative autonomy between the economic base and other features of society, but relative autonomy seems to be particularly running riot in Taylor's account. He moves on to consider a series of areas of society in the light of the change to post-Fordism. The first of these is youth and crime.[128] Whereas critical criminology was interested in youth subcultures, which were seen as a form of rebellion against the capitalist system in the relatively brief period between leaving school and setting up a new home after marriage,[129] the picture now is more of problematic youth transitions in which the difficulty of getting a satisfactory job leads to problems in leaving home or settling down with a partner. However, Taylor looks at this prolonged transition as an intolerable burden, whereas it is possible to see it in a more relaxed way, as I try to suggest above.

Taylor next considers the ecology of crime and provides a lengthy critique of the Chicago School's idea of a zone of transition.[130] He makes many very worthwhile points about the geography of crime in cities which have been settled since the Middle Ages or which grew with the industrial revolution. However, although these work very well as a critique of the Chicago School they do not relate particularly closely to the theme of post-Fordism. He does finally revert to the effects of post-Fordism by arguing that in England crime rose especially strongly in the late 1980s and early 1990s in industrial areas in which the post-Fordist economy failed to replace jobs lost.[131]

The next section of the book looks at financial crimes encouraged by a market society, starting with city scandals such as the Guinness affair or the collapse of Barings Bank, moving on to tax evasion, money laundering, where by 1990 over £1.8 billion of deposits in the United Kingdom were monies earned in the international drugs trade in the process of being laundered; insider trading; fraudulent stock-market manipulation; the selling of junk bonds.[132] There has also been substantial fraud in the financial-services market so that one in 20 mortgages in 1991 was estimated to be fraudulent; the fraudulent use of bank cards in the United Kingdom amounted to about £100 million a year; trade in counterfeit commodities such as pirate CDs appears currently to be worth around £3 billion a year globally. Taylor turns to a critique of Sutherland, making the point that the use of bribes to secure contracts outside the advanced capitalist countries is commonplace but not necessarily a crime committed against the firm for which the person offering bribes works.

It is certainly appropriate to describe all these phenomena as parts of the current criminal landscape. However, exactly how they fit into an analysis of post-Fordism or contemporary capitalism appears to me to be quite varied. The Guinness affair involved insider trading in an attempt to inflate the price of Guinness shares to facilitate the takeover of Distillers and was not primarily a matter of theft. The collapse of Barings bank was the work of one dealer, who was also not motivated by theft. Tax evasion is basically linked to the existence of tax rather than being a particular feature of post-Fordist society. Massive movements of money originating in the drugs trade is more a feature of globalization than of post-Fordism, and Taylor's analysis of globalization is relatively limited. The major UK issues in financial services have been the mis-selling of endowment policies and of pensions, both linked to neoliberal deregulation. The fraudulent use of bank cards is surely basically a product of this particular way of doing business rather than a result of post-Fordist enterprise. The trade in counterfeit commodities is linked to an aspect of post-Fordism, which is the promotion of brands as part of a consumer identity. However, it also links strongly to globalization, as much of this production is carried out by cheap labour in Third World countries attempting to make a profit for a Chinese businessman, for example, instead of Nike. These forms of white-collar crime fit quite well into a general Marxist analysis of the current stage of capitalism but are not adequately theorized by Taylor.

In the second half of his chapter on fraudsters and villains Taylor starts by pointing out that the rise of post-Fordism has also brought about the expansion of private policing, some of it of dubious probity. He then runs rather rapidly through a series of possible forms of criminal activity, concluding with a table in which he speculates on which will do better or worse in the near future. He thinks, for example, that the prospects for the theft of computer data are excellent whilst those for the smuggling of pornography are declining because of the rise of satellite television.[133] Although these speculations are perfectly sensible they are basically a series of ad hoc judgements. It would not, surely, make a major difference to post-Fordist society if thefts of computers were falling (he thinks the prospects are steady) while those of cars (falling, he thinks) were rising.

Taylor's next chapter is devoted to looking at the market in firearms in various market societies. Although he tries to make a case that firearms are used in Britain (e.g. in the Hungerford and Dunblane massacres) and not just in the United States, and that the increasingly free movement of goods in the European Union facilitates the smuggling of guns into Britain, most observers will surely still be struck by the contrast between the sheer ubiquity of firearms and very limited legislation in the United States and their rarity in Britain combined with very tight controls. Both may be market societies, but it is chiefly the difference between them that is striking.

Taylor's final substantive chapter concerns penality and policing. He spends some time in a discussion of Rusche and Kircheimer, then Foucault and then Stanley Cohen followed by Ulrich Beck's risk society before pointing out in a brief final section that the scope of private policing and prisons is greatly expanding. Some of Taylor's detailed observations offer insightful and acute ideas, but as in so much of the rest of his book the reader's impression is of a series of possibilities for integration into a proper analysis rather than such an analysis in itself. Perhaps it is the character of such detailed comments that some of them simply go wrong. Here is a particularly drastic example. Taylor disagrees with Foucault, who thinks that the future will see the development of some form of panopticon covering large areas of society. Instead, he argues:

> There is a powerful sense of the emergence of a new feudalism, in which, in effect, powerful private interests police the territory over which they have commercial hegemony, whilst leaving huge tracts of residual territory ('the territories beyond the walls') under generalised surveillance but substantially unattended.[134]

The quoted sentence is thoroughly misleading. Post-Fordist society is not static like feudalism; it is characterized by very rapid innovation. Personal ties are very flexible, and there is considerable social mobility. In the 'unattended' territory crime has fallen significantly since Taylor was writing. Two factors in this have been the extension of CCTV and the growth of community wardens, making the territory less unattended than in recent years.

My overall comment on Taylor's book is that although it contains many interesting insights overall it is too disjointed to give a fair impression of the possibilities for the Marxist analysis of crime today.

John Lea in *Crime and Modernity*,[135] the second text, is pursuing a basically Marxist approach. He describes his account as left realist, and starts by using the idea of the square of crime to argue that the nature of crime in any society is constructed and negotiated between the aspects of the square of crime we saw above.[136] He views premodern crime control as on the one hand communities policing themselves and on the other rulers trying to maintain their authority but not interfering particularly with local sanctions. Such societies are characterized by a particularly strong fear of strangers, of people who do not comply with the local rules. Within them both lords and peasants moved frequently between committing and denouncing crime.[137] Following Foucault and Elias he says that the development of capitalism leads to the development of governance, a parallel process in which people who become the working class are forced into appropriate behaviour by criminal sanctions and brutality, but in parallel to this also become the subject of attention by bourgeois reformers who aim to promote health, welfare education etc.[138] Initially the concept of police was much wider than modern policing, it was more a question of general social regulation.[139] Crime in the early modern period comprises a potentially confusing mixture between resistance to the new capitalist ways, most famously in Luddism; maintaining traditional ways which capitalists are trying to eradicate, for example rights to hunt or gather wood and crime on a more modern basis, for example wife murder or sheep stealing from ordinary people who cannot afford it, which was both illegal and popularly condemned.[140]

The police were initially seen by workers as alien enforcers of capitalist ways but then, in the second half of the nineteenth century in Britain, the working class got more of a stake in the system through the widening of the franchise, the legitimization and development of trade unions, the development of the welfare state etc. Except in the poorest working-class communities or in cases of industrial conflict the police were increasingly seen as legitimate, and conversely, police attention focused on the poorest rather than the working class generally.[141]

Lea then looks at three exceptions to this development of governance. First, crimes of the bourgeoisie – although there was some retreat from the initial role of capitalists as robber barons and a degree of intervention to protect the safety of workers and to protect other businesses and individuals from fraud there was a general doctrine that excessive interference in business is harmful. Thus capitalists were able to get away with things for which workers would probably be apprehended.[142] Second, the family, whose life became increasingly privatized rather than lived out on the street. The wife increasingly accepted a position of dependence and femininity, while her husband became the breadwinner. The role of the state became largely that of mediator, so that domestic violence was largely unpoliced.[143] Third, the colonies, which Lea sees as broadly similar to premodern societies in the early days of capitalism. Policing was a matter of the imposition of alien rule. There was an attempt to use the native population for slave or semi-slave labour; the economy was largely directed towards the production of agricultural or mineral raw materials. The native population was caught up in resistance based on the defence of their traditions and opposition to imperialist innovations. Its own crime control comprised a mixture of traditional methods and increasingly justice administered by national liberation movements.[144]

Lea is attempting to cover substantial areas in a few pages, but his treatment of colonies is far too cursory. No distinction is made between exploitation colonies such as sub-Saharan Africa where a small white colonial elite rules a native population and labour colonies such as Canada or Australia, where the native population is marginal to the colonial enterprise (and, obviously, many colonies were somewhere between these extremes). Lea seems to simply accept that colonies produce underdevelopment, whereas according to Lenin they produce rapid development.[145] No mention is made of the white man's burden, civilizing missions etc. A whole series of issues which require debate is simply assumed.

Lea argues that the general picture of the whole society accepting policing as legitimate broadly continued to develop in the twentieth century, reaching its culmination in the 1950s, during which working-class criminality became marginal, seen basically as a form of pathology.[146]

Lea says that by the end of the 1970s a second crisis of modernity had emerged. The first crisis was the global disruption which was solved by Keynesianism. This second crisis is an ever-deepening structural crisis which is chronic. There is a falling rate of profit, massive industrial overcapacity, the steady destruction of the social and economic infrastructure, growing unemployment and rising global poverty. Enormous funds of monetary capital seek speculative investments.[147] The increased mobility of capital enables corporations to get taxes which should have been destined for education and welfare reduced, because they can threaten to move elsewhere. Polarization is becoming much more acute, with the owners and managers of capital emerging as a mobile, global class, whereas the fastest-growing part of the working class is in low-wage, part-time and temporary employment, particularly in services. The bottom tenth of the population in Britain experienced a decline in income over the Thatcher years from a 4% share of national income to a 2% share, whereas the top 10% went from 21% to 27% over the same period. Leading sections of capital did not need to invest in the welfare and education of workers in the advanced countries, but instead sought out cheap labour overseas. People towards the top of the social scale were able to insulate themselves from public services, increasingly living in gated communities such as those now occupied by 10% of the population of the United States. Capital is unable to develop the Third World in spite of the global search for cheap labour, and inequality between the world's richest and poorest fifth of population rose from 30 times greater in 1960 to 60 times greater in 1990.[148] Instead of the integration of the population in the now 'decaying Keynesian welfare state' we have the assessment of risk from individuals who are members of groups that tend to become involved in crime.[149] Attempts to construct a personal identity combine a shifting gathering of elements from the global mass media and an aggressive masculinity.[150]

High rates of crime have become a standard background feature of life, and the boundaries of crime have become increasingly blurred: 'Anyone is likely to be aggressive, or to defraud or swindle you.'[151]

Likewise, date rapists or paedophiles are likely to be someone you know, ordinary people are increasingly drug users, low-paid workers move in and out of criminal economies without noticing, city dealers frequently ignore financial regulations.[152] Social crime as a form of resistance to capitalism has revived in poor communities. Activities include shoplifting, defrauding gas and electricity companies, social security fraud, alcohol and drug smuggling, buying stolen goods with money that gets spent on drugs. Marginalized poor youth engage in twocking and racing cars; more directly political youth protests at road construction, blood sports, meetings of the WTO.[153] International organized crime, based on activities such as drug smuggling and trafficking women for prostitution, is enmeshed with legitimate business; tobacco companies connive with smugglers.[154]

> ...the retreat of citizens behind locked doors and fortified estates leaves the streets, public parks and spaces to the criminal. The modern inner city housing estate and ghetto may become the equivalent of the Victorian rookery. Episodic and fractured governance by law enforcement agencies and private property interests leave large areas as social and economic rubbish tips create obvious sanctuary to petty and organised crime.[155]

Corruption might be thought a feature of backward states and areas, but has spread across the European Union to become a general character of political systems of the most advanced capitalist societies, although less in northern European democracies.[156] However, the gangster capitalism of Russia is the shape of the capitalist future:[157] 'the tendencies are clear:...the social relations of crime control, rather than being consolidated as in earlier periods of modernisation, are weakening and fragmenting'.[158]

Much of what Lea is describing points towards a more authoritarian style of policing, but of limited areas, reminiscent of premodern periods:

> The actuarial management of the dangerous classes or underclass suggests the image of policing in the eighteenth or early nineteenth centuries. Likewise, increased reliance by police agencies on technological surveillance rather than public communication and support suggests the fragmented and episodic policing based on an army of spies and informers characteristic of eighteenth-century England...increasingly autonomous private governance likewise

evokes the earlier stages of modernisation in which the propertied classes made their own arrangements for protection while the masses were left to their own devices.[159]

Lea's strategy for the revival of the social relations of crime control involves

a fundamental redistribution of economic and welfare resources to poor communities, both within advanced capitalist countries and on a global scale…. Relations of trust and solidarity will be enabled to replace those of risk and unpredictability. Social inclusion will enable robust communities to sort out a large proportion of their own disputes.[160]

'[T]he corruption and pillaging of the state by powerful interests must be curtailed, politics must be reinvented as a process of democratic involvement.'…'Most important is the development of real international institutions through which disputes can be resolved in the framework of the rule of law.'…'[T]here must be a re-marginalisation of crime.'[161]

If Lea's analysis of the present ills is accepted there can be no dispute as to the desirability of his aims. However, his general line of argument is that the nature of capitalism has shifted and that some truly massive force would be needed to restore something equivalent to the settled relations of the 1950s. What Lea has to offer is the 'new social movements against global capitalism', which he acknowledges are currently 'fragmented and episodic', although he does mention a 'global conflagration of class struggles' without any indication of how this would arise.[162]

The reader cannot fail to be struck by the disparity between the scale of the problems Lea is describing and the very limited and disparate agencies which are supposed to alleviate them. Although Lea is certainly describing some real phenomena, his analysis also omits aspects of contemporary reality which might offer more cause for hope. There are three main areas where Lea could be challenged.

First, his picture of a crisis of crime control. Although not all crime in Britain is captured by the British Crime Survey, the survey shows that crime in Britain peaked in 1995 and has since fallen by 44%. It is now at about the same level as in 1981, near the beginning of the Thatcher period.[163] The survey is based on the experiences of a sample of ordinary people, including those outside the gates of gated communities. A recent development has been the employment of community wardens to patrol the mean streets that Lea says have been abandoned. As it happens, my route to and from the University of Teesside passes through the second poorest postcode in the United Kingdom. The road is a reasonably pleasant one with fairly substantial terraced houses in a good state of repair and with small front gardens. I commute by wheelchair. Thus far, at least, I have had occasional joking comments about my driving, but more polite offers of help. The children who are playing football in the road are careful to avoid hitting me. Further down the road is a garage where I have serviced my car, and the main road into central Middlesbrough which is used by lots of people on foot. In this part of the main road are several restaurants where I have frequently eaten, the offices of Relate, and the bank I go to. It is not Hampstead, but neither is it remotely the war zone one would expect from Lea's book.

The second, and probably most important criticism is that he does not distinguish sufficiently between neoliberal state policies and the pressures of global capitalism. It obviously makes sense that if capitalists can readily move to countries offering cheap labour there will be a downward pressure on education and welfare facilities in the advanced countries. However, politicians such as Reagan, Thatcher and Bush Senior and Junior have exacerbated this tendency, whereas the core states of the European Union and Britain under New Labour have resisted it. The states which should be experiencing the pressure on the welfare state are members of the OECD. Over the years from 1980 to 2000 Public Social Expenditure as a percentage of GDP rose on average in these states by about 4%. The only states in which it fell were Ireland (because overall GDP rose sharply), Luxembourg and the Netherlands. Britain was very much in line with the average: social expenditure went from 17.9% GDP to 21.8%.[164] The years are not exactly the same, but average GDP per head in OECD countries rose from $7,670 in 1979 to $20,364 in 1996 (at 1996 prices). Over the same period that in the United Kingdom went from $6,889 to $19,153.[165] This does not, of course, belie the picture of increased inequality over that period. The general picture, however, would appear to be some trimming at the fringes of welfare states rather than their wholesale removal. The difference between a straightforward neoliberal government and a social democratic one can be seen more clearly in Britain once Labour got beyond its first term: '[Since 1997] spending on the NHS has more than doubled. There are now over 32,000 more doctors and 85,000 more nurses. We are engaged in the biggest hospital building programme the NHS has ever seen, delivering 100 new hospital schemes by 2010.'[166] These are admittedly Labour's own figures, but the main criticism of Labour's health record has been the wisdom of particular sorts of spending. Similar comments can be made about additional spending on education, Child Benefit and pensions. Starting from the analysis in his book Lea would obviously forecast that these improvements to the welfare state will damage Britain's economic performance against global competition, but it is clear that matters are more complicated than a straightforward economic determinism which dooms welfare states.[167]

Third, Lea consistently takes the position that global capitalism simply underdevelops Third World states. Although it is possible to derive this view from Marxism, there is the alternative possibility suggested by Lenin of rapid development. This issue requires a book to itself, but the experience of the Asian tiger economies such as Singapore, Taiwan, South Korea, Hong Kong and latterly and spectacularly China and least parts of India suggests that rapid development is indeed possible. It may not be egalitarian, democratic, balanced and ecologically sound, but it does seem to be happening.

Part III

The Toolkit: The Possibilities of Marxist Analysis

6
The Lumpenproletariat as the Criminal Class?[1]

Probably the simplest way of producing a criminological theory from Marx's writings is to take his account of the lumpenproletariat as, at least amongst other things, an account of a group of people in society many of whom are criminals. In this chapter I shall give a brief account of Marx's theory of the lumpenproletariat, but will then argue that it fails to produce an account of a coherent social group. I shall then argue that Marx uses the concept as a way of vilifying the part of the proletariat which supported Louis Napoleon Bonaparte on the one hand and vilifying and trivializing Bonaparte himself on the other. Finally I shall point out that there is a considerable similarity in both definition and function between Marx's view of the lumpenproletariat and Charles Murray's contemporary theory of the underclass.

The account of the lumpenproletariat which follows is not original, but is needed to make subsequent discussion clear.[2] Although possibly presaged in Engels's account of the Irish immigrants in *The Condition of the Working Class in England*, the lumpenproletariat make their initial appearance in the *Communist Manifesto*:

> The 'dangerous class', the social scum, that passively rotting mass thrown off by the lowest layers of old society, may, here and there, be swept into the movement by a proletarian revolution; its conditions of life, however, prepare it far more for the part of a bribed tool of reactionary intrigue.[3]
>
> Mobile Guards, each a thousand strong, composed of young men from fifteen to twenty years old. They belonged for the most part to the lumpenproletariat, which in all big towns forms a mass sharply differentiated from the industrial proletariat, a recruiting ground for thieves and criminals of all kinds living on the crumbs of society,

people without a definite trade, vagabonds, *gens sans feu et sans aveu* [men without hearth or home], varying according to the degree of civilisation of the nation to which they belong, but never renouncing their lazzaroni character – at the youthful age at which the Provisional Government recruited them, thoroughly malleable, as capable of the most heroic deeds and the most exalted sacrifices as of the basest banditry and the foulest corruption.[4]

From the aristocracy there were bankrupted roués of doubtful means and dubious provenance, from the bourgeoisie there were degenerate wastrels on the take, vagabonds, demobbed soldiers, discharged convicts, runaway galley slaves, swindlers and cheats, thugs, pickpockets, conjurers, card-sharps, pimps, brothel-keepers, porters, day-labourers, organ grinders, scrap dealers, knife grinders, tinkers and beggars, in short the whole amorphous, jumbled mass of flotsam and jetsam that the French term bohemian ...[5]

To summarize what emerges from these lively definitions, the lumpenproletariat is (i) apparently, a tightened-up version of the common ideas of the time about the 'dangerous classes'; although the proletariat itself tended to be identified in the terms reserved by Marx and Engels for the lumpenproletariat before socialists including Marx and Engels managed to revise common meanings;[6] (ii) people drawn from both precapitalist and capitalist social formations but who had left or been evicted from their previous social class; (iii) people who do not accept the idea of making their living by regular work; (iv) a source of criminals; (v) importantly, for Marx, comprised of people who are liable to be tempted by illicit pickings into the service of the right, particularly of the finance aristocracy, who share the approach to life and morality of the lumpenproletariat.

Anyone not totally degenerate would hate to be identified as a lumpenproletarian, which leads on to the use Marx makes of the concept. One way the concept functions is to dissociate the proletariat from supporting the bourgeoisie or Bonaparte: the Mobile Guards are lumpenproletarians, not proletarians;[7] proletarian support for the regime is actually lumpen elements; the members of the Society of 10 December are lumpenproletarians.[8] The other is to use the disreputable lumpenproletariat to impugn first the finance aristocracy:

The finance aristocracy, in its mode of acquisition as well as in its pleasures, is nothing but the rebirth of the lumpenproletariat on the heights of bourgeois society ... in 1847, on the most prominent stages of bourgeois society, the same scenes were publicly enacted that regularly lead the lumpenproletariat to brothels, to workhouses and lunatic asylums, to the bar of justice, to the dungeon, and to the scaffold.[9]

And also Bonaparte: the central puzzle of the *Eighteenth Brumaire* is how a swindling nonentity managed to become President of France and to get rid the National Assembly. Bonaparte's association with the Society of 10 December enables Marx to stress the shallowness of Bonaparte and the relative insubstantiality of his regime.[10] Take away his lumpen characteristics and other explanations have to be found, such as the ones put forward by Geoff Watkins and Roger Price, respectively, that the Bonaparte legend was very powerful in French politics, and that Bonaparte's regime offered an effective path to modernization.[11] Elsewhere Marx's conspiratorial rivals for leadership of the working class are tarred with the lumpenproletarian brush.[12] In a well-researched and comprehensive article Bovenkerk argues that a major function of the lumpenproletariat in Marx and Engels is to explain away parts of the proletariat which failed to behave in a proper revolutionary fashion.[13]

Let us move on to look at the problems with Marx's definitions above. To start with, we are left unclear who the lumpenproletariat really are. 'That passively rotting mass thrown off by the lowest layers of old society' sounds as though we might be dealing with, for example, peasants displaced from the land by enclosure or by the problems Marx charts in the *Eighteenth Brumaire*.[14] Historically these gravitated towards the cities and formed, often reluctantly, the beginnings of the industrial proletariat. So the difference between a recent ex-peasant who is becoming a proletarian rather than a lumpenproletarian seems to be a matter of attitude rather than of relation to the means of production: the proletarian has become more resigned to selling his labour power. Displaced peasants could also feature as 'people without a definite trade, vagabonds, *gens sans feu et sans aveu*', but again one would expect such people to turn into proletarians over time.

What about displaced proletarians – people whose industries have closed for one reason or another, people who cannot easily find work because they are old, sick, injured? These are definitely not the lumpenproletariat, we learn in *Capital*. The lumpenproletariat are 'vagabonds, criminals [and] prostitutes', the ' "dangerous" classes'; instead displaced proletarians are the 'lazarus-layers' of the proletariat.[15] And yet, mightn't at least some displaced proletarians turn to crime or to temporary jobs sometimes, particularly if the alternative was the workhouse? Marx is ambivalent about how easy it would be for a proletarian thrown out by one branch of industry to find employment in another. Some of his writing about the worker as a mere appendage of the machine suggests that one might turn easily from the appendage of one machine into the appendage of another; however, there are suggestions that people become so distorted by one machine that they are not suitable to work with another. Again, there may be problems about accepting factory life at all, which mean that one has to start life in a factory young, although perhaps moving to another factory might not be so difficult.[16] Perhaps this ambiguity corresponds to real life in the mid nineteenth century: one factory might involve more training or more distortion of the person or worse conditions than another, the demand for hands would be greater at one time than another. Any difficulties would surely lead some proletarians towards lumpen expedients.[17]

Coming to Marx's most detailed definition, 'porters, day-labourers, scrap dealers, knife grinders [and], tinkers' all make their living through labour. They are seen as lumpenproletarians because they are self-employed and because their forms of work are very easy to take up and abandon. The question of how easy it would be to take up proletarian employment is discussed in the previous paragraph. On the face of things, if it was easy to become a proletarian there is nothing to stop at least some lumpenproletarians making the transition; if it was hard to enter a new proletarian job then lumpenproletarians would be more stuck but would tend to be joined by displaced proletarians.

'Conjurers, card sharps and brothel keepers' and 'prostitutes' raise another question. Let us assume that card sharps are actually professional gamblers rather than fraudsters. Conjurers provide legitimate entertainment; professional gamblers are part of a substantial industry which is basically legal in modern Britain, although forms of gambling are certainly banned by some governments; and prostitution can be seen as sex work although, again, there is much debate about whether prostitution or forms of it is exploitative of women's sexuality. However, whether we use Marx's attempts at distinguishing productive and unproductive labour (see Chapter 8 below) or whether we rely on various arguments about the legitimacy of particular activities we are unlikely to get a list of illegitimate activities which would command widespread agreement, whether in the society generally or amongst socialists. As a personal example I would put people who slaughter animals and sell meat, estate agents, people who pressurize children to buy useless toys and people who send spam emails or do telephone cold calling and roofers from Hartlepool on my list of dubious characters deserving to be part of the lumpenproletariat, but remove from it people who offer useful services such as prostitutes and drug dealers. What is going on here seems to be that Marx is including an assortment of occupations which command widespread dislike to make the lumpenproletariat seem less reputable rather than engaging in any kind of serious social (or socialist) analysis.

Marx's account of the finance aristocracy is also problematical. Whilst manipulating large amounts of money can certainly spill over into gambling and into illegalities such as fraud, stealing pension funds or insider trading there is a legitimate function in capitalist economies for people who move capital from less to more profitable investments, assess levels of risk in investments, offer advice to others etc. In other words, this activity is part of the general evils of capitalism rather than a specially serious excrescence, and it is hard to see how a capitalist economy could function without at least some role for a stock exchange, futures markets, currency trading etc. There may well be scope for socialists to benefit from splits amongst the bourgeoisie. For obvious reasons they would tend to side with manufacturing capital which employs people and develops the forces of production against finance capitalists simply concerned with short-term profits. This presents a particularly difficult problem for British socialists given the size and relative success of the City of London compared with British manufacturing. But short of an unlikely worldwide revolutionary expropriation of capital the way forward would seem to be to try to reduce speculation (perhaps in the British case by joining the Euro), and encourage long-term socially and environmentally responsible investment rather than eliminating financial capital. In this context the simple identification of city financiers with lumpenproletarian pleasures and vices is not helpful.

My analysis of Marx's main definitions leads me to sympathize with Bovenkerk's conclusion, based on a wider range of references: 'In their [Marx and Engels's] more theoretical works, their definition of the term lumpenproletariat is unclear and inconsistent. Anyone who tries to base further study upon their interpretation of the term will soon be at his or her wits' end.'[18]

Marx has also been challenged on the grounds that the lumpenproletariat is not always associated with the right. Historically the workers most willing to engage in revolutionary activity have been those who have recently left the land and experience factory work as inhuman and unnatural. Thus revolutions have typically happened in newly industrialized countries rather than those which are more mature. A common observation in Russia was that the more established skilled workers supported the Mensheviks whilst more recent arrivals tended to support the Bolsheviks. And it would be the new arrivals whose relatives would tend to be living a hand-to-mouth urban existence as knife grinders and porters, but who would in many cases sympathize politically with revolutionary socialism. There are similar comments in Mao[19] and Fanon.[20] The most credible group of revolutionary socialists in the United States since the Second World War were the Black Panthers, who also thought of much of their following as lumpenproletarian, and even boasted a supporting rock group entitled the Lumpen.[21]

I now turn to a modern version of the idea of the lumpenproletariat, the idea of the underclass. I want to consider this idea as found in one of its most prominent exponents, Charles Murray. What sort of people, according to Murray, are the underclass? Murray says that he first noticed the underclass in the town where he grew up 'Their homes were littered and unkempt. The men in the family were unable to hold a job for more than a few weeks at a time. Drunkenness was common. The children grew up ill schooled and ill behaved and contributed a disproportionate share of the local juvenile delinquents.'[22] Murray sees this kind of person as distinct from blue-collar workers. This description lacks the picaresque features of Marx's definitions of the lumpenproletariat, but seems to be a description of a similar social group.

Murray made his reputation with analyses of the United States, but was then invited to the United Kingdom by *The Sunday Times*. He offered two accounts of the underclass here, which were published together with British criticisms of his ideas in *Charles Murray and the Underclass: The Developing Debate*. In brief, Murray argues that areas of Britain have come to be inhabited by an underclass. There are three interlocking features of his account, illegitimacy, crime and idleness. Illegitimacy has been increasing substantially. From the time of Henry VIII to that of Elizabeth II English illegitimacy rates stayed approximately 4.5%. They then moved up somewhat in the 1950s and 1960s, but went up dramatically in the late 1970s and after so that by 1994 they hit 31.2%. Alongside this the rate of divorce has increased to a record high, and the rate of marriage, particularly first marriage, has declined. People are setting less value on being married. Illegitimate children are concentrated in the poorest areas where there are most mothers from social class V, areas such as Middlesbrough. Obviously cohabitation has risen as an alternative to marriage, but Murray sees this as an unstable relationship, probably leading on to serial cohabitation. Murray argues that professional people are continuing to marry and that amongst professionals there will be a reversion to Victorian values and thus the 'new Victorians' will be surrounded by the New Rabble.[23] The decline in marriage has occurred because of a cultural assault from feminists and because state benefits have made it too easy to raise children outside marriage.[24] One might wonder to what extent this is a black problem: isn't there a tradition of illegitimacy amongst people who originate from the West Indies? Murray acknowledges that there is, but says there are so few blacks in Britain that this boosts the illegitimacy statistics by a mere 1%.[25] Apart from the general change in British culture a major reason for the increase in illegitimacy amongst the poorest is the benefit system which makes it easier to bring up children in the absence of fathers than it was in the past.

Murray's image of these families is that they essentially lack fathers. They thus tend to become unruly, and well-behaved children who live in communities where there are many single-parent families have to be violent in self-defence. This is all made worse by the other two features of the underclass.

Murray says that the prevalence of crime in areas where there is an underclass is damaging in two ways: it makes life difficult for law-abiding people who live there, and it gives children growing up there the wrong kind of socializing norms. One tends to think of England as more law-abiding than the United States, but it has a higher rate of burglary and probably of motor theft.[26] *Violent* crime in England is rising very rapidly even if the homicide rate is well below that in the United States, and overtook the United States in 1996.[27] This is not surprising because 'in every respect – the chances of getting caught, the chances of being found guilty and the chances of going to prison – crime has become dramatically safer in Britain throughout the post-war period, and most blatantly safer since 1960'.[28]

The third major feature of the underclass is the number of able-bodied young men unwilling to work. Young men see unemployment benefit as a 'right', and are not willing to work at realistic rates of pay. If offered work they tend to decline and are insufficiently self-disciplined to hold down a job. This is potentially a disaster as they are 'barbarians' who need the civilizing influence of work and supporting a wife.

For Marx the major immediate worry concerning the lumpenproletariat was that they might be used as foot soldiers by the right, notably by the finance aristocracy. Murray describes his politics as those of a Whig,[29] and not surprisingly his worries are different. The main concerns which come out of his British writings are that the underclass costs a lot in welfare benefits and in paying for police and prisons; that the underclass culture tends to spread and is pernicious: obviously most men need to work; and that underclass habits make life very difficult for people trying to bring up children well in areas where the underclass is the main class. He adds, but does not really explain, that the underclass is a threat to the survival of 'free institutions and a civil society'.[30]

Why has an underclass been developing in Britain? Murray's explanations are the increased cultural acceptability of illegitimacy; the way in which the welfare state makes it possible for single mothers to bring up children without fathers; the way that benefits make low-paid work unattractive, particularly for men and the way that crime has become an easier way of life. Murray's account obviously immediately raises many theoretical and empirical questions. As a matter of theory, do Murray's three aspects really hang together?[31] Would an underclass be pretty much the same thing as a lumpenproletariat, and if we wish to retain a Marxist framework of analysis but reject the concept of the lumpenproletariat, does this also point to rejecting the idea of an underclass? As a matter of fact, have we, as he claims, been developing an underclass in Britain? Is there really such a phenomenon in the United States?

A British empirical reply to Murray is easy to construct, and is politically important. The most important riposte is in terms of the relationship of cause and effect. Back in the 1960s Britain had virtually full employment. I can recall from my days in the student Socialist Society at Manchester University a leading light predicting in 1968 that unemployment was likely to go over 250,000 shortly and that this would lead to a revolutionary situation.... Unemployment at that level, before the numerous statistical adjustments of the 1980s designed to disguise the extent to which unemployment had grown, left little scope for an underclass. Unemployment then grew in the 1970s thanks to increased international competition, the oil crisis and, arguably, the unrestrained use of trade union power. Then came the Thatcher victory in 1979, followed by a range of specific policies which led to massive rises in unemployment: the vigorous application of monetarism even at the height of the 1983 recession; specific anti-union measures in a series of five Acts of Parliament; cuts in benefits and in higher rates of tax and the promotion of an individualist ideology most notoriously encapsulated in 'there is no such thing as society'. Thatcherite policies, which have continued in a less abrasive form under Major and Blair, left Britain more exposed than, for example, France, to increasing international competition and at least some shifting of manufacturing jobs to Third World countries offering cheap labour.[32]

Middlesbrough is specifically cited by Murray as a venue where the underclass has developed. The starting point of a local study fits the above analysis well: in the late 1960s there was a stable social structure underpinned by 'near full employment in relatively well paid, long-term and skilled jobs in Teesside's chemical, steel and heavy engineering industries'. However, 'between 1975 and 1986 one quarter of all jobs and half of all manufacturing jobs were lost on Teesside'.[33] This is at a time when living off the state was generally being made harder.[34] Indeed, by 2000 although overall unemployment on Teesside had fallen, in Middlesbrough those unemployed and claiming benefit, people on training schemes and people who would like to work but were not formally unemployed totalled some 35 %of the labour force.[35] In these circumstances it is plain that the major problem was unemployment facilitated by the policies of new right politicians. These same politicians found Murray's doctrines appealing in that they shift the blame for unemployment and deprivation to 'generous' welfare measures on the one hand and features of the communities suffering unemployment on the other.

There are a series of more general ripostes to Murray published alongside his articles and elsewhere which are worth rehearsing briefly.[36] He argues that illegitimacy is much greater in areas inhabited by the underclass than amongst the population generally and specifically amongst well paid young people who are in work, who, he says, are the 'new Victorians', whereas actually there has been a major tendency for couples to live together and have children across all social classes; and single mothers tend to remarry eventually.[37] The idea that there is a culture of deprivation which reproduces itself was a pet theme of an early adviser to Mrs Thatcher, Sir Keith Joseph (his eugenic ideas led to the nickname 'Sir Sheath'). A substantial research programme failed to produce much support for his views.[38] In fairness to Murray his American writings seem to be based more on the idea of the immediate rational choices of the poor than of a culture of poverty on the lines of Oscar Lewis.[39]

In the Teesside study there was strong evidence of the persistence of working class rather than underclass values amongst young people living in 'Willowdene', an estate which would certainly be a home of the underclass if one really existed on Teesside:

> a consistent finding of the research was that, whatever the nature of individual experiences, young people shared a conventional outlook and aspiration to marry, settle down and have children themselves.

This aspiration was found throughout the sample, including among persistent criminals and drug users who had had the least positive experiences of family life. For virtually all young people in the sample the future is seen conventionally as 'nice husband or wife, nice house and nice car'.[40]

Because getting a steady job was very difficult in the area

people worked outside the formal labour-market: caring for children and in the home, in more informal economic activities, on youth training schemes or New Deal programmes, or in a criminal enterprises. There was a general resistance to living a life on benefits.[41]

It was striking how far these values extended. Thus the sons of a heroin dealer unable to carry on because of imprisonment took over the family business; thieving is termed 'grafting', and often approached in the same way in the sense of establishing regular hours of work; one thief commented: 'I'm not a dole-waller. I never sign on. I was a thief, that's my own occupation.'[42]

A rather different analysis of the underclass is proposed by Jock Young.[43] He starts by pointing out that relatively few people in late modern societies can feel really secure: the possibility of unemployment and family breakdown lurks for much of the population. In turn this means that other people are willing to accept the denigratory account of the underclass as it reduces their insecurity. In addition, very many people in the 'underclass' actually work, possibly not in jobs that show up in the official figures. The work they do services the homes, restaurants, entertainment and so forth of dual career families who are doing well out of post-Fordist society. This is a very important riposte, because it breaks down the distinction between the underclass and the rest of society. Young's emphasis on the role of service work is worthy of careful empirical investigation. At first sight it would look more plausible in areas where the affluent and the impoverished live in close proximity, for example in London or New York, than in extensive areas where industrial jobs have vanished and alternatives are relatively scarce, such as Detroit or mining villages in Durham.

Thus although Murray comes from a very different part of the political spectrum from Marx, and the political impact of the idea of the underclass is very different from that of the lumpenproletariat, the same comment can be made on both of them: the concept is being used for its political impact rather than because it provides good explanations. The political impact of both concepts is pernicious and both are an obstacle to clear analysis.

This general rebuttal of Murray (and indeed, Marx on the lumpenproletariat) is not the end of the story because it leaves too many loose ends. Going back to the empirical account of Britain there may not be an underclass as a group sharply distinguished from the working class, but there are certainly geographical areas where the problems alluded to by Murray are experienced: there is such a level of crime that it is not possible to go out to work to acquire things in the normal way, because your house will probably be burgled in your absence;[44] where the schools are so bad that the chances of leaving literate, numerate and with a decent set of GCSEs is very low; and where the local economy provides so little demand that it is difficult to operate businesses successfully. In the same way, to the extent that there are people with lumpenproletarian characteristics that they might well present a problem under Marx's socialism in which all work and are paid accordingly. Here the discussion has basically moved from a discussion of the underclass to that of social exclusion, a situation where the impact of a whole range of poor facilities and problems interact to make for a poor quality of life and for difficulties in any attempts to ameliorate them.[45] Without commenting on Labour's actual attempts to deal with social exclusion the idea that it is a problem and that a coordinated solution is needed is plainly valid. A dimension of these problems which Murray does not discuss in his British writings is the problem caused by acquisitive crime aimed at keeping up addicts' drug supplies. In the Middlesbrough study the coming of heroin in the early 1990s was widely seen as worsening the quality of life on the estate, and plainly requires specific attention be it more effective policing or legalization.[46]

Moreover, there is such a lot more to Murray which relates to his ideas about the underclass and which would repay attention by socialists. To start with, his specific claim about the underclass in the United States is that it developed in the late 1960s and early 1970s at a time when the general economy was booming, so that the ready British answer above won't wash, although a very specific response discussing the job situation in the inner city might.[47] It is very important to get this right because Murray's claim is that enhanced welfare and less effective policing led to the growth of an underclass, and this idea has been used by the right in US politics as a justification for cuts in welfare and more imprisonment. Part of Murray's appeal is that he uses a very straightforward rational choice explanation for the choices of poor people. Thus men drifting in and out of work, women having children outside marriage on welfare and students failing at school are all explained by Murray in terms of changes in US state policy as they would impact on any ordinary person in that situation. For socialists there must be something wrong with these arguments, and it would benefit us to pinpoint what. And although there is some pleasure in reading Murray's recent arguments to the effect that the underclass has not gone away even though unemployment and crime in the United States have gone down very substantially, one feels that he may still be making some points worth discussing.[48]

Beyond this there is a range of claims about race made by Murray. In *Losing Ground* he claims that US blacks have been particular victims of foolishly generous welfare policies, compounded with the pernicious effects of affirmative action programmes which pass students and promote individuals beyond their current merits, thus discrediting blacks generally.[49] In *The Bell Curve* he claims that general intelligence or g is something real and measurable; that US society is increasingly meritocratic in that people's position in society is now closely aligned with their intelligence; that black people are on average less intelligent than whites; and that affirmative action frequently takes particular groups of blacks beyond their abilities in dangerous and discrediting ways. Apart from the pleasure of seeing someone dare to engage in so much political incorrectness in so many directions at once, Murray's obvious concern not to be thought simplistically racist, or simply hostile to welfare makes him someone worth attending to and criticizing. Equally, however, there is the problem that Murray makes three common sense assumptions about human nature: of rational calculation, chiefly in *Losing Ground;* of the idea of a dependency culture, as found in his British writings on the underclass; and of crime being linked to stupidity in *The Bell Curve*.[50] Then in *In Pursuit of Happiness and Good Government* we find Aristotelian ideas about happiness followed by the use of Maslow's hierarchy of needs analysed as preconditions of happiness, combined with explicitly classical liberal ideas about the role of the state.[51] It is difficult to make these compatible.[52]

Thus although the lumpenproletariat/underclass should be seen as invalid as a substantive concept, there are plenty of issues surrounding it which need attention. For socialists these include the following. Do people who have developed some lumpen characteristics simply get back to work when offered decent opportunities? If not, what should be done about it? How much does it matter if some unskilled people choose to live on welfare benefits rather than do boring jobs? Is it genuinely true that the services of some less skilled and less able people are becoming superfluous in capitalist society? What should socialists aim to do about this? Particularly if it is because unskilled manufacturing jobs have shifted to Third World countries which this work is helping to develop?

7
Alienation

The alienation theory was sketched briefly in the account of the main concepts of Marxism above. As was indicated there, considerable controversy surrounds the theory. The largest controversy concerns the role of the theory in the work of Marx from 1845 onwards, and I indicated my agreement with the view that it is basically dropped. However, there is also some debate as to whether the young Marx adopted the theory from Feuerbach or where he subscribes to a more historical version of the concept taken from Hegel. In what follows I shall simply assume that any version of the theory has some link with Marx. My focus will be on the possible usefulness of the theory for explaining crime.

The basic structure of the theory involves the idea that we can identify some central features of human nature. In Marx's version of human nature we are essentially loving, powerful, creative and communal. Various social arrangements – versions of religion, the market, the capitalist system or the state – separate these aspects of human nature from real human beings. In their alien form as God, commodities, capital or the state these features of human nature dominate people and divide them from one another. Alienated people have been denuded of aspects which properly belong to them. Thus, for example

> Just as in religion the spontaneous activity of the human imagination, the human brain, and the human heart, detaches itself from the individual and reappears as the alien activity of a god or of a devil, so the activity of the worker is not his own spontaneous activity. It belongs to another, it is a loss of his self.[1]

The result is that man (the worker) feels that he is acting freely only in his animal functions – eating, drinking, and procreating, or at most in his dwelling and adornment – while in his human functions, he is nothing more than animal.[2]

It is true that eating, drinking, procreating etc., are also genuine human functions. However, when abstracted from other aspects of human activity, and turned into final and exclusive ends, they are animal.[3]

A social system which alienates people in this way is plainly contrary to human nature. Fully achieved communism restores human nature to its proper state:

> (3) *Communism* as the *positive* transcendence of *private property* as *human self-estrangement,* and therefore as the real *appropriation* of the *human* essence by and for man; communism therefore as the complete return of man to himself as a *social* (i.e., human) being – a return accomplished consciously and embracing the entire wealth of previous development. This communism, as fully developed naturalism, equals humanism, and as fully developed humanism equals naturalism; it is the genuine resolution of the conflict between man and nature and between man and man – the true resolution of the strife between existence and essence, between objectification and self-confirmation, between freedom and necessity, between the individual and the species. Communism is the riddle of history solved, and it knows itself to be this solution.[4]

Numerous claims are being made in this passage. Possibilities which could be used in an analysis of crime include: solving the alienation between an individual and his or her proper nature; solving the alienation between the individual and other people; solving our alienation from nature; solving our alienation from our proper nature. Let us now consider some ways in which these might be applied to the understanding of crime.

One possibility which appears in the work of British radical criminologists is that of allowing individuals to express their sexual nature free of the restrictions imposed by capitalist society. Thus a desire for sex outside the bounds of marriage, or for homosexual sex could be realized.[5] There is no suggestion of this interpretation being followed up in Marx's manuscripts on alienation, or, indeed, elsewhere in Marx. However, there is a real sense in which a homosexual forced to deny his basic orientation is alienated from an important feature of himself, so it is worth pursuing this possible line of development. A desire for sexual closeness, and perhaps also for sexual variety, can be seen as fundamental to the human condition.

What about someone who is so ugly, or disabled, or unprepossessing that the only way he can achieve sexual closeness in capitalist society is by paying for it? There are various ways in which the alienation theory might deal with this. It might regard sex work as a legitimate form of work, in which case a socialist society would simply try to make sure that it is carried out in a non-alienated way, with sex workers properly rewarded, great care taken of their safety etc. A more ambitious version of this could be modelled on the ideas of Fourier, whose socialist utopia included an elaborate set of arrangements to make sure that all sexual needs were catered for.[6] Alternatively the theory of alienation could be linked with abolitionist views about prostitution which see it as such an alienated and degraded form of labour that it is not an acceptable activity for anybody.[7] Maybe the best that could be offered to the sexually undesirable would be advice on self-presentation and lines of chat, plus a socialist fashion makeover?

What about people who can only find sexual fulfilment in activities with children under the age of ten, or in non-consenting episodes of sadism and rape? One strategy would be to say that their sexuality has in some way become alienated. If only they could be brought to a recognition of non-alienated sexuality they and everyone else would be much happier. However, there is a problem with such an approach, which also applies to the discussion of prostitution in the previous paragraph. The alienation theory is not contributing anything significant. Paedophiles, sadists and rapists violate the consent of another human being in an area which is both central to a person's identity and which is capable of causing profound distress. The discussion of prostitution contributes nothing to a discussion which is already available within a debate between liberalism and radical feminism, with liberals asserting that people should be free to engage in activities which do not harm others and radical feminists asserting that women are harmed in the relations of prostitution however these are conducted.

Let us now move on to more standard Marxist terrain and consider workers who are alienated from the process of production and the product of their labour, who are deeply impoverished and thus are alienated from much that makes us distinctively human. Because they have to compete for work with other workers, such workers also suffer alienation from their fellow men. In this condition it is hardly surprising if some of them turn to acquisitive crime. Crimes carried out against the capitalists, such as burgling their houses, shoplifting from their shops or stealing things from places of work could be seen as individual attempts to reverse the alienation that they suffer. Insofar as these crimes are intended to feed their wives and children they could also be seen as an attempt to reduce the effects of alienation within the family. Marxists are unlikely to actually advocate thefts such as these because they do not undermine the capitalist system. They may, indeed, reinforce it by diverting attention from what the capitalists are doing to the workers in general.

Unfortunately, of course, workers who turn to crime do not restrict themselves to thefts from the capitalists. They also steal from their fellow workers, whose limited personal property is less well defended than that of the capitalists. They may also try to deaden the drudgery of their daily lives by getting drunk and thus engaging in fights, vandalism etc. This analysis of crime motivated by poverty is very similar to the account found in Willem Bonger, as described in Chapter 3. Does the alienation analysis add anything to it? The most obvious addition is a moral claim that the workers collectively create products which, if distributed according to need, would allow them to enjoy a more properly human existence. It does not, however, tell us exactly what is available for distribution to whom, or how we would reach a situation which would allow distribution according to need. It seems akin to the claim that the workers should enjoy the full fruits of their labour, which is criticized by Marx in the *Critique of the Gotha Programme* because it failed to deal with such matters as replacing the means of production used up, economic growth, collective and individual insurance, collective consumption for education or health services, funds for those unable to work etc.[8]

Let us turn briefly to the idea of resolving the conflict between man and nature, mentioned in the above extract. This is not a major theme of the *Economic and Philosophical Manuscripts*. The overall approach to the natural world in Marx is one which celebrates the increasing human ability to dominate, control and make use of the natural world. In that respect the major and controversial projects undertaken by communist regimes arguably link to Marx's own approach.[9] One example of a project involving the domination of nature would be the ploughing up of the virgin lands under Khrushchev, which initially produced a bumper harvest of grain but which subsequently degenerated into a catastrophic failure in which the fertility of the virgin steppe was not conserved and insufficient measures were taken to avoid soil erosion, with the result that grain yields fell dramatically and the Soviet Union had to import wheat.[10] A more current example would be the Three Gorges Dam project in China, with its massive ecological consequences.[11] Eastern Europe became notoriously polluted as a consequence of

Soviet industrialization policies which disregarded environmental degradation.[12] There is, however, the possibility within both the idea of resolving the alienation between man and nature and within the later Marx's analysis of the possibilities of communism as a system based on human need, of the understanding that this is only ultimately possible in a framework where care is taken to make sure that development is ecologically sustainable.[13] Indeed, the capitalist pursuit of profit arguably tends to disregard the ecological consequences of industrial expansion.[14] On this admittedly rather fragile basis it would be possible within the theory of alienation to think in terms of crime as the commission of wrong against the environment. Such wrongdoing might possibly be recognized as a crime within a capitalist society, but is more likely, if recognized at all, to be dealt with as an administrative misdemeanour.

What, finally, about solving the alienation between our current situation and proper nature? This line of thought offers numerous possibilities for the analysis of crime, but also displays the underlying problem of the alienation analysis. The alienation of workers under capitalism leading to the commission of crime is one possible example of this which we have already seen. Capitalists are alienated from other people because of their need to compete with other capitalists, and, flowing from this, their need to keep wages to a minimum, overwork and neglect the health and safety of their workforce, inflict damage on the environment, defraud investors, give short measure, sell adulterated goods, disregard the health of consumers, engage in false and exaggerated advertising etc. How much of this is actually regarded as crime as opposed to legitimate competitive practices or breaches of administrative regulations varies between one capitalist society and another. So far so Marxist.

Women are alienated from their loving, nurturing, communal and lesbian nature by patriarchy, which is itself intertwined with capitalism. They are constrained towards competition with other women for the benefits of marriage to men who enjoy power and either wealth or inflated wages, and because of this are slaves to the fashion and cosmetics industries. They are subordinated through domestic and sexual violence, which is justified and celebrated in pornography. Ideally they would live in lesbian communes, perhaps with a goddess presiding. Because of their alienated condition they are subject to a variety of crimes, some of which are recognized but not properly prosecuted, others of which are simply accepted or even celebrated: suttee, female circumcision, rape, pressure to have sex, harassment, objectification, prostitution, denial of the right to vote, grossly unequal education and pay, glass ceilings, abortion or abandonment of girl children, burning of witches, unequal sharing of housework and childcare, trafficking, double standards in marriage and divorce, dress codes imposed by mullahs and fashion magazines, hormone replacement therapy, exclusion from the Catholic priesthood – the list is very extensive.[15]

The previous paragraph fits a radical feminist account of women, but grates with the Marxian account of alienation. There is no suggestion in Marx and Engels that women are naturally lesbian, and there are some obvious criticisms of the picture of human nature and society that any critic influenced by the Marxist tradition would want to make. The list of crimes is excessively universal: women in the advanced capitalist countries do not normally suffer female circumcision, suttee or denial of the right to vote, and the extent to which they suffer the other crimes varies greatly between different classes and states. Linked to this, women themselves vary considerably, and thus do not all aspire to live in lesbian communes. Some women are quite happy as fashionable, heterosexual, stockbrokers etc. The account of alienation in the previous paragraph is based on a conception of human nature which is open to challenge.

The conception of human nature which underlies Marx's theory of alienation is also open to challenge, however. The particular challenge which appears to have led Marx to at least place much less emphasis on the theory if not to fully abandon it came in a book by the anarchist Max Stirner, *The Ego and His Own* (1845)[16]. This was the first major right-wing anarchist book. It took the idea of alienation one step further than Marx, and argues that the individual suffers alienation not just in the state or religion but also in human brotherhood and community, both of which are diversions from the proper focus of the individual on himself. The best way to answer this challenge was to try to develop a materialist account of human nature, based upon the way that real groups of people actually live. This is what Marx and Engels attempt in *The German Ideology*, particularly in the first section on Feuerbach. Their claim there that human nature and history is founded upon the mode of production is fundamental to the other theories that are characteristic of Marxism. This claim was also the basis of their response to Stirner: individuals simply don't and can't live on their own and solely consider their own interests in the way that Stirner assumes. The historical materialist picture of human nature would need to be developed into an account of gender to provide an adequate response to the radical feminists.

An account of alienation could also be written in terms of human beings' natural spiritual bent, from which they are diverted by a materialistic society, or in terms of our racial nature as – for example – Aryans, from which we can be diverted by Jewish conspiracies, cosmopolitanism, Negro culture and so forth. Some individuals are particularly aggressive, or competitive, or contemplative, and could argue that in a socialist society they were being alienated from their proper nature to which the human beings would also aspire if only they were not diverted by a misleading socialist ideology. An alienation theory is fundamentally a set of moral claims about the conditions in which human beings should properly live or in which they will flourish. The historical materialist analysis initiated by Marx and Engels provides a relatively thin account of human nature: we have a range of basic needs for food, warmth, shelter and sex, which can be satisfied in very diverse ways; and a range of abilities such as language, manual dexterity and an ability to conceptualize, which help to fulfil these basic needs.[17] Beyond this we are very flexible, and can live in a very wide variety of social formations and physical surroundings, and it is a matter of considerable debate in what way these relate to human flourishing, or indeed what counts as human flourishing.

Thus although a theory of alienation can be related to a wide range of possible crimes, the analysis of this chapter suggests that it does not contribute anything useful to our conceptualization of crime or our understanding of why it occurs or how it could be reduced. However, theories developed in some way from historical materialism would appear to be more promising.

8
Crime and the Reproduction Conditions of Capitalism

A philosopher produces ideas, a poet poems, a clergyman sermons, a professor compendia and so on. A criminal produces crimes. If we take a closer look at the connection between this latter branch of production and society as a whole, we shall rid ourselves of many prejudices. The criminal produces not only crimes but also criminal law, and with this also the professor who gives lectures on criminal law and in addition to this the inevitable compendium in which this same professor throws his lectures onto the general market as 'commodities'. This brings with it augmentation of national wealth, quite apart from the personal enjoyment which – as a competent witness, Professor Roscher, [tells] us ... the manuscript of the compendium brings to its originator himself. The criminal moreover produces the whole of the police and of criminal justice, constables, judges, hangmen, juries, etc.; and all these different lines of business, which form just as many categories of the social division of labour, develop different capacities of the human mind, create new needs and new ways of satisfying them. Torture alone has given rise to the most ingenious mechanical inventions, and employed many honourable craftsmen in the production of its instruments. The criminal produces an impression, partly moral and partly tragic, as the case may be, and in this way renders a 'service' by arousing the moral and aesthetic feelings of the public. He produces not only compendia on Criminal Law, not only penal codes and along with them legislators in this field, but also art, belles-lettres, novels, and even tragedies, as not only Müllner's *Schuld* and Schiller's *Räuber* show, but *Oedipus* and *Richard the Third*. The criminal breaks the monotony and everyday security of bourgeois life. In this way he keeps it from stagnation, and gives rise to that uneasy tension and agility without which even the spur of competition would get blunted. Thus he gives a stimulus to the productive forces. While crime takes a part of the redundant population off the labour market and thus reduces competition among the labourers – up to a certain point preventing wages from falling below the minimum – the struggle against crime absorbs another part of this population. Thus the criminal comes in as one of those natural 'counterweights' which bring about a correct balance and open up a whole perspective of 'useful' occupations. The effects of the criminal on the development of productive power can be shown in detail. Would locks ever have reached their present degree of excellence had there been no thieves? Would the making of bank-notes have reached its present perfection had there been no forgers? Would the microscope have found its way into the sphere of ordinary commerce (see Babbage) but for trading frauds? Does not practical chemistry owe just as much to the adulteration of commodities and the efforts to show it up as to the honest zeal for production? Crime, through its ever new methods of attack on property, constantly calls into being new methods of defence, and so is as productive as STRIKES for the invention of machines. And if one leaves the sphere of private crime: would the world market ever have come into being but for national crime? Indeed, would even the nations have arisen? And has not the Tree of Sin been at the same time the Tree of Knowledge ever since the time of Adam?[1]

This above extract is found in Marx's economic manuscripts of 1861–3. It forms a tiny part of his discussion of the work of other economists. Because it is one of Marx's most extended discussions of crime, as well as being entertaining in its own right, it is frequently quoted. As I indicated above, its initial purpose was not to provide an analysis of crime but to offer sarcastic comments on a flawed distinction, as Marx saw it, between productive and unproductive labour. Marx is arguing that for some economists virtually any labour is productive in the sense that it contributes to human achievements and indirectly to the production of profit. Marx himself argues that a proper conception of productive labour is restricted to labour which directly contributes to the production of profit, or in some of his formulations labour which directly contributes to a material product which is sold for a profit.

As I shall explain shortly, in my view Marx's own position on this issue is flawed. However, if we were going to follow Marx on this, the better of the two accounts would be that productive labour directly contributes to the production of profit. This can be seen most easily if we consider a product with a substantial intellectual content, such as a piece of software, a book or a DVD. The disc or the paper, the material vehicle on which the product is delivered, is very cheap to produce, whereas the content can be extremely expensive because it contains the labour of very many skilled labourers. The requirement for a material product seems unjustified: the price of any of these items is basically determined by the content rather than by the way it is delivered. If this argument is accepted we are left with a distinction between productive labour which contributes directly to the making of a profit, meaning that it forms part of a product which is sold, and unproductive labour which is paid for out of revenue. The same physical activity can fall into either category: a cook working to feed her family or to produce a meal in a household where she is a servant is an unproductive labourer because her work does not produce a profit; if she does the same work in a restaurant run by a capitalist she is a productive labourer. Similar comments could be made about an actor in a play put on within a household in contrast to the same play put on in a profit-making theatre. A particular point of this distinction is that government employees normally do not make a profit, so that the Queen, Cabinet ministers, state-employed road makers, admirals and generals are unproductive labourers. In a society which is run on capitalist lines the obvious aim is to reduce the number of unproductive labourers and boost the number of productive labourers.

The distinction which Marx is trying to make is one that he takes from classical political economy, and is reasonably clear. However, a brief consideration of the policy implications for advanced capitalist states suggests that the distinction breaks down. Such states employ very many people as teachers in schools and universities, neither of which are in business to make a profit. According to Marx's distinction a rational capitalist government would sack the unproductive labourers who research and teach science and technology. It would be better from a capitalist point of view if they were set to work producing hamburgers in a fast food chain run for profit. Mrs Thatcher's government actually came quite close to this.[2] However, a rational capitalist government aims to produce large numbers of highly skilled labourers who can help contribute to profit-making scientific and technological enterprises. This argument seems to me to be overwhelming. The major difference between the advanced capitalist countries and Third World countries is not the number of unskilled labourers available in each but the level of scientific and technical research and expertise available in the former and missing in the latter.

If we are willing to accept that researchers and teachers in science and technology make a massive difference to the profitability of capitalist enterprises, the flood gates are opened in principle for other unproductive labourers. Under the impact of second-wave feminism there was a debate amongst Marxists about the role of domestic labour. In terms of Marx's distinction it is definitely unproductive, but it is clearly necessary in order to reproduce workers on a daily and generational basis. Moreover the quality of domestic labour is arguably very important in some respects for profitability. Children who start school able to read and with an enthusiasm for learning have greater potential to become highly productive labourers in contrast to those who lack these qualities. Other aspects are less clear: a husband entertained by his wife to gourmet cooking and ecstatic sex might perform better at work than one provided with processed food and perfunctory sex, but he might be distracted by memories of the night's pleasures.

If scientific education and domestic labour have an impact on profitability, the same may be true of a range of less likely unproductive activities. Entertainers paid out of revenue by the BBC may help people to relax and therefore be more productive at work. Vicars may produce sermons encouraging perfection in everything, including work, and hence to contribute to profitability. The Queen helps to produce national unity and a calm atmosphere in which production can flourish, while her family keep the nation relaxed and entertained with a superb soap opera.

Moreover, productive labourers in one line of business can have deleterious effects on the productivity of labourers elsewhere in the economy. The argument that follows is rather simplistic, but readers will be able to devise ways of rendering it more sophisticated and satisfactory. Let us start with workers who produce legally available firearms in the United States. Although they help to produce a profit for their capitalist employers, the effect of firearms used on other citizens renders them less productive (injured) or terminally unproductive. Workers who produce alcohol and tobacco make a profit for their companies but have bad effects on the health and productivity of workers more generally. Similar comments can be made about workers who produce unhealthy food, making other workers overweight and under active. These are the more obvious examples, but the same sort of argument could be used about employees of companies offering cosmetic surgery, the producers of at least some legal and illegal drugs, the makers of some computer games, and the journalists on celebrity magazines which distract people from their work etc.

Even if it is not helpful to categorize labour as productive or unproductive, this discussion suggests a method of analysis which is genuinely useful in providing at least part of a Marxist account of crime. We can ask what role crime (or, in principle, any other social phenomenon) has in reproducing a capitalist economy, and whether or not it would have a different role in reproducing a socialist economy. A very extended model for this type of analysis may be found in *Capital* Volume 2, which comprises a discussion of the economic reproduction conditions of capitalism, based initially on the writings of the Physiocrats. Marx argues that there needs to be a balance between different sectors of the economy. This idea was followed up in a very influential essay by Althusser, 'Ideology and the State', in which he argued that in addition to economic reproduction a capitalist system requires the reproduction of labour power. He said that this occurs through a number of 'Ideological State Apparatuses', and gives as examples the school, the family, the legal system, the political system, the trade unions, the media, culture etc.[3] This idea was widely adopted in the 1970s by authors who were not remotely Althusserian.[4] Its popularity was doubtless helped by its similarity to the more familiar functionalist method of analysis characteristic of 1960s sociology. It also enabled radicals who were working in any of the 'state apparatuses' to argue that their attempts at being radical teachers or social workers were undermining the capitalist system by interfering with its reproduction conditions.

The popularity of the theory subsequently waned. One problem was that it fails to take account of the plural characteristics of the 'Apparatuses'. It is difficult to see Arthur Scargill, the President of the National Union of Mineworkers, who led a disastrous and lengthy strike in 1984–5 and who was referred to by Mrs Thatcher as 'the enemy within', or the leaders of Sinn Fein, who at that time were linked to the Provisional IRA and its armed struggle, as part of a 'state apparatus'. As the scale of Mrs Thatcher's assault on the trade unions and the welfare state became apparent, radicals working in parts of the state became more involved in trying to defend their institutions or welfare traditions or funding or their own jobs rather than attacking bodies which formed part of an 'ideological state apparatus'. The Conservatives kept winning electoral victories, the Soviet Union collapsed, and disaffected radicals became prone to adopt ideas drawn from postmodernism or Foucault.

However, if a Marxist account of crime and criminal justice is to be taken seriously an analysis of how these function to reproduce the capitalist system must surely be an important part of it. There are various levels at which this analysis will now be attempted. Certain basic features of criminal law are needed in any functioning society. Beyond this, some aspects of criminal law are necessary for the functioning of capitalism. The criminal justice system has a role in disciplining and channelling the reserve army of labour towards useful work and away from activities which interfere with capitalist reproduction. Criminal justice arguably has an ideological function in the reproduction of capitalism. The criminal justice system can also directly or indirectly generate a profit for capitalist enterprises.

In Chapter 2 the idea was accepted that there are 'consensus crimes' which are criminal in a wide variety of societies, although exactly how they are defined and the penalties they carry vary. The examples given were killing other members of the society without good reason, injuring other members of the society without good reason and stealing personal possessions. These acts are illegal because if they were decriminalized it would be very difficult to run a society. Even if most people continued to behave as if these acts were illegal, the knowledge that anyone that we meet could legally rob or kill us would mean that we would have to be constantly very much on our guard. These acts would plainly have to remain illegal in a socialist society, even if the procedures and penalties associated with them were changed.

The analysis in the previous paragraph can be seen as part of a general point, namely that amongst the reproduction conditions for capitalism are the more fundamental reproduction conditions needed for all human societies. These include breathable air, a way of maintaining tolerable temperatures which would probably include clothing, sources of food and some way of preserving language and transmitting culture. It is very difficult to imagine any sort of human society being preserved if these conditions were not met. It hardly needs pointing out that undermining these basic reproduction conditions of any society also undermines capitalism, but not in a way that is likely to lead towards a socialist society. The American occupation of Iraq from 2003 onwards involved an experiment with these conditions in which the policing and security arrangements of Saddam Hussein's regime were terminated without the substitution of any effective replacement. This led to widespread looting and disorder, which in turn started to undermine some of the basic requirements of continued life. Not surprisingly this led to the occupation becoming extremely unpopular, and also to groups of people setting up their own policing and security arrangements in the form of Shi'ite militias etc.

To some extent the legal reproduction conditions required by all human societies help to reproduce capitalism. If personal property cannot simply be stolen from someone, and particularly if there are no limits to the scale on which personal property may be accumulated, one of the requirements of capitalism is in place. There are, however, other legal requirements. Personal property must be alienable, not entailed. The purchase and sale of labour power must be allowed. It must be possible to make and enforce contracts, so that capitalists can make contracts with each other and also with consumers. A number of other provisions are not absolutely essential but are definitely helpful. It is probably better if workers are allowed to join unions to allow for the orderly negotiation of pay, but the powers of unions should be very limited. The more features of human life that are available for sale and purchase the better. Feudal limits on the sale of land or of labour power restrict the possibilities of capitalism. Moral limits on selling sexual services, drugs, slaves, body parts etc. are undesirable. It should be possible to form limited liability companies with shareholders.

For capitalism to flourish there must be as large a market as possible, and this will in turn lead to modifications in the criminal law. There should ideally be a common currency across as wide an area as possible, or failing that, it should be as easy as possible to exchange one currency for another. Weights and measures should be common across a wide area. There should be free movement of goods and people. This means that there should be no customs barriers and tariffs, no restrictions on movements of capital or labour. Intellectual property should be defended by the law. Improvements in transport obviously make the market work better. If particular states want to enforce standards, for example to make sure that cooking equipment is safe, that food is not adulterated, that medicines are pure, that electrical equipment does not interfere with radio transmissions etc., these should ideally be agreed internationally. This will allow capitalists to trade easily across national boundaries. Some of these features are typically defended by criminal law: forgery is normally a serious criminal offence. Other features such as the enforcement of standards for consumer products are more typically dealt with by administrative regulations.

So far we have been considering the legal underpinnings of capitalism, indicating both features that are logically necessary and those that help capitalism to function well and expand. We now move into areas which are much more contingent, starting with the issue of disciplining the working class. The early stages of the development of industrial capitalism involve massive changes for people who move from a peasant way of life to manufacturing. Instead of life governed by the hours of daylight, the weather and the seasons, the pattern of daily life is set by the demands of the manufacturing process. This is experienced as unnatural. Although some people leave the countryside attracted by the possibilities of life in the town others have been turned off the land, have no particular desire to work in industry and no aptitude or skill for life as workers. Even those attracted by urban life may well arrive in town without work arranged. There are thus likely to be large numbers of people drifting from one place to another with very limited means of support, and hence with a tendency to turn to crime. Urban workers who are thrown out of work generally lack the fallback resources which may be available in the countryside such as their own garden for growing vegetables, or common land where food can be gathered or hunted. They, too, may be driven towards crime as a way of surviving.

The perceived unnaturalness of factory life tends to generate various forms of Utopian Socialism, fuelled by a belief that this way of life cannot go on indefinitely. This is likely to lead to unrest, or, indeed, full-scale revolution. What is being described here is found in varying forms in different places: in England, Owenite socialism, Ricardian socialism, Chartism; in France the movements associated with Fourier, Saint Simon, Cabet; in Germany some Marxist socialism but also ideas associated with Weitling and Lasalle; in more backward areas such as Spain, Italy and Russia an assortment of anarchists and populists. A whole series of unsuccessful and successful revolutions in the nineteenth and early twentieth century testify to the instability associated with industrialization.

Overall, then, the strains of industrialization are liable to place demands on the criminal justice system. What about the reproduction requirements of a developed capitalist economy? In order to answer this question attention needs to be paid to the development of what David Garland calls the Culture of Control. In talking of this he is drawing a contrast between an era of penal welfarism which lasted from the late nineteenth century until the 1970s and the current period which has been characterized by much greater punitiveness and higher rates of imprisonment. Not everywhere has been afflicted by this culture, so that today we have a stark contrast between the Scandinavian countries with rates of imprisonment varying from 66 per hundred thousand in

Denmark, Norway and Finland to 82 per hundred thousand in Sweden on the one hand and the United States with 750 per hundred thousand on the other. There must obviously be some major differences between either the nature of capitalism in these two areas, or between aspects of the culture of the two sorts of society. Rates of imprisonment in Scandinavia are about as low as those anywhere in the world. They could thus be regarded as somewhere around the minimum level required to maintain a capitalist economy. Why are they so well below the rate in the United States? An immediate answer, based on a comparative analysis of the United States, France and Finland, is offered by Michael Tonry: 'Public officials in those countries chose the penal policies'.[5] His point is that changes in rates of crime over the latter years of the twentieth century are fairly similar between the three countries. What is different is the pressures on politicians who are in charge of criminal justice systems, and the strategies they adopted in response to these pressures:

> American politicians for thirty years competed with one another to show who was tougher on crime and in a wide variety of ways: requiring mandatory prison sentences, increasing the lengths of prison sentences, paying for a many-fold increase in the size of the prison establishment, campaigning for office on 'toughness platforms'.[6]

In contrast, in the mid-1960s Finnish policymakers decided that rates of imprisonment in Finland were too high, and stuck to this view over the next 40 years, producing several strategies to reduce numbers of prisoners. In doing this they were asserting that Finland is part of Scandinavia and of the West, sharply different from the Soviet Union.[7]

Why are Scandinavian rates of imprisonment so much lower than those in the United States? This is a question that would ideally have a very long answer, but some major factors in the low rate of Scandinavian imprisonment and very civilized conditions in Scandinavian prisons include the following. The Scandinavian countries for various reasons have very strong egalitarian traditions, various measures to discourage excessive consumption of alcohol, considerable emphasis on the importance of education and great respect for highly educated professionals such as academics and a correspondingly elevated tone in newspapers and television broadcasting. The countries enjoy excellent welfare states, political systems based on proportional representation and compromise. Because the societies were egalitarian there seems to have been less sense of difference between offenders and other citizens, leading to the early abandonment of corporal punishment and a strong tendency to keep prison sentences short. The aim of imprisonment was seen as reform, and loss of liberty was seen as enough of a punishment on its own. Because of respect for professional expertise the public was happy to leave the running of prisons to professionals. From the 1970s there came to be a greater emphasis on the rights of prisoners as opposed to prison as a welfare measure.[8] Some of what is being described here should be regarded as specific features of Scandinavian culture, but many features can be understood as aspects of a liberal and democratic variant of socialism, suggesting that a form of socialism achieved with a strong degree of consensus and without massive class struggle offers a good prospect for minimizing the role of the criminal justice system.

The United States stands at the opposite end of the capitalist spectrum, at least where imprisonment is concerned. As we have seen, from the 1980s onward the United States has been affected by the shift to an informational economy linked to globalization and a shifting of jobs to countries with cheaper labour. Pay and wealth differentials have expanded massively. Life for ordinary working people, already much less secure than in Europe because of the very limited US welfare state, has become still more risky. Politicians have emphasized the extent of crime and promised robust measures to deal with it. The war on drugs has greatly increased the rate of imprisonment, which has gone from approximately 100 per hundred thousand in the mid-1970s to some 750 per hundred thousand today.[9] The major question which this shift from penal welfarism to a culture of control raises for us is the extent to which it can be explained by the change in the nature of American capitalism as opposed to other changes in US society and culture which cannot be related directly to the economy. This is a difficult question: the economy on its own does not imprison people, but politicians seeking support against a background of worsening economic conditions for ordinary people can certainly present themselves as tough on crime, complete with measures which will increase the number of people being imprisoned. This is what Chambliss describes as the Republican Southern Strategy: winning votes which might otherwise go to the Democrats by raising fears of crime and disorder, aided by FBI manipulation of the crime figures to make them appear worse than they really are except after the application of zero tolerance policing, when figures are manipulated to show massive reductions of crime. Essentially the same process is described by Parenti (see Chapter 4 above).

This process fits very well with the role of the criminal justice system as part of the ideological reproduction conditions of capitalism. An ideological explanation of crime is used to raise fears amongst working people. These fears are then used as a justification for harsh penal measures against petty criminals, who are made to look much more threatening than they are in reality. The large numbers of criminals being dealt with by the criminal justice system provide the justification for additional spending on police, prisons etc. The additional police then justify their pay by finding still further criminals, and the vicious circle carries on.

A milder version of the same process has occurred in Britain, basically starting from Home Secretary Michael Howard's declaration in 1993 that 'prison works'. Together with various measures that have increased prison numbers and the Labour Party feeling itself constrained to adopt the slogan 'tough on crime, tough on the causes of crime', Britain's prisons have filled to bursting while the press continues, on the whole, to emphasize any aspects of crime statistics which suggest that crime, and particularly violent crime, is rising and getting out of hand. Labour's adoption of this basically Conservative approach has helped to procure an unprecedented three electoral victories for a Labour government which has been extremely relaxed about massive accretions of wealth,[10] a widening gap between rich and poor, and which has generally pursued very mildly left of centre policies.

The swollen criminal justice system in Britain and the totally out-of-hand situation in the United States thus certainly help to reproduce capitalism ideologically. It is by no means clear that expanding the criminal justice system in this way is necessary to preserve capitalism. Capitalism is reasonably stable in Germany and Italy, both of which have relatively low numbers of prisoners. Several features of the current situation mean that capitalism is not under serious threat. The working class is generally quite divided and industrially passive. Living standards have been tending to rise as the price of many commodities has fallen. There are worrying 'external' threats, notably from militant Islam and from climate change, but there is no reason to believe that existing governments or their rivals slightly to the left or right are incapable of responding to them. There is no obvious working model of socialism to attract workers in the advanced capitalist countries.

It therefore seems worth asking whether the culture of control is helping to preserve aspects of capitalism which might be under threat without it. Obviously some capitalists are doing very nicely out of the culture of control, be they firms building and running private prisons, suppliers of prison equipment, drug testing equipment etc., but I shall be arguing in a subsequent section that they are too small a sector to be essential to the overall welfare of capitalism. Similar arguments suggest that although the criminal justice system provides employment or alternatives to employment to a large number of people, the numbers are at best somewhat helpful to the overall capitalist system. Prison may be playing some very limited role in educating and reforming prisoners so that they become useful workers, but is probably encouraging recidivism at a much higher rate. Overall, then, the currently bloated criminal justice systems of the United Kingdom and the United States appear to be an excrescence on their respective capitalist systems rather than an essential feature of them. A minimalist system on Scandinavian lines would appear to be the essential minimum required to reproduce a capitalist system.

Criminal justice and economic reproduction

If the current swollen criminal justice systems of Britain and the United States are not essential to the ideological reproduction of their respective capitalist systems, is there a case that they are performing a vital economic role? Are they, for example, making a massive profit for particular capitalists? Or providing useful employment or activity for people who would otherwise have no useful economic role? Or perhaps providing vital benefits to depressed regions? As we have seen, the criminal justice system in the United States is very much larger than any other, and is probably also more open to profit-making by private companies. If, therefore, the economic argument is valid anywhere it should be valid in the United States.

Let us start with the profits made by particular capitalist corporations. There are three main corporations involved in providing and running privatized prisons in the United States. The largest of these is the Corrections Corporation of America, which houses 72,500 beds in 69 facilities in 19 states plus the District of Colombia.[11] The GEO Group has 49,300 prison and immigrant detention beds in 18 states.[12] Cornell Companies Inc. has 75 facilities in 15 states and has a service capacity of 18,465.[13] This would appear to amount to some 140,000 prisoners out of the US total of approximately 2,259,000, making up some 6% of the total, although some of the private numbers may be illegal immigrants awaiting deportation.[14] Private prisons are thus not by any means the main place where US prisoners are held, and although private prisoner numbers have tended to rise, the idea that the rise is solely driven by a search for profits from private prisons is too far fetched to take seriously. A more plausible theory is that the rise of private prisons is a consequence of factors that are increasing the number of prisoners in the United States because they appear to offer cost savings. Although the corporate websites make this claim,[15] along with claiming that the prisons perform well in terms of education programmes and prisoner welfare, the evidence seems to be equivocal at best. The most obvious source of cost savings is the employment of relatively unskilled and low-paid staff; a less obvious one is the shifting of costs which in public prisons would count as part of the cost of imprisonment into the public sector.[16]

What about the more plausible theory that the expansion of the US criminal justice system is driven by the possibilities of private profit-making? There are certainly very many companies which make a profit from building and/or running prisons. The Corrections Connection website, which acts as a noticeboard for people in the prison business, lists 2,700 companies who offer goods and services which are useful in running prisons.[17] *Correctional News Magazine* provides links from its website to more than 450 suppliers to the corrections industry, offering everything from access control systems to X-ray/screening by way of body armour, detention hardware, inmate management systems, perimeter fencing, precast cells, restraints, video motion detection, video visitation, weapons storage and numerous other headings.[18] The industry body, the American Correctional Association, solicits similar advertising for its magazine *Corrections Today*, its journal, *Corrections Compendium*, and for its annual *Buyers' Guide of Correctional Products and Services*.[19] Other money spinners include health care for prisoners, which is a major market even if the level of care provided is abysmal, prison brokers who sell bed spaces to states who need them,[20] and prison labour, involving 1,310 industries and annual sales of over $2 billion a year in 1998, with prisoners working directly or indirectly for Microsoft, IBM, Texas Instruments, AT&T and TWA.[21] There will also, of course, be lucrative markets for police and prison warder weaponry, cars, helicopters etc. With 2,259,000 prisoners, a substantial prison-building programme and the other personnel of the criminal justice system – police, judges, lawyers, probation officers and warders – we are obviously looking at a sizeable body of people.

Profits can also be made less directly from the criminal justice system. *Correctional News Magazine* is itself one example of this. Others include *SWAT Magazine*, which carries articles discussing weaponry, equipment and training for SWAT teams and, one suspects, those who admire them,[22] and *Guns and Weapons for Law Enforcement*, with reviews of – in the main – prototypes of assault rifles and sub-machine guns which will be suitable for US police officers once they go into production.

There is an annual mock prison riot at Moundsville, Virginia in May. Attendance is free, but the event provides marketing opportunities for assorted devices designed to temporarily disable prisoners.[23] Degrees in criminology and training for the various personnel of the criminal justice system are plainly thriving.

There is no doubt that collectively a very large number of people are involved in the US criminal justice system, and that catering to their need (or 'needs') is a major profit-making enterprise.[24] We should still not, however, conclude that this is an essential part of a capitalist economy. Other capitalist economies get along with a much smaller part of their activities devoted to the suppression of crime. This overall conclusion is similar to that of Christian Parenti:

> ... incarceration is a small-scale form of Keynesian, public-works-style stimulus. New penitentiaries can revive economically moribund regions and, acting as anchor industries, can bring in other employers such as medical services and retail chains.... The gulag provides opportunities for localised growth but it does not and will not assume the mantle of *de facto* industrial policy because it cannot and will not replace the role of military and aerospace spending.[25]

There is a strong argument that the gulag is a drag on the US economy in various respects. From about 1994 the United States has been spending more on prisons than it is on higher education, and there is a direct connection between excessive spending on prisons and relatively limited educational spending.[26] Castells presents very persuasive arguments to the effect that advanced scientific and technological education is crucial to maintaining the relative advantage of leading capitalist economies (see Chapter 1 above). There is certainly a substantial lobby for spending money on crime, of which more in the next section, but the lobby is there because spending in this area has been allowed to get out of hand. There are similar lobbies for other economic sectors such as agricultural or aviation.

The criminal justice system is one way of dealing with minorities who would otherwise be unemployed and perhaps disruptive. However, it would surely be possible to deal with black Americans in other, more humane and intelligent ways. Prison is plainly a damaging experience for most inmates. It is more difficult to obtain employment with a prison record. There is a high rate of recidivism. Family ties tend to break down. On the whole, private prisons appear to make this worse in the United States. Prison places are typically farmed out to surplus prisoners from other states, making travel distances for visiting relatives much greater. Arizona, for example, houses about 9,500 prisoners from other states in private prisons, including 850 from Alaska.[27] Dyer argues that this is a deliberate policy which enables the providers of private prisons to evade the regulations and inspection regimes which apply to prisoners in their home state, and which thus contributes to make prison an even worse experience.[28] One of the best ways to reduce recidivism is prisoner education, particularly higher education. Although some higher education continues in US prisons, higher education provision was basically terminated by the provisions of the 1994 Violent Crime Control and Law Enforcement Act. Prior to this Act about a tenth of 1% of Pell Grants (the basic Federal system of grant aid for poor students in higher education) were used to provide for the costs of higher education for prisoners. One of the provisions of the Act was to stop this practice. Higher education was very effective at lowering recidivism rates, and also had the potential to help prisoners become economically useful.[29] However, of course, higher recidivism provides more business for private prisons.

If it is simply a matter of preventing unemployed minorities from interfering with the reproduction of the capitalist system, prison is by no means the only alternative. In the 1960s disproportionate numbers of poor and black Americans were drafted into the Armed Forces to serve in Vietnam. However, in principle, it would surely be possible to employ potentially disruptive young men in other ways. At least a proportion of them could be educated to a point where they are useful in the informational economy. American cities could compete with each other in providing beautiful parks with labour-intensive floral displays, and the resulting expertise amongst minorities could have all sorts of useful spin-offs in the development of market gardening. Or they could compete in putting on elaborate musical performances, or displays of art. There is an almost infinitely large need for social care of the elderly, disabled and infirm, and young minority men could help to supply some of this. All of these possibilities could be seen as helping to reproduce capitalism. Of course, all of these sectors would provide opportunities for private enter-prise in much the same way as do prisons, and would generate lobbies devoted to persuading politicians and the general public that America needs better gardens, operas, social care etc.

Mass imprisonment as an economic option

The above argument that it is possible to run capitalist economies in ways that do not depend on mass imprisonment, together with the wide variation between the United States and other capitalist societies suggests that we should be looking at capitalist options rather than claiming that a particular level of imprisonment is an essential feature of capitalism, or an essential feature of some variant of capitalism. This makes it possible to produce theories which are much more plausible than claims about economic reproduction alone.

This approach is taken in slightly differing ways by William Chambliss, Jeffrey Reiman and Christian Parenti (see Chapter 4 above). Chambliss describes the expansion of the US criminal justice system. The central feature of his explanation is the Republican Southern Strategy. The earliest version of this was tried by Richard Nixon in 1968, but it really took off some time later. It involves appealing to voters' fears of social unrest and crime, and promising to be tough on crime. It was aided and abetted by the FBI acting as a lobby in favour of extra resources by manipulating the crime statistics so as to give the impression of crime getting out of control. He also mentions the war on drugs as a major source of expansion. A particular purpose of the war on drugs is to deal with the problem of surplus black Americans. Reiman talks of the theory of Pyrrhic Defeat, meaning that the goal of the American criminal justice system is to give the impression that there is a major threat from street crime perpetrated by poor Americans. This process is helped along by an emphasis on victimless crimes, particularly the war on drugs, which leads to other crimes committed to maintain drug habits. Black Americans are particularly likely to be sentenced to imprisonment, a process which they (reasonably) see as arbitrary and unjust. Prison is brutalizing, renders ex-prisoners difficult to employ and thus encourages further crime. Both Reiman and Chambliss argue that one of the functions of the criminal-ization of poor and black Americans is to deflect attention from rampant and extremely damaging corporate crime. The distinguishing feature of Parenti's account is his emphasis on the economic background. His argu-ment is that the United States ended the Second World War in a very advantageous position compared to the devastated economies of Europe and Japan. As these recovered their lower labour costs put them at a con-siderable advantage. American industry also had the problem of powerful trade unions and an increase in health and safety regulation. Parenti also talks about the Republican Southern Strategy, which he sees as a way of promoting the ideas of the New Right and thus rolling back regulation and union power. He puts rather more emphasis then Reiman and Chambliss on the policing aspect of the criminal justice system, but his approach is fully compatible with theirs.

Joel Dyer in *The Perpetual Prisoner Machine: How America Profits from Crime*[30] makes no claim whatsoever to be contributing to Marxist criminological theory, but his analysis can be seen as supplementing the above account. At first sight he is providing a strictly economic analysis:

> [T]he motive behind the unprecedented growth in the US prison population is the $150 billion being expended annually on the criminal justice, much of which eventually wound up in the bank accounts of the shareholders of some of America's best-known and most respected corporations.[31]

However, it soon emerges that his explanation is based on a vicious circle including aspects of the economy, developments in the media and developments in the political system. He starts with the media, which he says greatly increased its violent, crime-oriented content in the 1980s as a means of increasing ratings. News of violent crime is easy to gather from the law-enforcement agencies, which is handy for the trimmed-down staff of newspapers and television stations.[32] This in turn led members of the public to become fearful of crime, with 80% of the public believing in the late 1990s that crime is one of the biggest problems confronting America when actually crime has been falling and they are safer than in the 1970s.[33] Political consultants have picked up this fear of crime from the opinion polls and advise politicians from both parties that their popularity depends upon having a hard-on-crime position. This in turn has led to the war on crime that has so greatly increased the prison population, with policies such as mandatory sentencing, three-strikes laws and truth in sentencing, all of which greatly increase the length of prison terms and decrease judicial discretion. Some 70% of the massive increase in prisoner numbers from 1970 to 2000 is attributable to these changes together with the war on drugs, in other words to imprisonment which would not have occurred for the same offences back in 1970.[34] As prisons have expanded they have become a greater burden upon taxpayers.[35] This could have been expected to set limits to prison expansion, but the private corporations have found ways of circumventing such limits via lease-revenue bonds or by building prisons themselves and charging for their facilities.[36] Dyer notes the manipulation of crime statistics on the same lines as the critique we have already seen from Chambliss.[37]

Reiman, Chambliss, Dyer and Parenti produce between them an account of US prison expansion with its origins in the US economy but with an immediate basis in the political Republican Southern strategy, together with favourable lobbying by corporations which profit from expansion and a specific criminal justice system dimension in terms of particular laws and practices. Whilst this is not an exclusively economic or exclusively Marxist explanation it is certainly compatible with a Marxist approach and offers a credible and powerful set of theories.

It certainly provides a better explanation than the view of Hallsworth and others that we have entered an era of postmodern penality, an explanation too vague and generalized to make any sense of the varying rates of imprisonment discussed above.[38] It is also superior to the interesting analysis offered by Marie Gottschalk in *The Prison and the Gallows: The Politics of Mass Incarceration in America*.[39] Gottschalk offers what might be seen as a useful supplementary explanation. She calls attention to state structures and ideologies that facilitated the expansion of incarceration but which were in place well before the 1970s.[40] In a sense this must be valid, but, as was discussed briefly above, Finland had structures and ideologies facilitating mass incarceration following the Second World War, but actually went in the opposite direction from the United States and now has a low rate of incarceration. She argues that the movement in favour of victims of crime developed in the United States in the context of a limited welfare state into a movement for harsher sentencing.[41] Feminist campaigns against rape and domestic violence tended to be co-opted by the state and to advocate effective punishment rather than focus on welfare measures to assist victims.[42] All of this may be true, but US prisons are not generally bulging with rapists and wife batterers. The race and class dimensions of the gulag need to be accounted for, but Gottschalk fails to really come to grips with either.

Conclusion

Capitalism can be seen as having some necessary reproduction conditions. A supply of suitable labour, sufficient money capital and the enforceability of contracts are all prime examples of these. The criminal justice system has a role in maintaining these conditions. A certain level of imprisonment is doubtless necessary in order to preserve property and uphold contracts. It is possible to run a capitalist system with a much higher level of imprisonment, even though this is arguably less efficient. A bloated criminal justice system such as that in the United States, offers a way of reducing unemployment by mopping up people who are difficult to employ, notably the black minority. It makes considerable profits for some corporations. It is also part of an electoral and media nexus that helps to maintain right-wing policies which fit with an increasingly unequal and globalised informational society. Despite recent rises in the rate of imprisonment in the United Kingdom this American pattern is not an inescapable future for European states. Their superior welfare states and substantially lower rate of imprisonment also function to reproduce capitalism. The Scandinavian states in particular offer a dramatically different way of running what is still basically a capitalist society.

9
Marxism and Law

Introduction

This brief chapter starts by indicating, from Marx's own analysis of law, why law has historically been a problem for Marxist analysis. It moves on to consider the clear account of criminal law offered by Pashukanis, before making criticisms which broadly agree with E. P. Thompson, Douglas Hay and David Garland. These and other authors all consider that the law has a degree of autonomy from both the economic foundations of society and from the interests of the ruling class. The overall conclusion is that although there is certainly class bias in the criminal law and the law more generally, the law is effective as a defence of capitalism and the ruling class because it has a certain real degree of neutrality.

Law in Marx and Engels

As with many areas of social life, Marx and Engels do not attempt an extended systematic discussion of law,[1] but provide a general theory where law features. The clearest overall statement of the position of law comes from the famous passage in the Preface to the *Critique of Political Economy*, already quoted in Chapter 1:

> In the social production of their existence, men inevitably enter into definite relations, which are independent of their will, namely relations of production appropriate to a given stage in the development of their material forces of production. The totality of these relations of production constitutes the economic structure of society, the real foundation, on which arises a legal and political superstructure.... At

a certain stage of development, the material productive forces of society come into conflict with the existing relations of production or – this merely expresses the same thing in legal terms – with the property relations within the framework of which they have operated hitherto…. Then begins an era of social revolution. The changes in the economic foundation lead sooner or later to the transformation of the whole immense superstructure.[2]

The most fundamental social relations, according to this extract, are relations of production. The legal and political superstructure arises on top of this. Law is thus part of the superstructure, which according to the final sentence of the quotation changes following changes to the economic foundation. However, the relations of production constitute 'the economic structure of society', and the existing relations of production can be described 'in legal terms' as the 'property relations'. This appears to locate law in the economic foundation of society as well as in the superstructure. Part of the purpose of G. A. Cohen's *Karl Marx's Theory of History: A Defence*, briefly discussed in Chapter 1, is to solve this paradox by making the foundation of society the forces of production, which exist below the level where law is located and determine it.

As was also indicated in the introduction this is a very controversial area of Marxist theorizing. Where law is concerned the particular problem is that if relations of production have any degree of stability they would seem to have at least taken on a law-like character. Moreover, a legal framework can assist or impede the development and extension of a particular mode of production. This would be true, for example, of legislation to facilitate joint stock companies under capitalism, or to assist in enclosure at an earlier stage. In his Introduction to the *Grundrisse*, Marx attempts to argue that differing modes of production generate their own forms of law:

The bourgeois economists only have in view that production proceeds more smoothly with modern police than, e.g., under club-law. They forget, however, that club-law too is law, and that the law of the stronger survives, in a different form, even in their 'constitutional State'.

When the social conditions corresponding to a particular stage of production are just emerging or are already in a state of dissolution, disturbances naturally occur in production, although these may be of varying degree and varying effect.[3]

This argument that law has only a marginal effect on the constitution of stages of production gets revisited a little later:

> Laws may perpetuate an instrument of production, e.g., land, in certain families. These laws acquire economic significance only if large-scale landed property is in harmony with the mode of social production, as for instance in England. In France, agriculture was carried on on a small scale, despite the existence of large estates, which were therefore broken up by the Revolution. But can the small plot system be perpetuated, e.g. by laws? Property concentrates itself again despite these laws. The influence of laws aimed at preserving [existing] relations of distribution, and hence their effect on production, have to be examined specially.[4]

Marx now seems to be acknowledging that laws have some effect. We certainly need, as Hugh Collins argues, some explanation of the function of laws and why laws are needed to express the relations of production.[5] Moreover, as he suggests, this is going to be very difficult when it comes to the law on rape or laws aimed to penalize the pollution of rivers.[6]

Evgeny Pashukanis: law as an instrument of class oppression

An alternative approach, which we encountered briefly above in the discussion of Richard Quinney, can be found in Lenin[7] and more systematically in the writings of Pashukanis. Pashukanis was the leading figure of Soviet Marxist jurisprudence from 1924 to 1936. He was purged in 1937. His account of law is loosely modelled on Marxist analysis of the commodity. He argues that although legal forms existed before capitalism, even in mediaeval Europe they were extremely underdeveloped: 'only bourgeois-capitalist society creates all the conditions necessary for the legal element in social relationships to achieve its full realisation.'[8] For Pashukanis the fundamental social relationship 'whose inevitable expression is the form of law ... is the relationship of possessors of commodities'.[9] The products of labour become commodities under capitalism; with the development of socialism goods are distributed according to a social plan and commodities wither away. For Pashukanis a parallel process leads to the withering away of law as communism develops.

This analysis seems most obviously to apply to the law of contract, but Pashukanis argues that it also works for criminal law. It, too, is based on the exchange of equivalents: a crime is a contract concluded against one's will, and punishment is an equivalent of the harm done to the victim.[10] Initially this equivalent was removed in a blood feud; then blood money became an alternative; the state became involved by taking a share in compensation paid to the plaintiff.[11] When the state became the bourgeois state its system of criminal law developed initially to terrorize the pauperized part of the displaced peasant population, but then developed into an instrument to hold the exploited class in obedience: 'the criminal jurisdiction of the bourgeois state is organised class terror'.[12] Punishment remains an equivalent, but the victim becomes the state, and there is a gradation of liability depending on the degree of guilt.[13] The reduction of social wealth to labour time allows for a similar approach to criminal justice in which the punishment for a crime becomes the loss of a particular amount of abstract freedom.[14] Bourgeois justice takes the form of retributive equivalence: at the time of sentencing there is little interest in what will actually happen in prison or the criminal's subsequent career.[15] With the building of socialism the 'narrow horizons of bourgeois law' start to disappear. Instead of measures of punishment it will be a matter of symptoms characterizing a 'socially dangerous condition' and the development of methods of 'social defence'.[16]

There are a variety of problems with this analysis. Some sort of an account is needed of how the ruling class decide what is in their interests. This is not entirely straightforward. At a minimum there may be conflicts between different groups, different analyses and long- or short-term versions of the ruling class interest.[17] The idea of equivalence and the idea of class terror conflict with each other. Equivalence could just be seen as an ideological camouflage for class terror, but it seems to be more substantial than this in Pashukanis's text. In that case we need a clear explanation of when the criminal justice system is being used as an instrument of class terror and when it is operating on a pattern of equivalence. As Garland points out, various forms of sentencing such as indeterminate sentences and conceptions of irresponsibility have been used across Europe and in the United States – in other words bourgeois law is capable of moving away from the principle of equivalence without any suggestion of there being a crisis.[18] Equivalent amounts of harm might be expected to call forth equivalent amounts of punishment in legislation prevailing under capitalism, but this is debatable. Various activities – drug use, homosexuality between consenting adults, abortion, euthanasia, fox-hunting, various forms of betting – have been criminalized or decriminalized. At least until recently domestic violence and sexual violence on intimates have been punished much less severely than equivalent acts perpetrated on strangers. Capitalist societies are plainly capable of debating and altering what counts as equivalence.

The criminal law is certainly not just an instrument of class terror. It provides a degree of protection for working people against predatory criminals, including – to some extent – white-collar criminals. It also, however, provides some of the framework for the exploitation of labour.[19] The withering away of law and the idea of social defence under communism will be discussed below: a poignant instance would be Pashukanis's own fate, which could be categorized as social defence at the time but was reinterpreted as Stalinist paranoia by his rehabilitation.

The relative autonomy of law?

> It is similar with law. As soon as the new division of labour which creates professional lawyers becomes necessary, another new and independent sphere is opened up which, for all its general dependence on production and trade, still has its own capacity for reacting upon these spheres as well. In a modern state, law must not only correspond to the general economic position and be its expression, but must also be an expression which is *consistent in itself,* and which does not, owing to inner contradictions, look glaringly inconsistent. And in order to achieve this, the faithful reflection of economic conditions is more and more infringed upon. All the more so the more rarely it happens that a code of law is the blunt, unmitigated, unadulterated expression of the domination of a class–this in itself would already offend the 'conception of justice'.[20]

Engels' comment here is consistent with a recurrent idea in Marxism that the state has a relative autonomy and is capable of reacting back on the economy, and also with ideas taken from studies of the law in operation and the work of some Marxist historians. Hugh Collins simply looks at judicial reasoning in a case of marital rape in 1954. He comments of the reasoning of Lynsky J.

> There is no hint in the judgement of instrumental considerations being taken into account, either of a class nature of the protection of the interests of differently constituted groups. On the contrary the judge diligently searched for a consistent view about the appropriate

rule among the authorities without mentioning consequentialist considerations. He treated the mass of legal doctrine as a giant jigsaw puzzle which had to be fitted together to form a coherent picture ... Here the conflict lay between a general prohibition against rape and the institution of marriage ...[21]

The point Collins is making is that the behaviour of the judge in this case is fairly typical of judges, whereas the naked pursuit of class or group interest is not. The idea of legal autonomy, as found in Engels' letter, fits the behaviour of the judge much better. Legal autonomy fits particularly well with a conception of the state which allows that although it may in the last instance represent the interests of the capitalist class, it does so with quite an appearance of neutrality, as witness universal suffrage, social security payments, the National Health Service, free or very heavily subsidized education etc.[22] The idea of legal autonomy also features in Paul Hirst's criticisms of Pashukanis. Hirst denies that laws have one single origin or essence, or one unity of content. They are acted on from a variety of sources and have their own effects.[23]

A degree of state and legal autonomy also emerges from the work of Marxist historians. Douglas Hay and E. P. Thompson both considered aspects of law and order in eighteenth-century England.[24] Hay is interested in the persistence and extension of capital punishment in the law at a time when capital sentences were decreasingly carried out, and more generally in the mechanisms of rule in eighteenth-century England when feudalism had broken down and the apparatus of the modern state had yet to be constructed. Hay argues that legitimacy was achieved through the workings of the criminal law. Its inconsistencies facilitated its function as an ideological system, the central features of which were of the majesty and power of the law; the idea of justice, including a punctilious attention to legalism, a concern for property including the property of the poor and the occasional conviction and execution of men of property such as Lord Ferrers and the theme of mercy, which allowed the authorities to use the law as an instrument of class justice but with a sensitivity to public opinion. David Garland points out that criticism of Hay by other historians lays still greater emphasis on the willingness of the poor to make use of the law and their support for it.[25]

Edward Thompson reaches to similar conclusions as Hay in his analysis of the Black Act of 1723.[26]According to Thompson, the origin of the Act lay in the activities of groups of men: 'the middling orders of the forest: a few gentry sympathisers, more substantial farmers, more again of Yeoman and tradesmen or craftsmen, and a few of the poorer foresters.'[27] These people engaged in using forests in various ways, notably deer stealing, which people of their sort had either got away with for many years or which were not very severely penalized. In order to do this they intimidated gamekeepers and officials in charge of the forest. Their ultimate antagonists, however, were 'the great predators – Pepper, Chandos, Newcastle, Walpole – eager for office, perquisites, enclosure of Crown or public land. Their depredations were immeasurably larger and more injurious.'[28] The Black Act of 1823 introduced hanging for a wide range of offences, notably going armed and with a blackened face, hunting deer, poaching hares or fish, cutting down trees, or rescuing anyone from custody who was accused of any of these offences. It was, argues Thompson, introduced because the authorities were afraid of something close to class warfare:[29]

> The Act registered the long decline in the effectiveness of old methods of class control and discipline and their replacement by one standard recourse of authority: the example of terror. In place of the whipping-post and the stocks, manorial and corporate controls and the physical harrying of vagabonds, economists advocated the discipline of low wages and starvation and lawyers the sanction of death. Both indicated an increasing impersonality in the mediation of class relations, and a change, not so much in the 'fact' of crime as in the category – 'crime' – itself, as it was defined by the propertied. What was now to be punished was not an offence between men ... but an offence against property.[30]

Thompson then reviews how the Act came to be less used and eventually repealed, and moves on to some reflections about the law. It is, he says 'not possible to conceive of any complex society without law'. He notes that the ruled fought for their rights by means of law, and still felt a sense of legal wrong when it ceased to be possible to fight at law.[31] This, he says, is because the law is not just:

> a pliant medium to be twisted this way and that by whichever interests already possess effective power ... It is inherent in the special character of law, as a body of rules and procedures, that it shall apply logical criteria with reference to standards of universality and equity ... The essential precondition for the effectiveness of the law, in its function as ideology, is that it shall display an independence

from gross manipulation and shall seem to be just. It cannot seem to be so without upholding its own logic and criteria of equity; indeed, on occasion, by actually being just ... the rulers were, in serious senses, whether willingly or unwillingly, the prisoners of their own rhetoric; they played games of power according to rules which suited them, but they could not break those rules or the whole game would be thrown away.[32]

There were, in fact, several occasions when the government was defeated in the courts. 'Such occasions served, paradoxically, to consolidate power, to enhance its legitimacy and to inhibit revolutionary movements.'[33] Thompson sees these constraints on power as 'an unqualified human good '.[34] Thompson's approach to the role of law in the early eighteenth century must undoubtedly have been influenced by the events with which he opens his earlier masterpiece, *The Making of the English Working Class*, the arrest and trial for treason of leading members of the London Corresponding Society because they agitated for manhood suffrage, and their acquittal by a Grand Jury in 1794.[35]

The ideas about legal autonomy rehearsed in this section relate to the category of consensus crimes identified in Chapter 2, and to the ideas of left realism. In other words they relate to an acceptance of some crimes and standards as applying to everyone in a society whether the perpetrators are rich or poor, and to the use of law as a defence against these crimes even if the victims are poor and powerless.

They also relate to the possibility of using the law as a field of struggle against the state and against powerful corporations. This will be touched on in the next chapter. Possible examples include the role of juries in protecting whistle-blowers such as Clive Ponting (see next chapter), or of individuals and groups attempting to curb dubious state activities. Important examples of this include the work of Public Interest Lawyers and Phil Shiner, notably in calling the British government to account for human rights violations in Iraq,[36] lawyers defending the Fairford Five, who damaged B-52 bombers which were about to be used to bomb Iraq, claiming that the crime of aggression in war is far more serious than the damage they did,[37] and the activity of a whole variety of lawyers in making life difficult for the US government's prison at Guantanamo Bay.

10
Marxism, Justice and Criminal Justice

This chapter starts by considering the extensive debate as to whether or not Marx had a theory of justice. Although there are some good reasons for thinking that he did not, there are very powerful reasons for thinking that contemporary socialists *do* need a theory of justice. Over and above these, there are yet further reasons for anyone aspiring to develop a Marxist theory of criminology to make use of conceptions of justice, and, indeed, to have conceptions of criminal justice. These conceptions form a significant underpinning of the study of corporate and white-collar crime, which has been an area where Marxist criminologists have joined in a very important academic and public enterprise. They are also relevant to the issue of whether some more plebeian crimes can be regarded as forms of primitive rebellion, prefiguring more political activities. Finally there is the issue of whether trade union and socialist political activity has sometimes to engage in crime.

Marx and justice: the debate

There is an extensive debate as to whether Marx believed that the capitalist system was unjust. It would be neither possible nor appropriate to give a full exposition of this debate here. A very good introduction to the debate may be found in two articles by Norman Geras.[1] Geras starts by quoting and citing a series of passages which suggest that Marx did not have a theory of justice, followed by another series of passages which suggests that he did. In what follows I shall briefly indicate some of these passages but then indicate why modern socialists need a theory of justice. There will then be a brief account of the theory of justice that would be derived from Marx's works.

Many of the passages cluster around Marx's distinction between labour and labour power. In the sphere of circulation the capitalist purchases the labour power of the worker for its full equivalent. Capitalist and worker are equal individuals in capitalist society. Then, however, the capitalist sets the worker to work. In the first part of the working week the worker labours to produce value equivalent to the wage; in the second part of the week he or she labours to create surplus value, which is the foundation of profit, rent and interest. Thus in one sense the worker is paid the full equivalent of what he or she provides and in another sense the worker is exploited: 'laws that are based on the production and circulation of commodities, become by their own inner and inexorable dialectic changed into their very opposite.'[2] 'The relationship of exchange is therefore a mere semblance, which belongs to the circulation process.'[3] This paradox is central to much of the ambiguity.

Let us start with some passages which suggest that Marx does not operate with a theory of justice. The exploitation of labour, he says, is not unjust:

> The circumstance, that on the one hand the daily sustenance of labour power costs only half a day's labour, while on the other hand the very same labour power can work during a whole day, that consequently the value which its use during one day creates, is double what he pays for that use, this circumstance is, without doubt, a piece of good luck for the buyer, but by no means an injury to the seller.[4]
>
> If, therefore, the amount of value advanced in wages is not merely found again in the product, but augmented by a surplus-value, this is not because the seller has been defrauded, for he has really received the value of his commodity; it is due solely to the fact that this commodity has been used up by the buyer.[5]

He asserts that socialism is not a matter of better principles of distribution. In the *Critique of the Gotha Programme* there is the following well-known comment about the distribution of the 'proceeds of labour':

> What is 'fair' distribution? Do not the bourgeois assert that present-day distribution is 'fair'? And is it not, in fact, the only 'fair' distribution on the basis of the present-day mode of production?[6]

Marx was famously opposed to founding socialism on moral principles. He drafted the Preamble to the Rules of the International

Working Men's Association, and commented to Engels: 'I was, however, obliged to insert two sentences about "DUTY" and "RIGHT", and ditto about "TRUTH, MORALITY AND JUSTICE" in the preamble to the rules, but these are so placed that they can do no harm.'[7] The basis of this approach is that 'Right can never be higher than the economic structure of society and its cultural development which this determines.'[8] In other words Marx denies standards of justice which transcend particular epochs or mode of production.

Marx also considers that appeals to justice are linked to reformism, as in the well-known quotation from *Value, Price and Profit*: 'Instead of the conservative motto, "A fair day's wage for a fair day's work!" they ought to inscribe on their banner the revolutionary watchword, "Abolition of the wages system!"'[9]

Marx, it can be argued, is not actually proposing a superior principle of distributive justice, but arguing that a principle of distributive justice will not be needed in the higher stage of communist society. Indeed, communism is about self-realization or freedom rather than about distributive justice:

> In a higher phase of communist society ... after the productive forces have also increased with the all-round development of the individual, and all the springs of common wealth flow more abundantly – only then can the narrow horizon of bourgeois right be crossed in its entirety and society inscribe on its banners: From each according to his abilities, to each according to his needs![10]

In other words, in the higher phase of communism the means of production will be so productive that it will be possible to fulfil everyone's needs, rendering a principle of distribution otiose, just as it is for breathable air today.

However, in many other places Marx does seem to be appealing to principles of justice. At the core of his analysis of the capitalist system lies the extraction of surplus value from the worker, which belies the apparent equal exchange in the payment of wages:

> The means of production, with which the additional labour power is incorporated, as well as the necessaries with which the labourers are sustained, are nothing but component parts of the surplus product, of the tribute annually exacted from the working class by the capitalist class. Though the latter with a portion of that tribute purchases the additional labour power even at its full price, so that

equivalent is exchanged for equivalent, yet the transaction is for all that only the old dodge of every conqueror who buys commodities from the conquered with the money he has robbed them of.[11]

This use of the idea of robbery and booty to describe the transaction between the capitalist and the worker is not an isolated occurrence. Marx talks of: '... the question of how the booty is subsequently divided between the capitalist, the landlord and others'[12]; '... we treat the capitalist producer as owner of the entire surplus value, or, better perhaps, as the representative of all the sharers with him in the booty';[13] 'The learned disputation, how the booty pumped out of the labourer may be divided, with most advantage to accumulation, between the industrial capitalist and the rich idler, was hushed in face of the revolution of July.'[14] Elsewhere he talks of robbery.[15]

This is particularly true of the primitive accumulation which amassed the initial capital required for capitalism to get going: 'In actual history it is notorious that conquest, enslavement, robbery, murder, briefly, force, play the great part.'[16] '[C]apital comes dripping from head to foot, from every pore, with blood and dirt.'[17]

Whilst the cotton industry introduced child slavery in England, it gave in the United States a stimulus to the transformation of the earlier, more or less patriarchal slavery, into a system of commercial exploitation. In fact, the veiled slavery of the wage workers in Europe needed, for its pedestal, slavery pure and simple in the new world.[18]

Phrases such as the one above from the *Critique of the Gotha Programme*, 'narrow horizon of bourgeois right' suggest criteria of justice which go beyond particular modes of production. There are 'needs' that go beyond the capacity of any conceivable society to fulfil, so that the interpretation above in which a criterion of distributive justice is otiose must be wrong (this is more fully discussed in Chapter 11 below). Geras comments that 'Marx is clearly concerned with...the distribution of free time, of opportunities for fulfilling activity, of unpleasant or rebarbative work; with the distribution of welfare more generally, of social and economic benefits and burdens.'[19]

Geras continues to an elaborate discussion of how best to reconcile these opposing positions in Marx against and in favour of a theory of justice. He concludes that Marx does indeed have a theory of justice, but that 'Marx did think capitalism was unjust but he did not think he thought so'.[20] By this he means that Marx frequently considers 'the distribution of advantages and disadvantages quite generally, including here consequently the distribution of control over productive resources'.[21] It is plain that Marx finds this distribution under capitalism morally objectionable and considers the possible future distribution under communism morally superior. However, his official position when justice is directly discussed is that justice is an ideological support of particular modes of production; Marx's advocacy of communism is simply a matter of going along with the course of history.

For our present purposes there is no point in considering either the arguments Geras uses or those which are found in the substantial literature he discusses. We can short-circuit things by considering first, the situation of socialists today, and secondly the central issues facing aspiring Marxist criminologists.

As I indicated in Chapter 1, Marx believed that the growing size of the proletariat and its miserable conditions, together with the instability of the capitalist economy, would turn economic crises into political crises in which the workers and their allies would seize power. They would then set about constructing socialism and then communism. As I argued there, following the collapse of communism in the eastern bloc and the Chinese move to facilitate rapid capitalist growth, a series of revolutions with the aim of constructing communism can be regarded as highly unlikely. What is more plausible is some kind of mixture of trade union and social democratic campaigning and negotiations to secure basic welfare and working conditions together with lobbying by non-governmental organizations and the urging of anti-globalization protesters. The achievement of worldwide socialism is by no means the inevitable outcome of economic and political tendencies inscribed in the capitalist system. Instead the immediate prospect is at best a messy and uneven advance towards improved welfare for working people in underdeveloped countries and in the West. In this context arguments about justice are highly relevant.

What view of justice actually emerges from Marx? According to Geras: 'Denied publicly, repressed, his own ethical commitments keep returning: the values of freedom, self-development, human well-being and happiness; the ideal of a just society in which these things are decently distributed.'[22] These values, and particularly the idea of self-development through creative labour, are clearly very important in Marx. Because they are officially denied there is no attempt to prioritise them, or to consider situations in which they might conflict. In particular, apart from journalism in the early 1840s Marx does not seem to set a very high priority on free speech or the rights of minorities. This is not to say that he actively denies either of these other than the right to private property in the means of production, but he does not set a high priority on them. Thus there was not a significant legacy of texts where Marx defends free speech and minorities which could be alluded to by victims of communist regimes. Looking at existing capitalist societies and the principles of distribution that would flow from Marx's ideas it is difficult to be quite certain where the balance would be struck between providing better resources for low-paid workers, facilities for creative endeavours of various kinds, and resources for people such as pensioners, the long-term sick and disabled which would enable them to lead a better provided life and take part in creative enterprises. That said, it is clear that the distribution would be a much more egalitarian one than the present distribution, and in particular that the massive salaries and rewards going to the corporate rich and financiers would be very significantly reduced.

A switch from claiming that the victory of communism is inevitable to arguing for communism on grounds of justice also involves a reconsideration of the centrality of labour and of the working class. As we have seen, Marx rejects claims based on distribution or the idea of the right of labour to the full fruits of its product. Nonetheless it is clear in his writings both that the main force that makes the revolution is the working class, and that it is the interests of the working class which are seen as central in the building of communism. If Marxism is re-conceptualized as a doctrine based on justice, but one which includes a method of analysing the structure of societies and ways of transforming them, then it is not clear that justice demands the consideration of labour to the exclusion of everything else. In the Third World workers are generally better off than peasants, which is why peasants tend to migrate to urban areas. It may be that peasants generally have a future as workers, either in the countryside or having moved to towns, but it is not clear that the interests of justice always put workers before peasants.

Even if peasants have become a residual category as in Britain there are still many people who are not themselves directly workers or capitalists, including pensioners, people who are too sick or disabled to work, children and people (mainly women) who spend their time caring for people who cannot work. In current capitalist societies many of this substantial group are the poorest part of the population. As both Geras and Cohen point out, contributing labour to a commodity does not constitute a particularly good claim to the whole product. There are also claims based on the sorts of things capitalist apologists typically mention such as risk, enterprise, organization, inspiration, innovation etc. This type of argument points towards a generally more egalitarian pattern of distribution linked to need rather than to entitlement based on labour or enterprise, abstinence etc.[23]

It also points towards reformism. The advanced capitalist countries all have some form of welfare state, and the best of them have relatively comprehensive welfare states. According to Marx in the *Critique of the Gotha Programme*, in 'communist society, not as it has developed on its own foundations, but on the contrary, just as it emerges from capitalist society', each worker is remunerated according to the amount of labour he has performed: 'He receives a certificate from society that he has furnished such and such an amount of labour (after deducting his labour for the common funds), and with this certificate he draws from the social stock of means of consumption as much as the same amount of labour costs.'[24]

In a welfare state, however, there is a strange mixture when compared to this first stage of socialist society. Capitalists remain, including many idle rentiers, and the society is very unequal. The remuneration of workers is in terms of quality as well as quantity, and there are dramatic differences between the pay of workers on or below the minimum wage and those at the top of the scale. It is pretty clear that some of the 'quality' involved relates to factors such as trade union power, market position and gender. Indeed, if boardroom managing directors are considered as workers the quality of their work must be little short of miraculous to justify salaries in the millions of pounds. Alongside these disparate rewards, which are not remotely communist, there is quite a lot of reward according to need, in the form of health care, education, general social insurance to deal with disasters such as floods and individual benefits for sick and disabled people and for pensioners. Of course, it is possible to explain the welfare state in other terms such as its role in reproducing healthy, well educated workers, or the ideological benefits of a cradle-to-grave safety net, but level of need seems to be a major criterion of distribution. Someone who enjoys perfect health gets virtually nothing from the NHS, whereas someone who needs a heart transplant or expensive drugs gets quite a lot. People who are economically useless, such as pensioners and the severely disabled, nonetheless get significant health and personal care.

This in turn points to a form of class struggle which occurs in societies with a welfare state: the attempt to reduce the inequalities of the market and to expand the welfare state. As we saw in Chapter 1, thanks to the rise of informationalism and of new right politics, market inequalities have actually widened considerably since the 1970s. Alongside this, however, Britain has experienced a significant rise in spending on health and education, particularly under New Labour. Political parties, trade unions and interest groups all argue for or against particular ways of expanding or contracting the welfare state and the market. Thus recently in Britain we have had the issue of taxing non-domiciled plutocrats who enjoy the benefits of living in Britain for part of the time and making substantial profits here; the Liberals had a policy of taxing incomes over £100,000 at 50p in the pound, but dropped it. However various lobbies campaign for particular expensive drugs to be available on the NHS; the extension of the Scottish policy of paying for social care for the elderly to England; and similarly in the extension of the Scottish policy of not charging fees for students in higher education.

Many of the arguments are conducted in terms of justice. For example, the dividing line between health care and social care is a fine one, but health care in England is free from the NHS whereas social care is means tested. Is it fair for non-domiciled plutocrats to benefit from living in Britain without paying taxes which everyone else living here has to pay? What justifies the inflated pay of CEOs, footballers and rock stars compared to nurses? Why do executives get rewarded in substantial pay packages when they preside over companies that make a loss? Obviously issues of efficiency, for example, are balanced against issues of need. Thus it is argued that the massive remuneration of executives is necessary or they would go and work in the United States. More prosaically, and plausibly, people who undertake years of training are held to deserve higher pay than those in unskilled jobs. This type of argument over justice is much less exciting than a revolution in which the proletariat raises itself to become the ruling class,[25] and it can go backwards as well as forwards, but it can still take place in a society where the working class is relatively passive and significantly divided.

Where does criminal justice fit in to arguments about distributive justice? Writers on distributive justice tend to address criminal justice as a very minor afterthought. For example John Rawls in the classic *A Theory of Justice* has an extensive discussion of civil disobedience, which is a very special case of crime, but only a single page discussion of ordinary acquisitive crime in which he argues that it would be appropriate to maintain a just distribution by 'stabilising penal devices'. In other words, the task of a theorist of distributive justice is to work out a way of establishing a just distribution, and criminal justice would simply be a matter of restoring a just distribution.[26] The current distribution can be presumed to be imperfect on the basis of virtually any theory of distributive justice, and would certainly be imperfect on the basis of a Marxist theory. Where would crime fit into this? I want to distinguish crudely between corporate crime, other white-collar crime and street crime. White-collar crime pursued by individuals for their own individual interests may involve acts perpetrated against corporations, members of the public, the state or the environment. It tends to overlap with corporate crime when the leaders of corporations plunder shareholders, employees and governments with a view to enriching themselves rather than the corporation in question. Given that people who are in a position to carry out white-collar crimes are generally already relatively privileged it is in the interests of justice to pursue them. Criminologists and Marxists tend to argue that individual white-collar crime is not pursued as vigorously as it should be (although there are exceptions to this).[27] However, the criminal justice system and regulatory bodies do make some effort against individual white-collar criminals.

Corporate crime

Less effort is made against corporate crime. Corporate crime is carried out by people working for corporations primarily on behalf of the corporation rather than in their own interest. Its objective is to increase the profit of the corporation. It does this in various ways at the expense of consumers, other corporations or taxpayers. It may also involve harm to consumers, the general public or the environment. The people who benefit from corporate profit, shareholders and senior corporate executives, are in the main people who would tend to see their rewards going down in the pattern of distribution that would derive from Marxist principles. Some of the benefit, of course, goes to people saving for pensions or holders of insurance policies, and by no means everyone who is doing this is wealthy. However, these groups tend nonetheless to be at the better-off end of society. Corporate crime thus tends to make seriously unequal patterns of distribution still more unequal.

In Chapter 1 I indicated that Marxist criminologists would want to follow Sutherland in adopting a wider definition of crime than simply breaking a law, and would want to include seriously damaging breaches of administrative regulations and activities which are socially damaging and should be illegal. This would accord with the notion of crime as a 'serious wrong' which is, or should be, illegal. Taking this approach allows Marxist criminologists to work alongside others interested in corporate wrongdoing – there is no requirement of the adoption of a

Marxist framework in order to do useful empirical research in the area. This is just as well because of the scale of corporate crime and the relative paucity of research on it.

As I have indicated above in the discussion of Hirst in Chapter 1, and of Pearce, Chambliss and Reiman in Chapter 3, there is every indication that corporate and white-collar crime is much larger and much more damaging than street crime. Criminologists have written about corporate and white-collar crime to some extent, but surveys by scholars in the field indicate that it is underrepresented in criminology journals given its very major role in society.[28] A similar point can be made by using a website such as Amazon to search for corporate crime. It returns 187 books, in contrast to 1,324 for juvenile delinquency.[29] The study of corporate crime is generally held to have started with Sutherland.[30]

There is no suggestion that he was a Marxist. Apart from arguing for an extended account of crime (see Chapter 1 above) his main theoretical approach was to argue that his theory of differential association applies to corporate crime as well as to street crime, with young executives learning the techniques of corporate crime and attitudes favourable to it in small groups.[31] He argues that the financial cost of corporate crime is probably several times that of street crime,[32] and that

> This financial loss from white-collar crime, great as it is, is less important than the damage to social relations. White-collar crimes violate trust and therefore create distrust, and this lowers social morale and produces social disorganisation on a large-scale. Ordinary crimes, on the other hand, produce little effect on social institutions or social organisation.[33]

His study deals with 70 of America's largest corporations, each with one or more decision against it, and some guilty of serious recidivism, notably Armour and Company, Swift and Company, General Motors, Sears Roebuck and Montgomery Ward.[34] He argues that the corporations generally do not suffer serious sanctions from the criminal justice system partly because politicians depend upon contributions from corporations but more importantly because of the 'cultural homogeneity of legislators, judges, and administrators with businessmen'.[35] Corporate crime is, he says, both rationalized and highly rational in the sense that corporations choose crimes which are difficult to detect, where proof is difficult and where government officials can be induced not to investigate.[36]

As we have noted, Sutherland's book did not initiate a major area of criminological endeavour but there is a worthwhile tradition following on from his work. His collaborator Cressey followed his lead with a study of embezzlement.[37] The next major study was Frank Pearce's *Crimes of the Powerful* (see Chapter 5 above), first published in 1976. From the 1980s onwards the quantity of work on corporate crime has expanded considerably, although it is still relatively limited compared to other branches of criminology. In 1980 Marshall B. Clinard and Peter C. Yeager brought out *Corporate Crime*,[38] which follows in the footsteps of Sutherland but is more wide ranging and thorough. In 1983 Steven Box published *Power, Crime and Mystification*,[39] which pursued arguments about the definition and harm of crime similar to those of Sutherland. Frances T. Cullen and William J. Maakestad, *Corporate Crime Under Attack: The Ford Pinto Case and Beyond*,[40] discusses the Pinto case in detail and the prospects for prosecuting corporate crime more generally. John Braithwaite produced a more specialized study of the pharmaceutical industry in 1984, detailing a variety of fraudulent and dangerous practices, most seriously the systematic production of false data in drug trials, thus facilitating the marketing of dubious drugs.[41] Susan Shapiro's *Wayward Capitalists: Target of the Securities and Exchange Commission*,[42] should probably be mentioned as an account of episodes of insider dealing and financial fraud, but it lacks much depth of analysis – let alone Marxist analysis – and fails to consider seriously reasons why the regulatory framework is relatively ineffective. An early text for undergraduates, again definitely not from a Marxist point of view, was James Coleman's *The Criminal Elite: Understanding White-Collar Crime*.[43]

Moving on to the 1990s the volume of publication again expands. There is perhaps more of an attempt to theorize white-collar crime in another undergraduate text: Tony G. Poveda's *Rethinking White Collar Crime*,[44] but again definitely not from a Marxist point of view. Maurice Punch in *Dirty Business: Exploring Corporate Misconduct: Analysis and Cases*,[45] appears to set out to provide an analysis of why corporate misconduct happens, but his theorizing is relatively limited. There were enough authors in the field to produce conference volumes edited by Kip Schlegel and David Weisburd, *White-Collar Crime Reconsidered*,[46] and by Laureen Snider and Frank Pearce[47] which is heartening, but the volumes were not produced from any particularly systematic standpoint. Notable works include Calavita et al.'s *Big Money Crime: Fraud and Politics in the Savings and Loans Crisis*,[48] a detailed study of one of the biggest white-collar frauds in US history.

This improved, but by no means overwhelming rate of publication continues in the new century. Susan Simpson in *Corporate Crime, Law and Social Control*[49] presents an argument on empirical grounds for trying to regulate corporate misbehaviour rather than use criminal sanctions, although she bases her case on a period when criminalization was out of fashion.[50] Stephen M. Rosoff, Henry N. Pontell and Robert Tillman, *Profit without Honour: White-Collar Crime and the Looting of America*,[51] details an excellent range of examples but with a relative minimum of theory. Business academics such as Kenneth R. Gray, Larry A. Frieder and George W. Clark offer practical ideas to reduce corporate crime in *Corporate Scandals: The Many Faces of Greed, the Great Heist, Financial Bubbles, and the Absence of Virtue*.[52] Publication in the field has grown sufficiently to produce an international handbook[53] and textbooks.[54] A particularly exciting development links elite malfeasance at government and corporate levels.[55] Although it is chiefly about the staggering cost of George Bush's war crime, demonstrating that the Iraq conflict will cost the United States approximately 60 times as much as the initial administration estimate of $50 billion, Joseph Stiglitz and Linda J. Bilmes comment in *The $3 Trillion War* on: massive spending on security contractors, the allegations of overpayments to Haliburton, the company formerly headed by Vice President Dick Cheney, the 90 investigations opened by the Department of Defence into profiteering and corruption, and the use of 'sole source bidding' in which the government awards contracts to a single firm without competition, perhaps encouraged by campaign contributions, and the surge in profits for defence firms, leading to stock price increases of approximately 100%.[56]

Other works deal with corporate crime in Canada, India and Australia,[57] or are more to do with the relevant legal framework than criminology,[58] or are works of muckraking by journalists or practising lawyers.[59]

What about British criminologists? Apart from Steven Box mentioned above there is a small but productive group. Gary Slapper and Steve Tombs provide a general introduction to the field in *Corporate Crime*.[60] They document the difficulties in compiling statistics which show clearly that this area is not taken nearly as seriously as street crime. They then attempt to compare the cost of street crime and corporate crime towards the end of the 1990s. Adding together the cost of the police, Crown Prosecution Service, criminal courts, probation service, the prison service, Legal Aid and compensation to victims of crime, together with the costs of crime itself produces an annual total of around £50 billion. Sticking to the costs of particular categories of crime, the serious and complex frauds investigated by the Serious Fraud Office can amount to £5 billion at any one time. The annual cost of all burglaries was estimated to be around £1 billion in the 1990s, and with an average net loss of £370 per burglary. Hardly any burglaries, robberies or thefts caused losses sufficient to be of interest to the Serious Fraud Office, which in the 1990s had a threshold of £6 million. Pension misselling was estimated to affect up to 2.4 million victims and involve a total of £11 billion.[61] Deaths from safety crimes far outnumber deaths from homicide.[62] Frank Pearce and Steve Tombs investigated the deaths, injuries, ill health and environmental devastation caused by the chemical industry in *Toxic Capitalism: Corporate Crime and the Chemical Industry*.[63] Michael Levi and Alan Doig have produced investigations of fraud, extending beyond corporate crime to white-collar crime more generally.[64]

The literature on corporate crime has been listed in some detail to make the point that it is an established field, but one which is seriously under-researched compared to other areas of criminology, given the staggering scale of some of the harm involved. It is, moreover, an area where Marxist analysis offers a vital part of the explanation. As Slapper and Tombs make clear, the basic explanation for the large numbers of deaths and injuries from safety crimes is the competitive pressure and value orientation of capitalism:

> The preservation of human life and welfare is not the abiding, supreme governing principle of capitalism. Human welfare is a desideratum that prevailing ideology suggests must be sought as far as commercial considerations make this a realistic, achievable goal. Each year at least 400 people are killed and 50,000 seriously injured at work in Britain. Most of these are avoidable. They occur through economically-related courses concerning training, supervision, equipment and working environment. The degree of moral culpability (measured by the criminal law's criteria of gross negligence and recklessness as applied to the crimes of manslaughter and serious assault) from which the commercial carnage results is strikingly similar to that of conventional crime.[65]

Although Slapper and Tombs find some merit in more conventional criminological theories to explain corporate crime,[66] the above is overwhelmingly the best basic explanation. Thus we have an area in which Marxist theory works well, where the social damage is very considerable, and where neither the criminal justice system, the regulatory environment nor academic criminologists pay nearly enough attention to the mayhem being daily perpetrated by capitalist corporations. There are, furthermore, interesting ambiguities and theoretical issues within this promising approach. As Slapper and Tombs put it

> ... any full-blown theory of corporate crime will both encompass a range of elements and levels, and seek to represent the articulation of these elements and levels. Such a theoretical task would entail transcendence of the confines of both criminology and sociology. Key aspects of any such analysis would integrate understandings of the general state of national and the international economy, the nature of markets, industries, and in particular products or services with which particular corporations are involved, dominant ideologies and social values, formal political priorities and the nature of regulation, particular corporate structures, the balances of power within these, the distribution of opportunities within and beyond these, and corporate cultures and socialisation into these.[67]

This is, moreover, an area in which some genuine progress can be made, as witness increased resources for the Health and Safety Executive in the United Kingdom under the third Thatcher government or the belated and rather feeble Corporate Manslaughter and Corporate Homicide Act, 2007. Finally, Slapper and Tombs develop a critique of compliance-oriented regulation of corporations using a Marxist approach based on the work of Poulantzas and Gramsci,[68] which is also used as the basis for an approach based on enforceable punishments.[69]

Street crime

Is there a particular Marxist approach to street crime which might match the potential offered by corporate crime? One possibility is offered by Eric Hobsbawm's book *Primitive Rebels*.[70] In this classic history Hobsbawm considers a series of archaic types of protest which are on the boundaries of politics and crime: social bandits similar to Robin Hood, the Sicilian Mafia with their tinge of social protest, assorted millenarian sects, city mobs. All of these unite protests at the conditions of the poor with some kind of criminal enterprise. Are there still activities of this sort today – activities which combine criminal ways of acquiring resources with some degree of social protest? We have an immediate problem compared to Hobsbawm when he was writing in 1959. He could feel confident that progress towards socialism involved trade unions and a working-class political party (with issues, obviously, about the relative role of communist and social democratic parties).

Primitive rebels could thus be judged by how close they came to these models of socialist activity. Earlier in this book I suggested that if any sort of progress towards socialism is to occur it will be through some combination of the activities of very pragmatic politicians and trade unionists, non-governmental organizations and globalization protesters. The relative role played by each of these, and the value of what they do, is very much open to dispute, and the likely outcome is also much less clear. There are three categories of activity which will be briefly considered: political lawbreaking, victimless crimes and straightforward crimes which have a political edge. As we saw in Chapter 8, an important question in relation to these issues is an appropriate attitude to the law. It was argued there that if socialism is to be advocated using arguments based on justice then it should normally be advocated within a framework of legality, which also acts as a defence of socialists. For this reason support for breaking the law needs to be approached with considerable caution.

Political lawbreaking includes three aspects: illegal activities by political movements which ought to be legal, or which are in response to unreasonable behaviour by governments; lawbreaking by protesters linked to demonstrations and civil disobedience. The most obvious venue for illegal activities by political movements which ought to be legal is countries which are not properly democratic. Under apartheid in South Africa black people were not allowed to vote, the African National Congress was a banned organization, protest meetings could result in drastic repression as in the case of the Sharpeville massacre. Liberals, let alone socialists, would argue that attempting to continue legitimate political activity when it has been banned is acceptable. Further, if state repression makes legitimate political activity impossible it may be necessary to engage in civil disobedience and possibly also in military activity designed to overthrow the regime.

The banning of legitimate political activity is much less common in developed liberal democracies such as the United Kingdom. Restrictions tend to be imposed at the margins, such as the imposition of strike ballots and banning of secondary picketing by the Thatcher government, or the banning of some marches in Northern Ireland on the grounds that they might lead to violence. In these circumstances it is generally felt that the response should be an attempt to reverse the law, possibly matched with breaking or circumventing the law to see what happens. If the government has been properly elected and can be removed at the next election attempts at military overthrow are not appropriate. Another, similar, type of action is whistle-blowing. This will typically involve a civil servant who is bound by rules of secrecy revealing government actions which are themselves illegal: Clive Ponting leaking documents in 1984 which showed that the Argentinean cruiser of the Belgrano had been sunk whilst steaming away from the exclusion zone around the Falkland islands during the Falklands War of 1982; Sarah Tisdall, who leaked documents concerning the arrival of cruise missiles at Greenham Common in 1983; Katharine Gun, a GCHQ employee who was sacked in 2003 for revealing a US request to British intelligence agents to lend a hand in the illegal bugging of 'swing' nations at the United Nations to assist in the passage of a motion to authorize an attack on Iraq. Interestingly the Wikipedia list of US whistle-blowers is much longer than that for any other country, perhaps reflecting the US origins of Wikipedia, but also the extent of US corporate and governmental malfeasance.

Lawbreaking frequently accompanies the activities of protesters who tend to be known as anti-globalization protesters. It is generally either intended to publicize their cause, as in the trashing of global brand outlets such as Starbucks and McDonald's, or to attempt to interfere with the work of the G8 summits. It is not civil disobedience because the protesters do not wish to be caught, but it has a similar intention of publicizing their cause rather than seriously damaging the organizations targeted. Historically Marxists have been opposed to activities of this sort, which they associate with anarchists, but given the current situation with one superpower which has managed to impose neoliberal policies on most of the rest of the world they may well be willing to stretch a point. Civil disobedience is similar to this type of lawbreaking in that it is not genuinely intended to overthrow governments but to publicize and impede particular policies. Protesters are normally peaceful and are willing to accept the – normally modest – fines and imprisonment imposed for their actions.

The second main category requiring a brief comment is that of victimless crimes. These are particularly mentioned by the earlier critical criminologists. Their basic idea is that under socialism it will be possible for everyone to freely express their true nature. Thus people who want to engage in gay sex or the consumption of soft drugs should be able to pursue these activities without interference. This kind of view is no longer the exclusive purview of the left; at least some supporters of the New Right are happy to accept libertarian beliefs of this sort: Samuel Brittan is a well-known example. There is, obviously, much scope for debate about whether some crimes are genuinely victimless: the use of hard drugs or prostitution can be seen as victimless but can also be seen as harmful to some people. More traditional socialists and communists were less tolerant of this sort of free expression. Homosexuality was regarded as a form of capitalist decadence in Cuba and China. Whilst the acceptance of libertarianism may have been a distinguishing feature of 1960s new leftism, and remains rather more characteristic of those on the left of society than on the right it is no longer something which decisively marks off one from the other.

The third category, straightforward crimes with a political edge, harks back to the early stages of capitalism and people who felt deprived of, for example, access to game, timber or grazing available on what had been common land. There was widespread popular sympathy for people who broke the law to avail themselves of these things. Something of the same spirit attaches to attempts to avoid excise duty on tobacco and spirits, taxation on small jobs carried out by builders and craftsmen, modest amounts of working whilst claiming unemployment benefit and breaches of copyright on software, music and videos.[71] All of these are felt by many people to be relatively harmless and are seen as a way for people near the bottom of society to even things up somewhat. It is certainly worth debating what should be the socialist attitude to crimes of this sort. The reasons for socialists in liberal democracies to generally uphold the law rehearsed in the previous chapter are important in this context. As we shall see in Chapter 11 on communism, a communist society is likely to restrict ways in which people can make use of their money and resources in the public interest. The issues involved in these individually minor thefts are similar, making it debatable whether socialists should support this type of lawbreaking.

A better approach would be to consider whether the provisions which people are evading are just or not. For example, are there health grounds for Britain's relatively high taxes on alcohol and tobacco? On the whole there is a good case for arguing that people would be healthier if alcohol and tobacco became more expensive rather than less. What about the avoidance of taxation on small jobs? Many people benefit from home improvements and repairs which are cheaper because the workers carrying them out are evading income tax and VAT. However, there is no very strong case that small builders and craftsmen are victims of injustice compared to employees who are not in a position to evade PAYE. Indeed, many of the people who benefit from cheaper work on their houses will also be paying extra taxes to make up for those evaded. It is more difficult to reach a clear conclusion about modest amounts of paid work carried out by people on benefit because benefits in Britain are very low compared to wages. Nonetheless, the socialist emphasis should surely be on the desirability of improved benefits rather than the defence of benefit fraud. It is legitimate to point out that tax evasion, generally by people who are affluent, dwarfs benefit fraud. Estimated UK tax evasion in 2005 was somewhere between £97 and £150 billion, or 8% to 12% of GDP,[72] whereas benefit fraud costs some £900 million, yet the measures taken against the latter and the polemic against scroungers significantly outweighs measures against the former. Moreover, official estimates of unclaimed benefits for 2005–6 range from £5.7 billion to £9.37 billion.[73] That said, however, the socialist position should surely be in favour of justice rather than of limited theft. There is a still more ambiguous position when it comes to copyright evasion. It is hard to argue that Bill Gates deserves more money as a matter of justice, or to feel very sorry for the major corporate players in the entertainment industry. This is particularly true if the people benefiting from breaches of copyright are poor people in poor countries. A more vigorous defence of copyright needs to be matched by a more just distribution between rich and poor.

Overall the conclusions of this final section are on much the same lines as left realism: crimes against the public interest, even those with no immediate and direct victims, are against the interests of ordinary working people and should not be encouraged.

Conclusion

This chapter started by analysing Marx's position on justice. It endorsed the view that his account is irredeemably ambiguous, but moves on to argue that in a world where the onward advance to socialism is anything but certain socialists need to advocate their position in terms of a demand for distributive justice. It then moves on to consider the relationship between distributive justice and criminal justice, arguing that the role of criminal justice must be to preserve distributive justice. In this context corporate crime can be seen as producing a major exacerbation of distributive injustice. Marxist theory offers the best explanation of corporate crime, which massively outweighs street crime, and also points to a more promising approach to counteracting corporate crime than the predominantly fashionable one of compliance-oriented regulation. The final section considers whether there is a Marxist case for supporting some forms of street crime on the grounds that it represents primitive rebellion, but concludes that the crimes which could be defended are largely those which could also be defended from a liberal point of view. The advocacy of socialism based on justice points towards arguments for justice rather than a defence of certain forms of crime. The next chapter will extend this analysis by considering the Marxist account of communism.

11
Communism – The End of Crime?

A central claim of much of the writing discussed in Part II of this book is that communism would eliminate or greatly reduce crime. Bonger, for example, links a great deal of crime to absolute poverty which leaves individuals with a choice of stealing, starvation or suicide, and claims that a communist society would eliminate such poverty and the crime that it generates.[1] He linked poverty with alcoholism, prostitution, child labour and poor housing, considers that these would disappear with the building of communism, and that communism would also make it possible to raise the intellectual level of the proletariat, which would itself reduce the amount of crime.[2] Because he linked sexual crime with poverty and poor education he thought that sexual crime would also disappear under communism.[3] Communism would encourage altruism, which would also reduce crime because crime is linked to egoism.[4]

Turning to the American radicals, there is a specific claim in Quinney that a socialist society would be consonant with true human nature, which is not just interested in acquisition. In a socialist society there would be equality in decision-making, in material benefits and in the encouragement of fulfilling everyone's potential. The society would be democratic, and instead of law local committees would encourage people to conform to socialist customs.[5] Neither Chambliss nor Reiman discuss a specifically socialist society, but they share a very similar set of proposals for a much more egalitarian and rational society: the elimination of victimless crimes, a serious assault on corporate crime, increased honesty in public life, particularly in the compilation of statistics, stringent gun controls, the elimination of the features of the criminal justice system that railroad the poor into prison and a serious attempt to get rid of poverty. Plainly such a society would be intended to be much freer of crime than the present one.

The British radical criminologists also look to a socialist future to eliminate crime: 'the elimination of crime is possible under certain social arrangements'.[6] In the new society inequalities of wealth and power, of life chances and property would be eliminated.[7] 'The task is to create a society in which the facts of human diversity, whether personal, organic or social, are not subject to the power to criminalise'.[8]

In this chapter I want to assess these claims. The first step will be to give an account of Marx's own statements about communist society, which are notoriously guarded and thin. I shall make some comments about the interpretation of these and also about whether they remain realistic from a contemporary perspective even given a fair amount of goodwill in the setting up of a communist society. Following from this will come an assessment of whether a communist society would eliminate various forms of crime. I shall finish by making some comments about whether existing, or recently existing communist societies offer any valid guidance about crime.

Let us start from Marx's notoriously limited account, but flesh this out with some comments about what might be involved in the fulfilment of needs. From the *Communist Manifesto* we gather that the first step will be to 'raise the proletariat to the position of ruling class', in other words to install the dictatorship of the proletariat. In the *Critique of the Gotha Programme* Marx indicates that this new proletarian state installs socialism. Under socialism capitalists and landlords have been got rid of and everyone is rewarded according to their inputs of labour. Gradually society then moves on towards the higher stage of communism. Under communism

> In a higher phase of communist society, after the enslaving subordination of the individual to the division of labour, and thereby also the antithesis between mental and physical labour, has vanished; after labour has become not only a means of life but life's prime want; after the productive forces have also increased with the all-round development of the individual, and all the springs of common wealth flow more abundantly – only then can the narrow horizon of bourgeois right be crossed in its entirety and society inscribe on its banners: From each according to his abilities, to each according to his needs![9]

In fleshing this out let us start briefly with labour becoming 'life's prime want'. Is it realistic to expect all labour to be life's prime want for everyone all the time? There is another suggestion in *Capital* Volume 3:

> The actual wealth of society, and the possibility of constantly expanding its reproduction process, therefore, do not depend upon the duration of surplus labour, but upon its productivity and the more or less copious conditions of production under which it is performed. In fact, the realm of freedom actually begins only where labour which is determined by necessity and mundane considerations ceases; thus in the very nature of things it lies beyond the sphere of actual material production. Just as the savage must wrestle with Nature to satisfy his wants, to maintain and reproduce life, so must civilised man, and he must do so in all social formations and under all possible modes of production. With his development this realm of physical necessity expands as a result of his wants; but, at the same time, the forces of production which satisfy these wants also increase. Freedom in this field can only consist in socialised man, the associated producers, rationally regulating their interchange with Nature, bringing it under their common control, instead of being ruled by it as by the blind forces of Nature; and achieving this with the least expenditure of energy and under conditions most favourable to, and worthy of, their human nature. But it nonetheless still remains a realm of necessity. Beyond it begins that development of human energy which is an end in itself, the true realm of freedom, which, however, can blossom forth only with this realm of necessity as its basis. The shortening of the working day is its basic prerequisite.[10]

The straightforward meaning of this passage is that although attempts should be made to render production 'favourable to, and worthy of ... human nature' the 'true realm of freedom' occurs outside necessary production and requires the shortening of the working day. This suggests that the labour necessary to keep social life going would still be disagreeable under communism, at least for some people some of the time.

The previous discussion points towards a consideration of alienation in a communist society. The passage from *Capital* Volume 3 suggests that a degree of alienation would persist in a communist society. Alienation might also be expected to persist for some time during the transition towards a communist society, given that the revolution would be made by alienated workers who would become less alienated only gradually. As we saw in Chapter 7 there is good reason to think that alienation tends to cause crime, so that crime would at least persist until a fully communist society had been attained. Another theme relating to alienation needs to be mentioned here. The young Marx's critique of alienation points towards some kind of face-to-face society in which I produce things for you because I know you need them and because I care for you, and you do the same for me. This is very different from the picture painted by the older Marx in which communism follows on from an advanced capitalist society, which would be characterized by a worldwide division of labour and advanced industrial techniques. The sort and amount of crime that could be expected in a face-to-face society would naturally be different from that in communism developed from advanced capitalism.

In what follows I propose to accept the view that the older Marx dropped the concept of alienation for good reasons in favour of the view that human nature is very flexible and adapts itself to the existing mode of production. Similar problems arise within this perspective. People at the time of the revolution would have the characteristic virtues and vices of people under capitalism and would only gradually adapt to a socialist and then communist society. And capitalist vices such as egoism and cupidity would lead some people to commit crime.

A much worse problem than the persistence of some labour dominated by necessity concerns 'to each according to his needs'. I shall start by assuming that this means 'his or her' needs. I find Cohen's claim that this is unsustainable, given the resources of the planet, thoroughly plausible.[11] For example, in the United Kingdom we have a fairly typical European level of car ownership, at approximately 419 per thousand inhabitants.[12] Chinese car ownership recently raced past the 10 million mark,[13] taking China to approximately 0.76 cars per thousand Chinese. European and American levels of car ownership are already making a significant contribution to global warming. North America and Europe have been responsible for about 70% of the growth in CO_2 emissions since 1850.[14] If the United Kingdom entirely stopped using fossil fuels to generate heat and electricity, its consumption would be replaced by the Chinese within a year at current rates of expansion. Current levels of consumption in the advanced countries threaten a crisis due to global warming. Bringing the rest of the world up to the level of the advanced countries would speed up the crisis considerably, and replace deprivation due to underdevelopment with devastation caused by climate change. Worse still, bearing in mind Marx's comments about 'the springs of common wealth...flowing more abundantly' there is an implicit promise that consumption in the advanced countries will also rise. Reverting to cars, three British households in ten do not own a car. For some of these, such as people too infirm to drive or young people living in city centres car ownership is not appropriate. However, this still leaves a lot of households which would really enjoy extra mobility and comfort.

It could be argued that things are not necessarily as bleak as this. It may be possible to replace fossil fuel with renewable energy, and some developments which meet human need do not use up natural resources any worse than now. For example, improved computer software or more powerful chips may well save energy and other natural resources rather than expend them. However, things may well also have been worse all along. Many people would love to write and direct an epic film, design a major experiment to alter the climate of Australia, travel to the moon, consume items such as genuine champagne and caviar which are naturally scarce etc. All of these activities should, in my view, take place in a socialist society, but would have to be rationed out as part of the overall plan. A further major category of human need is the need for various forms of care, particularly emotional care.[15] It is possible to provide physical care at least partly by improved equipment – a mobile hoist, for example, can be used for one helper to lift a disabled person into a bath, which is then chemically cleaned and disinfected before the next disabled person is bathed, or various forms of electronic monitoring can make sure that an old person who is living alone has not collapsed. However, emotional care basically needs to be provided by other people, and requires considerable amounts of time and effort. 'The springs of common wealth' may 'flow more abundantly', but the only ways that this will help with emotional care are marginal – we might need less of it if we are physically healthy, and people who are spending less time providing themselves with the necessities of daily life will have more leisure to devote to others.

We have thus identified two reasons for thinking that any reasonably likely socialist society would need criteria of distributive justice, namely that some people would have to work at things which they found disagreeable at least some of the time, and there would need to be a degree of rationing of scarce resources. How serious these constraints would be obviously depends on technological developments, but I am pessimistic that problems of distributive justice would altogether go away. The obvious consequence of scarcity is that at least some people would want to do things or use things beyond their allocation according to the plan, which in turn means that some of the people wanting to use resources beyond the constraints of the plan would probably do so by criminal means. This problem might be considerably less than its equivalent in current society. There would be a much greater degree of equality, so that fewer people would be left with a strong sense of unfairness. Presumably advertisers would stop stoking up artificial needs and heightening real ones. Presumably the marketing of brands would cease. Nonetheless, there is every reason to think that at least some problems of distributive justice and of attempts to evade distributive justice would remain. Indeed, this is probably true by definition. A theory of distributive justice is a theory about distributing scarce goods. If there are scarce goods then there is the possibility of crime because some people want goods to which they are not entitled under the scheme of distributive justice which the society has adopted, and are sufficiently motivated to get hold of them by illicit means.

A society planned according to need might generate more crime in another way. There would likely be debate about the best ways of meeting need. For example, the countryside in Britain functions as agricultural land to meet the need for food and as a park for the recreation of town dwellers, some of whom like to walk peacefully whilst others prefer to ride around on scrambler motorcycles. Some country people enjoy sports which most town dwellers regard as cruel such as fox-hunting, hare coursing etc. Town dwellers may well want to live in houses built on what was rural land. There is thus much scope for argument about the use of the countryside in order to meet rival legitimate needs. The same sort of issues are starting to arise about green ways of generating power. Local people tend to feel that wind turbines spoil their amenities; a plan to use the tidal power of the River Avon is upsetting other river users. One would hope that these issues would be dealt with by debate and compromise. This already happens to some extent in current day society, but those who are disgruntled can often resort to the market in order to go and hunt animals in places where it is allowed, buy houses which do not look out over wind turbines etc. As a socialist society would typically allocate resources according to need rather than leaving things up to the market this safety valve would tend to be closed, leaving people to take direct action against aspects of the social plan which left them disgruntled.

So far we have been looking at the strongest claim that socialism would eliminate crime, namely that crime based on limited resources would be unnecessary, and have found good reason to believe that it would not do so fully. Indeed, as we saw in the last paragraph, the diminution or elimination of the market might actually make some sorts of crime more common. This is disappointing, as it will be recalled from the section on definitions that the most obvious claim for a Marxist approach to crime is that communism would eliminate the second category of crimes, those based upon the requirements of a particular mode of production. Communism, one might hope, would eliminate scarcity of material things and therefore eliminate crime based upon unfulfilled need. Although it seems reasonable to expect that it would eliminate gross need, and therefore be better than capitalism for many people, there is every reason to believe that there would still be a considerable amount of unmet need, which would serve as a motive for crime.

Let us move on to looking at the other varieties of crime identified in Chapter 2. The first was consensus crimes, such as murder or robbery. Murder and robbery based on sheer deprivation of resources, or on felt relative deprivation fuelled by advertising and conspicuous consumption should go down considerably, although, as we have seen, might well not be eliminated. One of the standard criticisms of Marxism is that it does not have much to say about patriarchy or about divisions based on race. To some extent both of these divisions are also the basis of interpersonal crimes. It is very much to be hoped that a move to socialism would reduce antagonisms based on patriarchy and race, but there is no reason to believe that these would automatically disappear as the consequence of the rise of socialism.[16] Crimes linked to them would also remain to some extent. What about murder motivated by sexual jealousy? Fourier's version of socialist society in which one of the needs fulfilled under socialism would be sexual need, and in which 'all perversions are equal under the law', would perhaps have the best hope of eliminating sexual jealousy. However, the availability of sex with someone else might well not make it fully acceptable to find one's partner in bed with one's best friend, and Marx makes no particular claims that his sort of communism fulfils needs of this sort.

Over the past 30 years domestic and sexual violence have moved into the area of consensus crimes in most of the advanced societies. Although these crimes are basically universally deplored they remain very common. There would appear to be at least 60,000 cases of rape annually in England and Wales.[17] Of these some 13,000 are reported to police, and a little over 5% of reported cases end in a conviction. Is there any reason to believe that the rate of rape would go down in a socialist society? Much of the literature argues that rape is a crime of violence where the motive is to dominate the victim rather than to have enjoyable sex. Perhaps in a socialist society fewer people would want to dominate others. Maybe a socialist society would offer greater legitimate access to sex, and thus reduce the motive for rape to the extent it is a sexual one. However, neither of these claims is particularly central to Marx's conception of communism. Looking at things another way, there is a fundamental human need not to be a victim of domestic or sexual violence. It is to be hoped that a socialist society would recognize this need. Some of it would be fulfilled through programmes of education, for example through aspects of sex education and citizenship education in schools. Nonetheless, some level of domestic and sexual violence might well continue, and one would hope that a socialist society would take it more seriously and prosecute it more effectively than is the case in current day society. Here again there is reason to expect more prosecutions and convictions for crime in socialist society rather than less, but in my view that would make it a better society.

What about thefts based on boredom, such as stealing cars, racing them and ending the evening by destroying them and cutting down on the forensic evidence in a really exciting blaze? Or vandalizing public property such as public toilets, bus shelters etc.? Would life in a socialist society be more exciting? Perhaps a socialist society would lay on more things for young people to do? However, if some of the motive for vandalism is rebellion against the constricting norms of a suffocatingly stable and peaceful society a socialist society might have more problems with vandalism than we have today.

To some extent murder and interpersonal violence have a technological basis. A major factor in the higher rate of homicide in the United States than in Canada or Western Europe is the American habit of shooting family members, fellow citizens etc. To people in Britain this appears to have an obvious solution. Following a particularly serious shooting using handguns in a primary school in Dunblane, the possession of handguns was made illegal for everyone except the armed forces and the police in some circumstances, to the extent that even the British Olympic pistol team has to practice abroad. Currently the major British worry is that many young people carry knives, which tends to result in stabbings with serious consequences, and various measures are being taken to try to reduce this problem. It is to be hoped that a move to a socialist society would be accompanied by greater feelings of community and security so that people would have less desire to possess offensive weapons, but there is surely every reason to think that this would be more difficult in a society with a tradition of carrying arms such as the United States.

Our third category of crimes was those based on the enforcement of religious and moral ideals. A major foundation of religious faith is insecurity, and as European societies have become more secure they have tended to become more secular. Many people still have some degree of religious faith, but it becomes much less of a basis for serious social divisions. England is an officially Protestant society, but there is very little antagonism towards Catholics except when they try to drastically curtail women's right to abortion. Catholics elsewhere in Europe, such as in Spain and Italy, have basically accepted the legalization of contraception, abortion and divorce, and taken to having much smaller families. Even if a communist society took no measures to reduce or eliminate religion, European experience would suggest that religious faith would tend to decline, or at least to be less socially significant, as people became more secure. However religious faith has diminished much less in the United States, which also enjoys the security which comes with affluence.

More extreme views about moral ideals tend to have religious foundations, but there is nothing to prevent people who take a secular approach from disagreeing about particular issues. At what age are most people able to consent to having sex? What level of learning difficulties renders a person unable to consent to having sex? How drunk does somebody have to be before she is unable to consent to having sex? Most people would accept the validity of consent to mild sadomasochism, such as being spanked with a paddle, but what about more extreme activities such as nailing someone's foreskin to a coffee table (which led to a prison sentence in the Spanner case)? If foreskin nailing is all right, what about cannibalism, again with consent? Is voluntary euthanasia acceptable, and if it is, what safeguards should there be to prevent someone being pressurized into agreeing to it? Many people would accept that a woman has a right to choose whether or not to have an abortion, but have substantial reservations about infanticide. At what point does the former turn into the latter? The answer to this question is likely to vary as medical technology advances. Is it acceptable to grow foetuses deliberately for experimental or therapeutic purposes? Should the age limit for this be the same as that for abortion? Should people be able to use any drugs they desire, with resources in this area being channelled into health education and rehabilitation, or do some drugs lead to such bad behaviour that they need to be restricted – obvious candidates might be alcohol and crystal meth. Is sex work a legitimate form of work which meets some people's needs? Or are communists constrained towards the abolitionist perspective on prostitution? It is possible to have quite a range of disagreement about all these issues within a secular perspective. Still remaining within a secular perspective, most people would agree that there is a spectrum of legitimate disagreement about these issues, but that at a certain point it is appropriate to have criminal sanctions. Thus, for example, someone who thinks that the age of sexual consent should be 18 is likely to be willing to engage in polite and constructive disagreement with someone who thinks it should be 14 but will want to invoke criminal sanctions on someone who thinks he is having consenting sex with 7-year-olds. As I indicated above, Marxists will be keen to ensure that no one is pressured into making decisions on these issues through poverty, but this is by no means the only matter at stake. And a communist society should certainly ensure that there are no economic pressures on these issues, but this will hardly stop paedophiles from being attracted to children, exhausted carers from being attracted at least in some part of their thoughts to euthanasia and so forth. Thus a communist society could be expected, one way and another, to have less of a list of crimes in these areas and less occurrence of such crimes, but overall the picture might not differ very dramatically from more tolerant societies such as Holland today.

What about our fourth category, derivative offences? A communist society which was serious about eliminating domestic and sexual violence might well find it necessary to introduce rather more secondary offences in these areas. For example, it is emerging that under current English laws and practices drunken women have very little protection from rape. Thus a specific offence of having sex with someone who is having difficulty speaking, has serious motor difficulties, or who is intermittently unconscious through drink or drugs might be a sensible addition to laws on sexual violence. It is difficult to be sure, but a communist society might thus have rather more derivative offences.

Finally, offences linked to maintaining the authority of the state would hopefully wither away in a communist society, but might actually be rather more necessary shortly after decisive moves away from capitalism at a time when supporters of capitalism would feel a real chance of moving back to their preferred society.

My overall conclusion is thus that a communist society might actually define more acts as crimes and encounter a higher rate of criminal behaviour, at least in some respects, than capitalist society, but that it would also be a better society for most people to live in. This conclusion of course also entails of that neither the state nor law would entirely wither away in a communist society. This is contrary to the ideas of Engels and of Lenin in *The State and Revolution*.[18] However, as we saw in Chapter 9, there are good reasons for understanding law as a basic feature of a civilized society and a bulwark against oppression.[19]

Let us finally turn briefly to existing or recently existing communist societies. Do they provide us with any guidance about what a communist society might or might not achieve by way of eliminating crime? Some scholars take the view that Marx's account of communist society is so remote from the Soviet Union, China, Cuba etc. that it is not appropriate to refer to them for any sort of guidance. This seems to come from the same stable as claims that Islam and Christianity are peaceful religions and never cause wars or persecutions if they are properly interpreted. Those who conduct wars and persecutions in the name of Allah or God are said to be not real Muslims or Christians and can therefore be discounted. For me this is unrealistic and discounts too big a slice of history. However, there are obviously peaceful Christians and tolerant Muslims, and it is worth considering how these religions can be compatible with a peaceful and tolerant society. It is therefore my view that for analogous reasons a brief consideration of crime and punishment in existing (or recently existing) communist societies is appropriate.

It has to be acknowledged that the societies have had to cope with very difficult circumstances. The Soviet Union was the consequence of the revolution of October 1917, which came at the end, for Russia, of a devastating war. It led on to the Civil War and intervention from the leading capitalist powers, which remained a serious threat up to the actual German invasion in the Second World War. When this was repulsed at the cost of some 21 million lives and 5 million dead soldiers the Soviet Union faced a nuclear threat of varying intensity until its demise. The Chinese revolution came after the Japanese occupation and the Civil War. The possibility of invasion by other powers has remained an ongoing threat. Cuba has faced the US embargo and assorted US sponsored dirty tricks etc. since the revolution with particularly devastating consequences in the Special Period following the collapse of the Soviet Union in 1989. Marx's original assumption was that communism would emerge in the leading capitalist countries rather than relative backwaters, and that it would rapidly spread from one country to another. Some of the difficulties experienced by existing communist countries can therefore be attributed to their relative backwardness and isolation.

Despite these difficult circumstances, all three communist societies chalked up major achievements. Here is a summary from Makoto Itoh, writing about the Soviet Union:

> Soviet society had achieved economic growth higher than most advanced capitalist countries, despite heavier military burdens. It had removed the threat of unemployment and guaranteed relatively egalitarian living conditions, including pensions, medical care and child care, and an extended education system that produced the largest number of engineers in the world, and greatly expanded jobs for women, enhancing their positions at workplaces in accord with the socialist idea. So long as there was relatively easy access to rich natural resources and to mobilisable workforces in the process of industrialisation to construct heavy industries on a large scale, the Soviet economy could grow suitably within the form of central planning based on the co-operation of workers, who were motivated by improving living conditions in the spirit of socialism.[20]

He argues that this process reached its limits in the 1970s and that the Soviet bureaucracy was unable to replace it with anything more effective. Much of the above description would also apply to China and Cuba. For China one would add that in recent years it is famous for double digit economic expansion and for taking a large swathe of its population out of poverty, and for Cuba its level of literacy and its health system represent major achievements. On the face of it societies fitting this description should be able to fulfil at least some of the possibilities for eliminating crime described above.

The available empirical evidence is rather ambiguous. The Soviet Union, particularly, generated a massive amount of low level (and probably high level) fraud and corruption, in which people exploited their occupational positions in order to get bribes or backhanders or to use work materials and facilities for private purposes.[21] This led people to distinguish between two broad categories of crime:

> The concept of a criminal ... has various meanings for the Soviet citizen. There are private criminals and public criminals. One who robs, rapes, or murders is a private criminal: one who has done wrong to another person .... The Soviet citizen will condemn criminal activity directed against individuals. Crimes against the person have a quality that permits universal condemnation. The other type of crime, that which permeates the USSR because it is 'the land of kleptomania,' as Simis describes it, evokes only token social control.[22]

Thus private crime involved the type of wrongdoing which would also be seen as criminal in most other societies. Public crime was also illegal, but almost everyone became involved in it, and thus liable to criminal sanctions if they were unlucky or fell foul of the wrong official. Indeed, whistle-blowers who complained about public corruption were likely to face sanctions of one kind or another, such as short jail sentences, loss of job or loss of pension.[23] Something similar – doubtless with 'Chinese characteristics' – must have applied in China prior to 1978; since then there has been the complication that with the turn to capitalism under Deng Xiaoping there have been opportunities for private profit-making so that corrupt state officials can use their position to provide advantages of one kind or another for entrepreneurs.

The interpretation of crime statistics in Western democracies is notoriously problematical, but is quite plain sailing compared to communist countries.[24] Official crime statistics are heavily dependent on leadership decisions about what to present to the public. An announcement that there is rising crime thus probably corresponds to real events in the society, but may include a leadership decision that the public would benefit from witnessing a crackdown on crime. The next comment must therefore be regarded as tentative. It would seem generally that moves towards a market society lead to a rise in important sorts of crime. Thus in China we have President Jiang Zemin launching a Yanda (strike hard) campaign against crime in 2001 stating

> the number of non-violent crimes, such as theft, and violent social crimes, such as murder, armed robbery and kidnapping, as well as crimes committed by 'mafia-style' Chinese syndicates were on the increase in a dramatic way. Only 'striking severe blows' would curb rising crime rates: crimes registered by police had reportedly increased by 50 per cent over 1999 figures and, over the past 20 years, mafia-style gang crimes had increased sevenfold and crimes involving bombings had increased 2.6-fold. Only 9 per cent of registered crimes in 1985 were considered major crimes. By 1990, the figure had climbed to 21 per cent and by 1995 it had risen to 42 per cent.[25]

This tallies with Wong's comment:

> There are many reasons for the rise in crime [since 1978]. The transformation of the Peoples Republic of China from a society driven by spirituality (socialism) to one of materialism (capitalism) provided the motivation for deviance. The ready availability and abundance of goods and materials in big cities heightened temptation

and increased criminal opportunity ... also, with a new freedom of movement previously static local communities disintegrated and along with this went their traditional social control and crime prevention capabilities.[26]

It is widely recognized that crime rose dramatically in the territory of the former Soviet Union following its collapse,[27] but this process seems to have been under way to a lesser extent under perestroika.[28] Anecdotal evidence certainly suggests that there was a very low level of public crime in the Soviet Union under Brezhnev. Ordinary Russians had various worries but crime did not rank highly among them.[29] On the face of it this is evidence that crime – largely meaning consensus crime which is criminal under socialism or capitalism – increases with the growth of the market.

Why, then, did the Soviet Union have an extensive system of repression and a socialist economy? How extensive was the repression is a major topic of debate, which reappears regularly in *Europe Asia Studies*. A sober estimate is given by Stephen Wheatcroft. At the end of 1938 Soviet labour camps held 1.3 million people. Another 300,000 were held in prison and a further 300,000 in labour colonies. An additional million people were held in special exile. This would mean that the entire repressive system held some 2.9 million people or 2.5% of the population.[30] Wheatcroft's estimate is considerably lower than that of some other commentators, but hardly suggests a society with no problem of crime, particularly when one adds in his estimate of one million executions during the Stalin years. Also, of course, the population of the repressive system was not static, so that a much higher percentage of the Soviet population than 2.5% were affected at one time or another. Given that many of the victims of the repression have since been rehabilitated, a further issue is obviously state crime against Soviet citizens, making the compilation of figures even harder.[31]

Neither China nor Cuba have experienced quite the Soviet level of repression, but Cuba's 487 prisoners per hundred thousand of population is very high by world standards although not at the level of the United States. China's 118 prisoners per hundred thousand of population is lower than that in the United Kingdom and lower than the world average. It would rise somewhat if China abolished the death penalty. China currently executes nearly 10,000 people per annum according to Amnesty International. Some 68 offences can carry the death penalty, including tax fraud, embezzlement and corruption, which at least shows that white-collar crime can be taken very seriously in China.[32] In the run-up to the 2008 Olympics there are suggestions that China is scaling back on executions. However, recent investment in mobile vans equipped to carry out lethal injections, claimed to be better on human rights grounds than the more traditional bullet in the back of the head, but actually probably intended to facilitate a lucrative trade in organs, suggests that the ultimate penalty will remain for some time.[33]

We do not seem to be looking at societies where crime has virtually vanished. The most difficult case is clearly the Soviet Union under Stalin. Were there special factors at work which could leave us more optimistic about a communist future? There were undoubtedly special factors at work, but there is also much dispute about how they should be interpreted. Marx plainly expected that a communist revolution would be led by the working class. The working class was a (significant) minority of the Russian population in 1917. Over the course of the revolution and the Civil War it was seriously eroded. Many workers, particularly those who had only recently stopped being peasants, went back to their villages and resumed peasant life. Workers who were more enthusiastic supporters of the revolution either joined the Red Army, many perishing in the Civil War, or became part of the Bolshevik administration. By the end of the Civil War there were relatively few workers remaining. The number of workers subsequently rose with increasing industrialization, but these new workers were generally recent ex-peasants. The majority of the population of the former Russian empire were peasants. To the extent that they supported the revolution it was because they wanted more land. Under War Communism the Bolsheviks, desperate to feed the cities and the army, took the class struggle to the countryside. They promised poor peasants who did not have sufficient land on which to make a living that they would redistribute land if the poor peasants would help them extract surpluses of grain from the kulaks or rich peasants. By the end of the Civil War in 1920 almost all the peasantry had become middle peasants who basically aspired to engage in subsistence farming. The Bolsheviks were thus left as the representatives of the proletariat in a country where there was very little proletariat remaining, and where the peasants had no particular desire to contribute to the building of a socialist future.

It was in this situation that Lenin introduced the New Economic Policy in 1921, allowing a limited reversion to capitalism with a view to building up the means of production. At the same time he proposed the ban on factions in the Communist Party. The Communist Party had been left as the only legal party because all the other parties in Russia had at one stage or another attempted to mount a coup against the government. This is not surprising because the Tsars had never taken democracy seriously, so that no tradition of loyal opposition had been established. Instead, any party which meant business had to prepare for some kind of revolution against Tsarism. The Bolshevik leadership was faced with a country which did not support its aspirations, surrounded by states which regarded it as a menace and which had intervened on the White side in the Civil War. In this situation paranoia was quite a rational frame of mind. Opposition was seen as objectively treasonable, as giving assistance to the enemies of the state. The use of the secret police, of camps and of trials which did not match Western norms had been established in the Civil War period and now continued.

Things became much worse with the starting of the Five Year Plans in 1928. The central feature of the first plan was the collectivization of the peasantry, which was supposed to be matched by the rapid development of industry and hence the mechanization of agriculture. According to official theory only the kulaks would oppose the Plan. In fact, however, the peasants had largely remained middle peasants in the aftermath of land redistribution during War Communism, and resisted collectivization en masse. Stalin was almost certainly paranoid by disposition, but had plenty to be paranoid about, and it is in this situation that the gulag expanded to its maximum. The security apparatus took on a dynamic of its own, working to plans which detailed numbers of arrests and provided labour for development projects such as building canals, forestry, opening up Siberia etc. It is difficult, given this situation, to produce a sensible discussion of the effect of the introduction of a communist economy on crime. Many people were simply swept up by the secret police with no justification; others engaged in mild forms of resistance which were exaggerated because of the overall situation; others engaged in economic crimes by doing things such as selling grain, which a few years earlier would have been legal.

Followers of Trotsky claim that things would have been different if revolution elsewhere had been pursued more vigorously: revolution in Germany particularly, but also in other Western countries would have made the Soviet Union more secure and provided the capital and expertise for Russian industrialization. I am inclined to think that the failure of revolutions elsewhere is chiefly down to the lack of revolutionary situations rather than the bungling of Stalinist leadership. As I remarked in the general discussion of Marxism at the beginning of this book it is in any case now very unlikely that people in other countries will want to attempt revolutions on the same lines as those which introduced

Communism in Russia, China, Cuba, Vietnam etc., given that the short-term result is likely to be massive disruption and bloodshed, and the end result seems likely to be a reversion to capitalism in one guise or another.

Future movements towards socialism are likely to comprise a combination of three rather disparate phenomena. First, some individual states will introduce socialist measures. There are various examples of this. The Scandinavian countries typically have excellent welfare states, high rates of taxation, and greater social equality than most other states. The core states of the European Union have a tradition of Rhineland capitalism in which workers and capitalists are regarded as social partners and there is a tradition of having workers on company boards. This functions against a background of generous welfare states. In Latin America there have been recent movements towards socialism, most notably in Venezuela. Second, the institutions of global capitalism such as the meetings of the G8 and the WTO are now regularly disrupted by a motley grouping of anti-globalization or anti-capitalism demonstrators. These comprise a mixture between anarchists, Greens, trade unionists, anti-poverty protesters and so forth. It is very debatable that the protesters would share an image of a desirable future, let alone be able to bring it about, but some of the protests have an effect. We thus find the G8 making pledges on world poverty and the environment, firms committing themselves to fair trade, unit trusts being set-up for ethical investors etc. The third phenomenon was at one stage advancing quite strongly at a European level: a move to set minimum standards for working hours and holidays accepted across national frontiers so there would be no point in capitalists relocating from Germany to France in search of an easier target for exploitation. This has been very much threatened by the possibility of moving operations to countries with substantially cheaper labour and less bureaucratic regulation. However, all workers want reasonable pay, leisure, health insurance, medical treatment and education for their children. In the longer term, therefore, it should be possible to introduce some minimum standards on a worldwide basis.

None of the three movements towards socialism listed in the previous paragraph is incompatible with liberal democracy. For that reason they are all also liable to erosion when pro-capitalist parties win elections, neoconservative ideologists persuade workers that they do not need trade unions, coalitions of anti-globalization protesters fall apart etc. But because advances towards socialism of this sort can be reversed quite easily they do not need to be defended by a military build-up, the secret police, a ban on other parties and groupings etc., and are therefore not likely to lead to substantial criminalization and incarceration on the Soviet model. Good social democratic institutions are perfectly compatible with relatively low levels of crime and incarceration in the Scandinavian countries, which have on average numbers in the 1970s per 100,000 in prison.[34] However we saw a whole series of reasons above for thinking that a move to socialism would produce some of its own forms of criminalization. This provides an independent reason for seeking humane but effective alternatives to incarceration.

Conclusion: Is There a Future for Marxist Criminology?

A viable Marxist criminology emerges from this book. It is not as dramatic and exciting as the original critical criminology, but it stands on reasonably firm theoretical and conceptual foundations.

The version of the general theory of Marxism that was found to be best supported was a social democratic vision which does not seek to change capitalist democracies by violent revolution. The ideas of informationalism offer a supplement to historical materialism which enables it to make sense of the modern world. However, the features of Marxism which led Marx and others to claim that a communist future is inevitable do not work. Some of them have been conceptually flawed since their inception, notably the features of the economic analysis of capitalism which are supposed to lead to an inevitable economic breakdown. Others have not fared well with the passage of history since Marx's day. When Marx was writing most capitalist states were not democracies, the only significant exceptions being Britain, the United States and Holland. In contrast the more advanced capitalist states today are all democracies, flawed though they may be. There is nothing institutional that prevents electorates from voting in socialist governments. Obvious problems include the shrinkage of the industrial working class and the extent to which people who depend on work for a living have different interests both within and beyond advanced capitalist nations. The collapse of the Soviet Union and of communism in Eastern Europe is widely felt to have discredited the cause of rapid revolutionary advance. In these circumstances socialist advance needs to be linked to a theory of distributive justice. Such a theory also needs to incorporate people who are incapable of working for various reasons. International socialist advance is not a matter of worldwide revolution but of the gradual development of forms of cooperation and of economic regulation in the interests of working people.

Against this background it is possible to develop a well supported account of crime, but in order to do this crime needs to be subdivided into different categories. Consensus crimes such as murder, assault and the theft of personal property are widely recognized in different societies. It is possible to some extent to provide a Marxist explanation of these in varying capitalist societies. There are also reasons for thinking that the prevalence of these crimes will diminish under communism, but it is utopian to expect them to disappear altogether. Marxist criminology can offer a good account of a second subdivision: crimes linked to a particular mode of production, and can be at the cutting edge of analysing and combating the corporate crime which is so prevalent under capitalism. It can offer some insightful ideas on the third category, crimes based on religious and moral values, particularly where these have a significant economic dimension, and is no worse than any other sort of criminology in discussing victimless crime. The fourth category was derivative offences, where the explanation would be as good as the explanation of the main offence. The final category was offences against the state, which might be expected to increase with any transition towards communism, although a reversible, social democratic transition would be less likely to provoke a criminal response.

The critique section of the book showed a considerable amount of very solid analysis produced by criminologists influenced by Marxism. Obviously some features of past work need to be abandoned or modified because of subsequent changes, notably the collapse of the Soviet Union and the resultant accelerated globalization. I argued against the notion that Marxist initiatives would permit much greater libertarian freedoms than are possible under capitalism, and criticized the ready acceptance of the symbolic interactionist view that crime has no ontological reality so that anything can be decriminalized, preferring the five-fold categorization mentioned above. The economic analysis of the criminal justice system begun by Rusche and Kircheimer, and continued particularly by American Marxist commentators, is a worthwhile beginning but needs further development, as discussed in the Toolkit section. The brief discussion of constitutive criminology demonstrated pretty conclusively the superiority of Marxist analysis to this weird and wonderful attempt at superseding it.

My review of the equipment available in the Marxist toolkit began with two approaches which I consider to be unhelpful. The location of crime in the lumpenproletariat suffers from foggy definition of this category combined with an unwarranted denigration of its historical role. It involves, moreover, an acceptance of the presentation of crime as found in official statistics. Although some of this street crime is genuinely harmful to ordinary working people, much of it simply leads to relatively minor claims against insurance. It certainly pales in comparison with corporate crime, from which the offences of people at the bottom of society are a distraction. There is also a more specific political reason for caution in that the link between crime and the lumpenproletariat is very similar to that identified by Charles Murray and others between crime and the underclass. This link is empirically debatable and has the effect of blaming the victims of new right deindustrialization and offshoring for the resultant unemployment and social disruption. The second unhelpful approach was that based on alienation. Whilst many commentators find the young Marx's advocacy of creative labour and condemnation of stultifying and monotonous work inspiring, the alienation theory lacks a clear focus for the analysis of concrete social problems. Moreover it is based on assertions about human nature which are impossible to justify in any definitive way: rival assertions by, for example, radical feminists are just as plausible but point in different directions.

The idea of the reproduction conditions of capitalism provides a much firmer foundation for the analysis of crime and criminal justice system. Indeed, some version of this analysis must work if any kind of Marxist criminology is viable. At a fundamental level, laws which are necessary for any kind of orderly society, such as those against consensus crimes, are also necessary for the reproduction of capitalism. Aspects of these, such as the prohibition of theft, provide the beginnings of the legal foundations of capitalism once precapitalist restrictions on the freedom to exploit labour have been done away with. During the painful birth of capitalist social relations the harsher penalties imposed by the criminal justice system are an essential instrument for turning serfs, peasants and vagabonds into labourers. Subsequently these can be reduced in severity until a reformist penal welfare emerges to complement the welfare state which accompanies the development of Fordist mass production. More recently the economy has shifted towards globalization, with the accompanying stresses of deindustrialization in the advanced countries. One solution to this is the growth of mass incarceration as found in the United States and to a much lesser extent in Britain. However, this is not the only possible solution, as witness other capitalist societies which have much lower levels of imprisonment.

Indeed, there are good reasons for thinking that the excessive use of imprisonment is actually damaging not just to those who suffer as prisoners but also to the overall health of a capitalist economy. It thus makes sense to struggle for a more humane and productive version of capitalism.

The analysis of law is another area which must work in some way if Marxism is to have any chance of making sense of crime. I started by briefly discussing the long-standing difficulty that law seems to be part of both the economic foundations of society and the ideological superstructure. A really thorough analysis of this would need to be much longer than appropriate for this book, but the likely direction would be to see law as a substantive area of society in its own right, with continuities historically across different social systems. The relative continuity of the criminal law can be seen to have its foundations in consensus crimes. An alternative analysis of law as simply an instrument of class terror suffers from several major objections. The empirical analysis of law by Marxist historians supports the idea of law as a substantive area. If law is relatively autonomous from the mode of production it is capable of offering a degree of protection to subordinate classes. The acceptance of the rule of law is an aspect of this protection, and is worthy of support by socialists. The overall conclusions of this analysis are congruent with the generally reformist tenor of my overall account of Marxism, and with the left realist version of Marxist criminology.

The reformist motif also emerges from the next item in the Toolkit, which was a consideration of justice: socialist advance in the real world depends upon an egalitarian account of distributive justice. This is because, as we saw, the inevitable triumph of socialism is by no means inevitable seen from the perspective of the twenty-first century. Moreover an overall account of social justice points to claims from some categories other than workers. Criminal justice forms an aspect of distributive justice. In particular white-collar and corporate crime has devastating social effects and has been too little analysed and pursued by criminologists. Marxist criminologists have played an honourable role in this area, which has much scope for further development. The generally reformist approach taken in this book led to a fairly cautious account of street crime. Supporting street crime as a form of resistance against capitalism involves undermining the rule of law and possibly undermining socialist advances in the development of the welfare state. The best hope lies in community solutions to crime and the avoidance of the growth of mass imprisonment, as already concluded in the discussion of the reproduction conditions of capitalism.

The final item in the Toolkit is appropriately the concept of communism. Some aspects of Marx's definition of communism imply the availability of indefinitely large amounts of labour power and were never viable; others are ecologically problematic. However, the ideal of a society based on human need remains very desirable. Such a society would have to be based on a conception of distributive justice, which in turn opens the possibility of crimes committed by people who do not accept the chosen pattern of distribution. The development of such a society would reduce crimes based on poverty but might increase corruption and crimes based on people wanting to use some of their resources to circumvent the social plan. The acknowledgement of some activities as crimes is definitely the sign of a more civilized and advanced society, so that this need not render socialism invalid. A brief account of the experience of crime in existing or recently existing communist societies, flawed although they may be, also suggests that communism actually generates some varieties of crime but that this may be a price worth paying.

Far from having died in the late twentieth century, Marxist criminology has a real and vibrant future in the globalizing world of the twenty-first century.

Notes

Introduction

1. MECW 3, 442; 4, 366, 425. This is a reference to: Karl Marx and Friedrich Engels, *Collected Works*, Vol. 3, p. 442; Vol. 4, pp. 366, 425. This abbreviation and convention will be followed throughout.
2. MECW 11, 497.
3. MECW 35, 488.
4. MECW 6, 494; 10, 62; 11, 149.
5. MECW 16, 489.
6. MECW 30, 389.
7. Willem Bonger, *Criminality and Economic Conditions*, London: W. Heinemann, 1916.
8. Goerg Rusche and Otto Kirchheimer, *Punishment and Social Structure*, New York: Columbia University Press, 1939.
9. William Chambliss, *On the Take: From Petty Crooks To Presidents*, London; Bloomington, IN: Indiana University Press, 1978; William Chambliss, *Power, Politics, and Crime*, Boulder, CO: Westview Press, 2001; William Chambliss and Milton Mankoff, *Whose Law, What Order? A Conflict Approach To Criminology*, New York: Wiley, 1976; William Chambliss and Robert Seidman, *Law, Order, and Power*, Reading, MA: Addison-Wesley Pub. Co., 1982.
10. Jeffrey Reiman, *The Rich Get Richer and the Poor Get Prison: Ideology, Class, and Criminal Justice*, Boston, MA: Allyn and Bacon, 1998.
11. Ian Taylor, Paul Walton and Jock Young, *The New Criminology: For a Social Theory of Deviance*, London: Routledge and Kegan Paul, 1973; Ian Taylor, Paul Walton and Jock Young, (eds), *Critical Criminology*, London: Routledge and Kegan Paul, 1975; Stuart Hall, Charles Critcher, Tony Jefferson, John Clarke and Brian Roberts, *Policing the Crisis: Mugging, the State, and Law and Order*, London: Macmillan, 1978.
12. Ian Taylor, *Crime in Context: A Critical Criminology of Market Societies*, Cambridge: Polity, 1999; John Lea, *Crime and Modernity: Continuities in Left Realist Criminology*, London: Sage, 2002; See also the collections: Paul Walton and Jock Young, (eds), *The New Criminology Revisited*, Basingstoke: Macmillan, 1998; Kerry Carrington and Russell Hogg, *Critical Criminology Issues, Debates, Challenges*, Cullompton: Willan, 2002.
13. See, for example, Evgeny Pashukanis, *Pashukanis: Selected Writings on Marxism and Law*, London: Academic Press, 1980.

1 Marxism in the Twenty-First Century

1. See Eduard Bernstein, *The Preconditions of Socialism* (trans. and ed. Henry Tudor), Cambridge, Cambridge University Press, 1993; Peter Gay, *The Dilemma of Democratic Socialism: Eduard Bernstein's Challenge to Marx*, New York: Octagon Books, 1979.

2. See Neil Harding, *Leninism*, Basingstoke: Macmillan, 1996; Neil Harding, *Lenin's Political Thought*, Vols 1 and 2, London: Macmillan, 1977, 1981.
3. See Joseph V. Stalin, *Foundations of Leninism*, Peking: Foreign Languages Press, 1976, p. 37, see: http://www.marx2mao.com/Stalin/FL24.html
4. Lev D. Trotsky, *The Revolution Betrayed*, 1936, see: http://www.marxists.org/archive/trotsky/1936/revbet/index.htm
5. See: http://www.marxists.org/archive/trotsky/germany/index.htm
6. See particularly Herbert Marcuse, *Reason and Revolution*, London: Routledge, 1986; *One Dimensional Man*, New York: Sphere, 1972.
7. This idea is pursued in the interesting collection: Daryl Glaser and David Walker (eds), *Twentieth Century Marxism: A Global Introduction*, London: Routledge, 2007.
8. For a well-argued account which emphasizes links with Hegel instead of Feuerbach, see Chris Arthur, *Dialectic of Labour*, Oxford: Blackwell, 1986. For my account of why Arthur is wrong see 'Marx's Conceptual Framework From 1843–5: Hegelian dialectic and historical necessity versus Feuerbachian humanistic materialism?' *Studies in Marxism*, Vol. 2, Dec. 1995.
9. *Economic and Philosophical Manuscripts of 1844*, MECW 3, 274.
10. Ibid., p. 275.
11. Ibid., p. 277.
12. Ibid., p. 275.
13. *Contribution to the Critique of Hegel's Philosophy of Law*, MECW 3, 175.
14. For example 'On the Jewish Question', MECW 3, 155.
15. For example 'Comments on James Mill', MECW 3, 217.
16. *Economic and Philosophical Manuscripts of 1844*, MECW 3, 309.
17. Ibid., MECW 3, 238–9, 240, 270, 296.
18. L. Althusser, *For Marx*, London: Allen Lane, 1969.
19. See Mark Cowling, 'The Case for Two Marxes, Re-stated' in *Approaches to Marx*, Milton Keynes: Open University Press, 1989, pp. 1–32. I also argue that the retention of the alienation vocabulary does not generally imply the retention of the analysis founded on alienation – see 'Alienation in the Older Marx' *Contemporary Political Theory* Vol. 5, part 3, August 2006, pp. 319–39.
20. MECW 29, 263.
21. G. A. Cohen, *Karl Marx's Theory of History: A Defence*, Oxford: Oxford University Press, 1978.
22. MECW 6, 167.
23. For example Balibar in Louis Althusser and Etienne Balibar, *Reading Capital*, London: New Left Books, 1970, p. 304, cf. Barry Hindess and Paul Q. Hirst, *Pre-Capitalist Modes of Production*, London: Routledge, 1975, pp. 12, 68.
24. For example William Shaw, *Marx's Theory of History*, Hutchinson: London, 1978.
25. Engels to J. Bloch, 21–22 Sept. 1890, Marx and Engels, *Werke*, Berlin: Dietz Verlag, 1956–62, Vol. 37, p. 463.
26. See, for example, Barry Hindess and Paul Hirst, *Mode of Production and Social Formation*, London: Routledge, 1976; Anthony Cutler, Paul Hirst, Barry Hindess and Athar Hussein, *Marx's Capital and Capitalism Today*, London: Routledge, 1977, Vol. 1. These interpretations and some others are discussed more fully in Mark Cowling and John Manners, 'Pre-History: The Debate

before Cohen' in Paul Wetherly (ed.), *Marx's Theory of History: The Contemporary Debate*, Aldershot: Avebury, 1992, pp. 9–29.

27. Paul Baran and Paul Sweezy, *Monopoly Capital: An Essay on the American Economic and Social Order*, New York: Monthly Review Press, 1989.
28. See: http://en.wikipedia.org/wiki/Consumer_goods_in_the_Soviet_Union
29. *Manifesto of the Communist Party*, MECW 6, 485.
30. *The Class Struggles in France*, MECW 10; The Eighteenth Brumaire of Louis Napoleon Bonaparte, MECW 11.
31. Bernstein, *The Preconditions of Socialism*.
32. For a discussion of the New Middle Class see N. Poulantzas, *Classes in Contemporary Capitalism*, London: New Left Books, 1975; E. O. Wright, *Class, Crisis and the State*, London: New Left Books, 1975 and *Classes*, London: Verso, 1985; Guglielmo Carchedi, *On the Economic Identification of Social Classes*, London: Routledge and Kegan Paul, 1977.
33. MECW 6, 496.
34. V. I. Lenin, *The Right of Nations to Self Determination* (1914), in *Collected Works*, Moscow: Progress Publishers, 1972, Vol. 20, pp. 393–454; Joseph V. Stalin, *Marxism and the National Question*, 1913 see: http://www.marxists.org/reference/archive/stalin/works/1913/03.htm; Otto Bauer, *The Question of Nationalities and Social Democracy*, Minnesota, MN: University of Minnesota Press, 2000; H. B. Davis, *Toward A Marxist Theory of Nationalism*, New York: Monthly Review Press, 1978.
35. MECW 6, 486.
36. Eugen von Böhm-Bawerk, *Karl Marx and the Close of His System*, trans. Alice M. Macdonald, London: T. F. Unwin, 1898; Ian Steedman, *Marx after Sraffa*, London: New Left Books, 1977; Geoff Hodgson, *Capital, Value and Exploitation*, Oxford: Blackwell, 1982; Alan Freeman, 'Marx after Marx after Sraffa', 2002 at: http://ideas.repec.org/p/pra/mprapa/2619.html; Andrew Kliman, *Reclaiming Marx's 'Capital': A Refutation of the Myth of Inconsistency*, Lanham, MD: Lexington Books, 2007.
37. See Martijn Konings, 'Simon Clarke's Theory of Crisis: A Critique', *Studies in Marxism*, Vol. 11, 2007, pp. 5–20; Ernest Mandel, 'Marx's Theory of Crises' at: http://www.isg-fi.org.uk/spip.php?article140
38. Rosa Luxemburg, *The Accumulation of Capital*, London: Routledge and Kegan Paul, 1951.
39. Chris Harman, *Explaining the Crisis – A Marxist Re-Appraisal*, London: Bookmarks, 1999; Michael Kidron, *Western Capitalism Since the War*, Harmondsworth: Penguin Books, 1970.
40. A useful starting point for this is the Wikipedia article at: http://en.wikipedia.org/wiki/Moore%27s_Law
41. See: http://www.littletechshoppe.com/ns1625/winchest.html
42. MECW 5, 35.
43. MECW 29, 263.
44. For a careful elaboration of this version of the theory see Joe McCarney, *The Real World of Ideology*, Brighton: Harvester, 1980.
45. Engels, *Anti-Dühring*, MECW 25, 120.
46. MECW 25, 124.
47. See Mark Cowling, The Dialectic in the Later Works of Marx and its Relation to Hegel, University of Manchester, PhD, 1975.

48. There certainly remains a strong level of interest in Marx from journalists, academics and the general public. Despite the existence of extensive editions of his collected works quite a lot of material remains unpublished. On these themes see Marcello Musto, 'The Rediscovery of Karl Marx', *International Review of Social History*, Vol. 52, 2007, pp. 477–98, particularly p. 496.

49. The three volumes of *The Information Age: Economy, Society and Culture* are the following: Manuel Castells, *The Rise of the Network Society*, Vol. 1 Oxford: Blackwell, 1996; *The Power of Identity*, Vol. 2 (second edition), Oxford: Blackwell, 2004; *End of Millennium*, Vol. 3 (second edition), Oxford: Blackwell, 2000.

50. Castells, *The Rise of the Network Society*, p. 14.

51. Ibid., p. 17.

52. Ibid., p. 471.

53. Ibid., p. 472.

54. Ibid., p. 168.

55. Ibid., p. 171.

56. Ibid., p. 172.

57. Ibid., p. 192.

58. Ibid., p. 205.

59. Ibid., p. 473.

60. Ibid., p. 474.

61. Ibid., p. 476.

62. Ibid., p. 92.

63. Ibid., p. 93.

64. Ibid., p. 97.

65. Ibid., p. 99.

66. Ibid., pp. 107–8.

67. Taylor, *Crime in Context*.

68. For example David Held and Anthony McGrew, (eds), *The Global Transformation Reader*, Cambridge: Polity, Cambridge, 2001, p. 4; Anthony McGrew, *The Transformation of Democracy*, Cambridge: Polity, 1997, p.8; Giddens, Jameson and Wallerstein, severally quoted in John Beynon and David Dunkerley, (eds), *Globalisation: The Reader*, New York: Routledge, 2000, p. 4; Stephen Gill, 'Globalisation, Market Globalisation and Disciplinary Neo-Liberalism', *Millennium, Journal of International Studies*, Vol. 24, 1995, Pt. 3, pp. 399–423, p. 406.

69. Castells, *The Rise of the Network Society* , pp. 217–8.

70. Ibid., p. 229.

71. Ibid., p. 237.

72. Ibid., p. 247.

73. Ibid., pp. 257–61.

74. Ibid., p. 265.

75. Ibid., pp. 196–281.

76. Ibid., p. 274.

77. Ibid., p. 275.

78. Castells, *End of Millennium*, p. 130.

79. Ibid., p. 132.

80. Ibid., pp. 134–5.

81. Ibid., p. 136.

82. Ibid., p. 137; 12% in 2006 according to Bureau of Labor Statistics – see Center for Economic and Policy Research at: http://www.cepr.net/index.php?option=com_content&task=view&id=1019&Itemid=138
83. Castells, *The Power of Identity*, p. 313.
84. Ibid., p. 314.
85. Ibid., p. 314.
86. Ibid., p. 315. See also Manuel Castells and Pekka Himanen, *The Information Society and the Welfare State : The Finnish Model*, Oxford: Oxford University Press, 2004.
87. Castells, *End of Millennium*, p. 160.
88. Ibid., p. 143.
89. Ibid., p. 146.
90. Ibid., p. 148.
91. Ibid., p. 150.
92. Ibid., p. 151.
93. Ibid., p. 152.
94. Ibid., p. 8.
95. Ibid., p. 10.
96. Ibid., p. 26.
97. Ibid., p. 30.
98. Ibid., p. 36.
99. Castells, *The Rise of the Network Society*, p. 105.
100. Ibid., pp. 134–5.
101. Castells, *End of Millennium*, pp. 83–90.
102. Ibid., p. 92.
103. Ibid. p. 96.
104. Ibid. pp. 212–330.
105. Figures from Sarah Anderson, 'Wal-Mart Pay Gap' Institute for Policy Studies, Washington, DC, at: http://www.ips-dc.org/projects/global_econ/Wal-mart_pay_gap.pdf , 2005.
106. A contemporary example would be the January 2007 lobbying of the World Economic Forum in Davos by trade union leaders seeking corporate responsibility. See: http://www.ituc-csi.org/spip.php?article604
107. See Castells, *The Power of Identity*, p. 331.

2 Marxism and the Definition of Crime

1. Paul Q. Hirst, 'Marx and Engels on Law, Crime and Morality' in, I. Taylor, P. Walton and J. Young (eds), *Critical Criminology*, first edition, London: Routledge and Kegan Paul, 1975, pp. 203–32.
2. Ibid., p. 203.
3. Ibid., p. 204.
4. Louis Althusser, *For Marx* [Pour Marx], London: NLB, 1977. See particularly the essay 'On the Young Marx'.
5. Hirst, 'Marx and Engels on Law, Crime and Morality', pp. 215–17.
6. Ibid., pp. 217–19. I argue below that this is a valid interpretation of Marx, but not at all helpful as an explanation of crime – see Chapter 5.
7. Hirst, 'Marx and Engels on Law, Crime and Morality', pp. 220–1.
8. Marx's Economic Manuscript, 1861–3, MECW 30, 389.

9. Hirst, 'Marx and Engels on Law, Crime and Morality', pp. 221–7.
10. Cutler, Hirst, Hindess and Hussein, *Marx's Capital and Capitalism Today*.
11. Hirst, 'Marx and Engels on Law, Crime and Morality', p. 228. The comment was not particularly accurate when Hirst wrote. Two years previously Taylor Walton and Young were commenting on the huge scale of corporate and white-collar crime in contrast to relatively minor thefts such as the Great Train Robbery. Ian Taylor, Paul Walton and Jock Young, *The New Criminology*, London, Routledge and Kegan Paul, 1973, p. 35.
12. United Nations Office on Drugs and Crime, 'United Nations World Drugs Report 2005, Executive Summary,' United Nations, http://www.unodc.org/pdf/WDR_2005/volume_1_ex_summary.pdf
13. T. Burke, 'Warning: Drugs Cost the Earth', *New Statesman*, 30 June 2003.
14. T. A. Obaid, 'Statement, Panel on International Migration and the Millennium Development Goals', http://www.unfpa.org/news/news.cfm?ID=685
15. United Nations Office on Drugs and Crime, 'World Drugs Report 2005', http://www.unodc.org/pdf/WDR_2005/volume_1_web.pdf
16. BBC News 13 February 2001, http://news.bbc.co.uk/1/hi/uk/1169049.stm; http://www.politics.co.uk/issue-briefs/economy/taxation/alcohol-duties/alcohol-duties-$366621.htm
17. A good starting point on this would be Jeffrey Reiman, 'Paul's Justice Page', http://www.paulsjusticepage.com/reiman.htm The general idea expressed in the text can be widely found in the literature on corporate crime or on globalization. One book which sums up the links between neoliberal deregulation and crime well is Robert Tillman and Michael Indergaard, *Pump and Dump: The Rancid Rules of the New Economy*, New Brunswick, NJ; London: Rutgers University Press, 2005.
18. For a brief but compelling account of the link between Vice President Dick Cheney, Halliburton and Iraq contracts see Corpwatch, 'Corpwatch: Halliburton', at: http://www.corpwatch.org/article.php?list=type&type=15 The figure of 10,000 relates to the immediate effects of the US invasion. How much the invaders are responsible for the further 100,000 to 1 million deaths is open to debate – see Jonathan Steele and Suzanne Goldberg, 'What Is the Real Death Toll in Iraq?', *Guardian*, 19 March 2008.
19. Castells, *End of Millennium*, ch. 3.
20. Emile Durkheim, *The Division of Labour in Society*, Basingstoke: Macmillan, 1984, p. 73.
21. Paul W. Tappan, 'Who is the Criminal?', *American Sociological Review*, Vol. 12, 1947, p. 100.
22. For details, see Home Office, 'What is the British Crime Survey?' at: http://www.homeoffice.gov.uk/rds/bcs1.html
23. On an attempt to deal with this problem, see A. Myhill and J. Allen, 'Rape and Sexual Assault of Women: The Extent and Nature of the Problem. Findings from the British Crime Survey', London: Home Office, 2002.
24. Alvin Gouldner, quoted in David Downes and Paul Rock, *Understanding Deviance: A Guide to the Sociology of Crime and Rule Breaking*, third edition, Oxford: Oxford University Press, 1998, p.183.
25. See George H. Mead, *Mind, Self and Society from the Standpoint of a Social Behaviorist*, Chicago, IL: Chicago University Press, 1967.

26. Howard S. Becker, *Outsiders Studies in the Sociology of Deviance*, New York: Free Press, 1991.
27. Ibid., p. 9.
28. Ibid., ch. 7.
29. John Muncie, 'The Construction and Deconstruction of Crime' in John Muncie and Eugene McLaughlin (eds), *The Problem of Crime*, London: Sage, 2001.
30. Richard Quinney, *The Social Reality of Crime*, Boston, MA: Little, Brown and Co, 1970, p. 15.
31. Ibid., p. 302. A similar approach may be found in John Lea, *Crime and Modernity*, London: Sage, 2002, p. 24.
32. Quinney, The Social Reality of Crime, p. 223.
33. See, for example, Nick Davies, *Guardian*, 22 and 23 May 2003.
34. For a good recent exposition and discussion of this debate see G. Slapper and S. Tombs, *Corporate Crime*, Harlow: Longman, 1999, pp. 3–8.
35. Edwin Sutherland, *White Collar Crime: The Uncut Version*, London: Yale University Press, 1985, p. 5.
36. Edwin Sutherland, 'Is "White-Collar Crime" Crime?', *American Sociological Review*, Vol. 10, 1945, p.139.
37. Cf. Slapper and Tombs, *Corporate Crime*, p. 4.
38. Tappan, *Who is the Criminal?*, p. 99.
39. Slapper and Tombs, *Corporate Crime*, p. 17.
40. Sutherland, 'Is "White-Collar Crime" Crime?', pp. 137–8
41. Slapper and Tombs, *Corporate Crime*, p. 15
42. Ibid., p. 19
43. Paddy Hillyard and Steve Tombs, 'Beyond Criminology?' in *Criminal Obsessions: Why Harm Matters More than Crime*, Paddy Hillyard, Christina Pantazis, Steve Tombs, Dave Gordon and Danny Dorling (eds), London: Crime and Justice Foundation, 2005, pp. 5–22.
44. Ibid., p. 6.
45. Ibid., p. 7. This comment links to the earlier theme that deregulation encourages crime: the Health and Safety Executive has been starved of funds and constrained to adopt an approach based on encouragement rather than inspection.
46. This is why successful British prosecutions for corporate manslaughter could be counted on the fingers of one hand and have applied only to small firms. The act passed in 2007 will make prosecution easier but would result only in a fine, which in the case of public bodies would involve the State fining itself – see Corporate Manslaughter and Corporate Homicide Act 2007.
47. Hillyard and Tombs, 'Beyond Criminology', p. 10.
48. Ibid., pp. 12–13.
49. Ibid., p. 14.
50. Ibid., pp. 19, 56, 64.
51. Danny Dorling, 'Prime Suspect: Murder in Britain', in Paddy Hillyard, Christina Pantazis, Steve Tombs, Dave Gordon and Danny Dorling (eds), *Criminal Obsessions: Why Harm Matters More than Crime*, pp. 23–38.
52. Ibid., p. 38.
53. Hillyard and Tombs, "Beyond Criminology?" p. 8.

54. Herman and Julia Schwendinger, 'Defenders of Order or Guardians of Human Rights?' in Ian Taylor, Paul Walton and Jock Young (eds), *Critical Criminology*, London: Routledge, 1975, pp. 113–146.
55. Ibid., p. 132.
56. Ibid., p. 137.
57. It might be necessary to make an exception to the above critique of a human rights approach in the case of dictatorships. If a dictator has taken the sensible precaution of making laws which define everything he does as legal, the obvious framework within which to condemn some of his acts as criminal is one based on an assertion of human rights, but these would need to be tightly drawn up. The list of crimes in the early articles of the Rome Statute of the International Criminal Court is an example of the sort of obvious violations of human rights that I have in mind – see: http://www.icc-cpi.int/library/about/officialjournal/Rome_Statute_English.pdf
58. Nils Christie, *A Suitable Amount of Crime*, London: Routledge, 2004, p. 4.
59. Ibid., p. 5.
60. Ibid., p. 7.
61. See also his excellent: Nils Christie, *Crime Control as Industry: Towards GULAGS, Western Style*, London: Routledge, 2000.
62. John Hagen, *Crime and Disrepute*, Thousand Oaks, CA: Pine Forge Press, 1994, p. 12.
63. Cf. James Q. Wilson, *Thinking about Crime*, Rev. ed., New York: Vintage Books, 1985, p. 5.
64. See, for example, the graphic description in Rusche and Kirchheimer, *Punishment and Social Structure*, p. 19.
65. For a useful discussion of this issue, mainly in relation to Canada and the United States, see Richard V. Ericson and Aaron Doyle, 'Criminalization in Private: The Case of Insurance Fraud', in Law Commission of Canada (ed.), *What is a Crime?.*, Vancouver, BC: University of British Columbia Press, 2004, pp. 99–124.
66. Steven Penney, 'Crime, Copyright, and the Digital Age' in Law Commission of Canada (ed.),*What is a Crime?*, Vancouver, BC: University of British Columbia, 2004, pp. 61–98.
67. For these sexual issues see Mark Cowling and Paul Reynolds, *Making Sense of Sexual Consent*, Aldershot: Ashgate, 2004.

3 The Classics – Criminology Encounters *Das Kapital*

1. Willem Bonger, *Introduction to Criminology*, London: Methuen and Company, 1936, p. 82.
2. W. A. Bonger, *Criminality and Economic Conditions*, Boston, MA: Little, Brown and Company, 1916.
3. For more detail see Jakob M. Van Bemmelen, 'Pioneers in Criminology: VIII Willem Bonger', *The Journal of Criminal Law, Criminology, and Police Science*, Vol. 46, 1955, pp. 293–302.
4. W. Bonger, *Race and Crime*, (1943), [1939], New York: Columbia University Press, 1943.

5. See John H. Wigmore, 'Willem Bonger', *Journal of Criminal Law and Criminology*, Vol. 31, Part 5, 1941, p. 657.
6. Bonger, *Criminality and Economic Conditions*, p. 378.
7. Ibid., p. 382 et. seq. See also Bonger, *Introduction to Criminology*, ch. 4.
8. Bonger, *Criminality and Economic Conditions*, p. 379.
9. Ibid., p. 380.
10. Bonger, *Introduction to Criminology*, pp. 2–3.
11. Bonger, *Criminality and Economic Conditions*, p. 389.
12. Bonger, *Criminality and Economic Conditions*, p. 394.
13. Ibid., p. 397.
14. Ibid., pp. 398–9.
15. Ibid., p. 401.
16. Ibid., p. 403.
17. Ibid., p. 404.
18. Cf. Bonger, *Introduction to Criminology*, pp. 95–6.
19. Bonger, *Criminality and Economic Conditions*, pp. 407–10 .
20. Ibid., p. 433.
21. Ibid., p. 434.
22. Ibid., p. 435.
23. Ibid., p. 448.
24. Ibid., pp. 464–8.
25. Ibid., p. 462–3.
26. Ibid., p. 473.
27. Ibid., pp. 507–8.
28. Ibid., pp. 483–4.
29. Ibid., p. 487.
30. Ibid., p. 487.
31. Bonger, *Introduction to Criminology*, p. 88.
32. Bonger, *Criminality and Economic Conditions*, pp. 516–7.
33. Ibid., p. 518.
34. Ibid., p. 545.
35. Ibid., pp. 625–8.
36. Ibid., pp. 546–55 .
37. Ibid., p. 556.
38. Ibid., p. 561.
39. Ibid., p. 564.
40. Ibid., p. 572.
41. Cf. Bonger, *Introduction to Criminology*, p. 94; *Criminality and Economic Conditions*, p. 574.
42. Ibid., pp. 590–1.
43. Ibid., pp. 594–5.
44. Ibid., p. 599.
45. Ibid., p. 600.
46. Ibid., p. 601.
47. Ibid., p. 603.
48. Ibid., p. 605.
49. Ibid., p. 607.
50. Ibid., p. 608.
51. Ibid., pp. 609–11.

52. Ibid., pp. 612–21.
53. Ibid., p. 621.
54. Ibid., p. 626.
55. Ibid., pp. 626–8.
56. Cf. Bonger, *Introduction to Criminology*, p. 104; *Criminality and Economic Conditions*, pp. 635–6.
57. Ibid., pp. 637–8.
58. Ibid., pp. 639–43.
59. Ibid., pp. 644–7.
60. Ibid., pp. 648–50.
61. Ibid., pp. 650–1.
62. Ibid., p. 659.
63. Ibid., pp. 660–2.
64. Ibid., p. 670.
65. Ibid., p. 671.
66. Ibid., p. 672.
67. Bonger recognized some of this type of dispute in the Holland of his day in his defence of homosexuality – see Van Bemmelen, 'Pioneers', p. 301.
68. See: http://news.bbc.co.uk/1/hi/magazine/3251725.stm
69. See, for example: http://www.sussex.ac.uk/Units/spru/publications/imprint/sewps/sewp61/sewp61.htmlb
70. Gresham M. Sykes, and David Matza, 'Techniques of Neutralization', *American Sociological Review*, Vol. 22, 1957, pp. 664–70.
71. Rusche and Kirchheimer, *Punishment and Social Structure*.
72. Rusche and Kircheimer, *Punishment and Social Structure*, p. 5.
73. As David Garland puts it, 'this perception of punishment as being aimed at the control of the lower orders...pervades [*Punishment and Social Structure*]', *Punishment and Modern Society: A Study in Social Theory*, Oxford: Clarendon Press, 1990, pp. 91–2.
74. Ibid., p. 11.
75. Ibid.
76. Ibid., p. 18.
77. Ibid., p. 19.
78. Ibid., p. 20.
79. Ibid., pp. 20–1.
80. Ibid., p. 25.
81. Ibid., p. 49.
82. Ibid., p. 50. Garland argues that the house of correction and transportation were actually mainly an expense rather than a source of profit – see *Punishment and Modern Society*, p. 106.
83. Ibid., p. 65.
84. Ibid., p. 60.
85. Ibid., p. 120.
86. Ibid., p. 96.
87. Ibid., pp. 105, 112, 132.
88. Ibid., p. 95.
89. Ibid., pp. 129–30. The idea of prison as an institution which trains prisoners to adapt to the workplace is a recurrent subordinate theme in the book. See also pp. 63– 107.

90. Ibid., pp. 147, 159, 167.
91. Ibid., p. 153.
92. Ibid., p. 161.
93. Ibid., p. 76.
94. Ibid., p. 78.
95. Ibid., p. 85.
96. Ibid., pp. 78–9.
97. For details see Garland, *Punishment and Modern Society*, p. 106, Raymond J. Michalowski and Susan M. Carlson, 'Unemployment, Imprisonment, and Social Structures of Accumulation: Historical Contingency in the Rusche-Kirchheimer Hypothesis', *Criminology*, Vol. 37, No. 2, 1999, pp. 217–49, p. 218.
98. B. Laffargue and T. Godefroy, 'Economic cycles and punishment: Unemployment and imprisonment, A time-series study: France, 1920–1985', *Contemporary Crises*, Vol. 13, 1989, pp. 371–404.
99. Ibid., p. 373.
100. Ibid., pp. 383–4.
101. Michalowski and Carlson, 'Unemployment, Imprisonment, and Social Structures of Accumulation', p. 228.
102. For a good summary of these see Taylor, *A Critical Criminology of Market Societies*, pp. 190–96.
103. See: https://www.cia.gov/cia/publications/factbook/print/us.html
104. See the database at the International Centre for Prison Studies, King's College, available at: http://www.prisonstudies.org/ (18 February 2008).
105. Charles Murray: 'The Underclass Revisited', American Enterprise Institute Short Publications, at: http://www.aei.org/publications/pubID.14891/pub_detail.asp
106. All figures are taken from the database at the International Centre for Prison Studies, King's College, available at: http://www.prisonstudies.org/ (18 February 2008).
107. David Garland, *The Culture of Control: Crime and Social Order in Contemporary Society*, Oxford: Oxford University Press, 2001.
108. Garland, *Punishment and Modern Society*, p. 107.

4 Radical US Criminology

1. Robert K. Merton, 'Social Structure and Anomie', *American Sociological Review*, Vol. 3, 1938, pp. 672–82.
2. Richard Cloward and Lloyd E. Ohlin, *Delinquency and Opportunity: A Theory of Delinquent Gangs*, New York: Free Press, 1960.
3. For a very good and basically favourable account of Merton's strain theory see Steven F. Messner and Richard Rosenfeld, *Crime and the American Dream*, Belmont, CA: Wadsworth Publishing Company, 1997.
4. Ibid, p. 73.
5. Ibid., p. 99.
6. Ibid., p. 101.
7. Ibid., p. 103.

8. As well as the major figures discussed in the main text several articles were published in the 1970s and early 1980s exploring the possibilities of a Marxist analysis of crime. One example is Stephen Spitzer, ' Toward a Marxian Theory of Deviance', *Social Problems*, Vol. 22, June 1975, pp. 638–51. This is best seen as an exploratory article looking at possibilities. Another is Mark Colvin and John Pauley, 'A Critique of Criminology: Toward an Integrated Structural-Marxist Theory of Delinquency Production', *American Journal of Sociology*, Vol. 89, No. 3, 1983, pp. 513–51, a massively ambitious piece which attempts to develop a substantially modified Marxist analysis of class and correlate it with empirical findings about delinquency.

9. R. Quinney, *Crime and Justice in Society, The Problem of Crime*, New York: Dodd, Mead, 1970.

10. Quinney, *The Social Reality of Crime*, Boston, MA: Little and Brown, 1970.

11. R. Quinney, *Critique of Legal Order*, New Brunswick and London: 2002. (Originally Boston, MA: Little, Brown and Company, 1974).

12. R. Quinney, *Criminal Justice in America: A Critical Understanding*, Boston, MA: Little and Brown, 1974.

13. R. Quinney, *Class, State and Crime*, New York: David McKay, 1977.

14. Quinney, *Critique of Legal Order*, p. 13.

15. Ibid., p. 97.

16. Ibid., p. 145.

17. Ibid., p. 16.

18. Ibid., p. 26.

19. Ibid., pp. 57, 59–68, 71–3, 76–80, 83, 89–91.

20. Ibid., pp. 35–42, 49, 124–9.

21. Ibid., pp. 52, 55.

22. Ibid., p. xxi.

23. Ibid., p. 156.

24. Ibid., pp. 160–1.

25. Ibid., pp. 75, 104, 110, 112–19, 131.

26. President's Commission on Law Enforcement and Administration of Justice, 1967, quoted on p. 172.

27. President's Crime Commission, p.181, cf. the quotation from President Nixon on prison reform, p. 185.

28. Ibid., pp. 167, 189.

29. Ibid., p. 187.

30. Ibid., p. 188.

31. Ibid., pp. 190–1.

32. Frank Pearce, *Crimes of the Powerful*, London: Pluto, 1978 (first published 1976).

33. Ibid., pp. 26–48.

34. Ibid., pp. 34–48.

35. Ibid., pp. 41–2.

36. Ibid., pp. 47–8.

37. Ibid., pp. 52–55.

38. Ibid., pp. 59–61.

39. Ibid., pp. 63, 66.

40. Ibid., pp. 63–4.

41. Ibid., p. 67.

42. Ibid., p. 67. The quotation from Taylor Walton and Young comes from a rejoinder to reviewers of *The New Criminology* in the *British Journal of Criminology*, Vol. 13, No. 4, 1973, pp. 401–3, p. 401.
43. Ibid., p. 77.
44. Ibid., p. 78.
45. Ibid., p. 81.
46. Ibid., esp. pp. 84, 90.
47. Ibid., p. 98.
48. Ibid., p. 104.
49. Ibid., p. 114.
50. Ibid., pp. 120–1.
51. Ibid., pp. 121–130, cf. p.157.
52. Ibid., pp. 131–46.
53. William J. Chambliss, 'Toward a Political Economy of Crime', *Theory and Society*, Vol. 2, 1975, pp. 149–170.
54. Ibid., pp. 150–1.
55. Ibid., pp. 153–4.
56. Ibid., p. 158.
57. Chambliss, *From Petty Crooks to Presidents*, 1978.
58. Ibid., p. 2, cf. p. 180.
59. Ibid., p. 2.
60. Ibid., p. 9.
61. Ibid., p. 62.
62. Ibid., p. 74.
63. Ibid., ch. 6.
64. Ibid., p. 151.
65. Ibid., p. 156.
66. Ibid., p. 183.
67. Ibid., pp. 184–5.
68. Chambliss, *Power, Politics, and Crime*, 2001.
69. Ibid., p. 1.
70. Ibid., p. 2.
71. Ibid., p. 5.
72. Ibid., p. 20.
73. Ibid., pp. 35–8.
74. Ibid., p. 47.
75. Ibid., pp. 50–4.
76. Ibid., pp. 55–9.
77. Ibid., pp. 41, 46.
78. Ibid., pp. 42–3.
79. Ibid., pp. 43–4.
80. Ibid., pp. 67–71.
81. Ibid., p. 80.
82. Ibid., pp. 94–5.
83. Ibid., ch. 5.
84. Ibid., p. 134.
85. Ibid., p. 137.
86. Ibid., p. 138.
87. Ibid., pp. 139–40.

88. See also pp. 148–51.
89. See also pp. 153–5.
90. See also pp. 155–65. I suspect the extensive charge sheet of the US state is well known to readers of this book. One particular point is that the CIA has frequently been accused of drug smuggling in order to finance other activities. Much of the smuggled drugs end up in the ghetto, where they contribute to the problems already mentioned.
91. Ibid., p. 141.
92. Ibid., p. 166.
93. Ibid., pp. 166–70.
94. Ibid., pp. 170–2.
95. Reiman, *The Rich Get Richer and the Poor Get Prison.*
96. Ibid., p. 1.
97. Ibid., p. 2.
98. Ibid., p. 14.
99. Ibid., p. 19.
100. Ibid., p. 3.
101. Ibid., p. 55.
102. Ibid., p. 4.
103. Ibid., pp. 51–91.
104. Ibid., p. 7.
105. Ibid., p. 42.
106. Ibid., p. 170.
107. Ibid., p. 156.
108. Ibid., p. 8.
109. Ibid., p. 8.
110. Ibid., pp. 19–20.
111. Ibid., pp. 20–3.
112. Ibid., pp. 23–6.
113. Ibid., pp. 26–8.
114. Ibid., pp. 29–31.
115. Ibid., pp. 31–3.
116. Ibid., pp. 33–40.
117. Ibid., p. 51.
118. Ibid., p. 61.
119. Ibid., p. 62.
120. Ibid., p. 63.
121. Ibid., pp. 65–8.
122. Ibid., p. 68.
123. Ibid., p. 69.
124. Ibid., pp. 69–70.
125. Ibid., pp. 74–5.
126. Ibid., pp. 76–7.
127. Ibid., pp. 80–1.
128. Ibid., pp. 81–7.
129. Ibid., pp. 87–90.
130. Ibid., p. 102.
131. Ibid., pp. 104–5.
132. Ibid., p. 105.

133. Ibid., pp. 106–7.
134. Ibid., pp. 111–13.
135. Ibid., pp. 114–15.
136. Ibid., pp. 116–19.
137. Ibid., pp. 128–9.
138. http://paulsjusticepage.com/RichGetRicher/Fraud2004/TaleOf2Criminals. htm
139. http://www.paulsjusticeblog.com/2006/08/ebbers_25_year_sentence_for_ worldcom_fraud.php
140. Reiman, *The Rich Get Richer and the Poor Get Prison*, pp. 179–92..
141. Ibid., pp. 209–11.
142. Ibid., pp. 212–15.
143. Reiman ,'The Rich (Still) Get Richer:... Understanding Ideology, Outrage and Economic Bias" at: http://paulsjusticepage.com/elite-deviance/reiman. htm
144. Christian Parenti, *Lockdown America: Police and Prisons in the Age of Crisis*, London: Verso, 1999.
145. Ibid., p. xii.
146. Ibid., p. 5.
147. Ibid., p. 6.
148. Ibid., p. 7.
149. Ibid., p. 9.
150. Ibid., p. 14.
151. Ibid., pp. 18–23.
152. Ibid., p. 31.
153. Ibid., p. 34.
154. Ibid., pp. 36–7.
155. Ibid., pp. 38–9.
156. Ibid., pp. 40–1.
157. Ibid., pp. 42–3.
158. Ibid., p. 44.
159. Ibid., p. 47.
160. Ibid., pp. 51–2.
161. Ibid., p. 57.
162. Ibid., p. 58.
163. Ibid., p. 65.
164. Ibid., pp. 74–83.
165. Ibid., pp. 84–9.
166. Ibid., pp. 90–110.
167. Ibid., pp. 111–38.
168. Ibid., ch. 7.
169. Ibid., pp. 168–9.
170. Ibid., p. 173.
171. Ibid., ch. 11.
172. Ibid., pp. 175–81.
173. Ibid., ch. 10.
174. Ibid., pp. 242–4.
175. The argument of this section is a summary of my: 'Postmodern Policies? The Erratic Interventions of Constitutive Criminology', *Internet Journal of*

Criminology 2006 at: http://www.internetjournalofcriminology.com/ Cowling%20-%20Postmodern%20Policies.pdf

176. Stuart Henry and Dragan Milovanovic, *Constitutive Criminology: Beyond Postmodernism*, London: Sage, 1996.

177. Stuart Henry and Dragan Milovanovic, *Constitutive Criminology at Work: Applications to Crime and Justice*, New York: State University of New York Press, 1999.

178. Notably Dragan Milovanovic, *Postmodern Criminology*, New York: Garland Publishing, 1997; Dragan Milovanovic, (ed.) *Chaos, Criminology, and Social Justice: The New Orderly (Dis) Order*, Westport, CT: Praeger 1997; Dragan Milovanovic, *Critical Criminology at the Edge: Postmodern Perspectives, Integration, and Applications*, Westport, CT: Praeger, 2002; Bruce A. Arrigo, Dragan Milovanovic and Robert C. Schehr, *The French Connection in Criminology: Rediscovering Crime, Law and Social Change*, Albany, NY: State University of New York Press, 2005; Christopher R. Williams and Bruce Arrigo, *Theory, Justice and Social Change: Theoretical Integrations and Critical Applications*, New York: Kluwer, 2004.

179. Henry and Milovanovic, *Constitutive Criminology: Beyond Postmodernism*, pp. 4–11.

180. (e. g. Alex Callinicos, *Against Postmodernism: A Marxist Critique*, Cambridge: Polity, 1989; Norman Geras, *Discourses of Extremity: Radical Ethics and Post-Marxist Extravagances*, London: Verso, 1990; Christopher Norris, *What's Wrong with Postmodernism: Critical Theory and the Ends of Philosophy*, London: Harvester Wheatsheaf, 1990; Paul R. Gross and Norman Levitt, *Higher Superstition: the Academic Left and its Quarrels with Science*, Baltimore, MD and London: Johns Hopkins University Press, 1994; Alan Sokal and Jean Bricmont, *Intellectual Impostures*, London: Profile Books, 1999).

181. Thorstein Veblen, *The Theory of the Leisure Class*, London: Allen and Unwin, 1925 (First published 1899).

182. Vance Packard, *Status Seekers*, London, Longman, 1959.

183. Sue Penna and Majid Yar M., 'From Modern to Postmodern Penality? A Response To Hallsworth', *Theoretical Criminology*, Vol. 7, No. 4, 2003, 469–82.

184. Milovanovic, *Chaos, Criminology, and Social Justice*, p. 207.

185. Milovanovic, *Critical Criminology at the Edge*, p. 125.

186. The quoted passage is from: Stuart Henry and Dragan Milovanovic, 'Constitutive Criminology: Origins, Core Concepts, and Evaluation', *Social Justice*, Vol. 27, No. 2, 2000, p. 268. Questia. 9 Nov. 2006, http://www. questia.com/PM.qst?a=o&d=5001793345

187. Benoît Mandelbrot, *The Fractal Geometry of Nature*, New York: W. H. Freeman, 1983; H. Gregerson and L. Sailer, 'Chaos Theory and Its Implications for Social Science Research', *Human Relations*, Vol. 46, 1993, pp. 777–802; C. Pickover, 'Pattern Formation and Chaos in Networks,' *Communication of the ACM*, Vol. 31, 1988, pp. 136–51.

188. Niklas A. Luhmann, 'Operational Closure and Structural Coupling: The Differentiation of the Legal System', *Cardozo Law Review*, Vol. 13, 1992, pp. 1419–41; Gunther Teubner, *Law as an Autopoietic System*, Oxford: Blackwell, 1993.

189. Giyatri Spivak, 'Can the Subaltern Speak?' in Cary Nelson and Lawrence Grossberg (eds), *Marxisms and the Interpretation of Culture*, London:

Macmillan, 1988; Bob Jessop, *State Theory: Putting the Capitalist State in Its Place*, Cambridge: Polity Press, 1990.

190. Alan Hunt, *Explorations in Law and Society: Toward a Constitutive Theory of Law*, New York: Routledge, 1993.

191. Mari J. Matsuda, Charles R. Larence, Richard Delgado and Kimberle W. Crenshaw, (eds) *Words That Wound*, San Francisco, CA: Westview Press, 1993.

192. Teubner, *Law as an Autopoietic System*; Gunther Teubner, 'The Two Faces of Janus: Rethinking Legal Pluralism', *Cardozo Law Review*, Vol. 13, 1992, pp. 1443–62; Drucilla Cornell, *Beyond Accommodation: Ethical Feminism, Deconstruction, and the Law*, New York: Routledge, 1991.

193. Karl Marx, *Early Writings*, (trans. Rodney Livingstone and Gregor Benton), New York: Random House, 1975; Derek Sayer, *Marx's Method*, New York: Humanities Press, 1979.

194. Jacques Lacan, *The Seminar of Jacques Lacan: Book IX: Identification 1961–1962*, (trans. Cormac Gallageur) (unpublished), 1961; Dragan Milovanovic and Ellie Ragland, (eds) *Topologically Speaking*, New York: Other Press, 2001; Dragan Milovanovic, 'Postmodern Criminology', *Justice Quarterly*, Vol. 13, 1996, pp. 567–610.

195. Mark Cowling, 'Postmodern Policies? The Erratic Interventions of Constitutive Criminology', *Internet Journal of Criminology*, 2006..

196. For example in Milovanovic, *Chaos, Criminology, and Social Justice*, pp. 6, 19.

5   British Critical Criminology

1. Jean Francois Lyotard, *The Postmodern Condition*, Manchester: Manchester University Press, 1984.

2. Taylor, Walton and Young, *The New Criminology: For a Social Theory of Deviance*.

3. Ibid., pp. 26–7.

4. Ibid., p. 29.

5. Ibid., p. 33.

6. Ibid., pp. 37, 40–1, 45.

7. Ibid., pp. 50–1, 61, 147, 178.

8. Ibid., pp. 118–19.

9. Ibid., p. 132.

10. Ibid., p. 34.

11. Ibid., pp. 78, 83, 87.

12. Ibid., pp. 94–5.

13. Ibid., p. 101.

14. Ibid., p. 106.

15. Ibid., p. 139.

16. Ibid., p. 145.

17. Ibid., pp. 145–6.

18. Ibid., p. 155.

19. Ibid., p. 164.

20. Ibid., pp. 209–10.

21. Ibid., p. 213; see Chapter 8 below.

22. Ibid., pp. 214–5.
23. Ibid., p. 216.
24. Ibid., pp. 216–7.
25. Ibid., p. 217.
26. MECW 3, 275.
27. Taylor, Walton and Young, *The New Criminology*, pp. 219–20.
28. Ibid., p. 220.
29. Ibid., p. 221.
30. Ibid., pp. 222–8.
31. Ibid., p. 230.
32. Ibid., p. 231.
33. Ibid., p. 233.
34. Ibid., p. 234.
35. Ibid., pp. 235–6.
36. Ibid., pp. 251, 266.
37. Ibid., p. 267.
38. Ibid., p. 270,
39. Ibid., pp. 270–7.
40. Ibid., p. 280.
41. Ibid., p. 281.
42. Ibid., p. 281, cf. Taylor, Walton and Young, *Critical Criminology*, p. 44.
43. Taylor, Walton and Young, *The New Criminology*, p. 282.
44. Taylor, Walton and Young, *Critical Criminology*, pp. 6–8.
45. Ibid., pp. 12–13.
46. Ibid., p. 14.
47. Ibid., p. 15.
48. Ibid., pp. 16–17.
49. Ibid., pp. 18–19.
50. Ibid., p. 23.
51. Ibid., p. 30.
52. Ibid., pp. 31–3.
53. Ibid., p. 33.
54. Ibid., p. 34.
55. Ibid., p. 35.
56. Ibid., p. 42.
57. Ibid., p. 45.
58. Ibid., p. 47.
59. Ibid., p. 52.
60. Ibid., p. 54.
61. Ibid., p. 55.
62. Ibid., p. 67.
63. Ibid., pp. 68–9.
64. Ibid., p. 71.
65. Ibid., pp. 71–2.
66. Ibid., p. 72.
67. Ibid., p. 73.
68. Ibid., p. 74.
69. Ibid., p. 75.
70. Ibid., pp. 77–8.

71. Ibid., p. 79.
72. Ibid., pp. 77–80.
73. Ibid., p. 82.
74. Ibid., p. 83.
75. Ibid., p. 86.
76. Ibid., p. 87.
77. Ibid., p. 88.
78. Ibid., p. 89.
79. Ibid., p. 90.
80. Ibid., pp. 150–1.
81. Ibid., p. 152.
82. Ibid., p. 164.
83. Paul Walton and Jock Young, (eds), *The New Criminology Revisited*, Basingstoke: Macmillan, 1997; Kerry Carrington and Russell Hogg, (eds), *Critical Criminology: Issues, Debates, Challenges*, Cullompton, Willan, 2002.
84. Jock Young, 'Breaking Windows: Situating the New Criminology' in Walton and Young, *The New Criminology Revisited*, pp. 14–46.
85. Jock Young, 'Critical Criminology in the Twenty First Century: Critique, Irony and the Always Unfinished', in Carrington and Hall, *Critical Criminology*, pp. 251–74, for the ten ironies see pp. 254–5.
86. Ibid., p. 258.
87. Ibid., p. 259.
88. See, for example, Frances Heidensohn, *Women and Crime*, Houndmills: Macmillan Press, 1995, p. 22.
89. See Ruth Chigwada-Bailey, *Black Women's Experiences of Criminal Justice: A Discourse on Disadvantage*, Sherfield-on-Loddon ,Waterside Press, 1997.
90. Hall et al., *Policing the Crisis*, 1978.
91. Ibid., pp. 201–6.
92. Ibid., pp. 263–72.
93. Ibid., pp. 212–3, 230, 237.
94. Ibid., p. 222.
95. Ibid., pp. 261–2.
96. Ibid., p. 221.
97. Ibid., p. 305.
98. Ibid., p. 309.
99. Ibid., p. 316.
100. Ibid., p. 16.
101. See, for example, Kenneth Thompson, *Moral Panics*, London: Routledge, 1998, p. 89.
102. Hall et al., *Policing the Crisis*, pp. 38–41.
103. Ibid., p. 37.
104. Ibid., pp. 57–60.
105. Ibid., p. 68.
106. Ibid., ch. 4.
107. Ibid., ch. 5.
108. Ibid., ch. 6.
109. See, for example, Bo Särlvik and Ivor Crewe, *Decade of Dealignment*, Cambridge, Cambridge University Press, 1983.

110. For example, John Gray, 'Blair's Project in Retrospect', *International Affairs*, Vol. 80, 1, January 2004, pp. 39–48.
111. Hall et al. *Policing the Crisis*, p. 11.
112. Ibid., p. 11.
113. Interview, 23 September 1987, see: http://www.margaretthatcher.org/speeches/displaydocument.asp?docid=106689
114. For accounts of Thatcherism see, for example, Dennis Kavanagh, *Thatcherism and British Politics: The End of Consensus*, Oxford: Oxford University Press, 1987; Eric J. Evans, *Thatcher and Thatcherism*, (second edition) London: Routledge, 2004.
115. James Q. Wilson, *Thinking About Crime*, New York: Vintage, 1985.
116. For an example of a critique see Jock Young, 'Left Realist Criminology' in Maguire et al., 1997, *The Oxford Handbook of Criminology*, Oxford: Oxford University Press, pp. 473–95, critique at pp. 475–78.
117. Young in Jock Young and Roger Matthews, (eds), *Rethinking Criminology: The Realist Debate* London: Sage, 1992, p. 15.
118. Ibid., pp. 27–9.
119. Ibid., p. 34.
120. Ibid., p. 50.
121. Taylor, *A Critical Criminology of Market Societies*.
122. Ibid., pp. 9–10.
123. Stuart Hall and Martin Jacques, *New Times: The Changing Face of Politics in the 1990s*, London: Lawrence and Wishart, 1990.
124. Taylor, *Crime in Context*, ch. 2.
125. Adapted from ibid., p. 11.
126. Taylor was writing when the current fall in the level of crime had only been going on for about three years.
127. Ibid., ch. 1.
128. Ibid., ch. 3.
129. See particularly Stuart Hall et al., *Resistance through Rituals*, London: Hutchinson University Library, 1976.
130. Ibid., ch. 4.
131. Taylor, *Crime in Context*, p. 134.
132. Ibid., ch. 5.
133. Ibid., p.172.
134. Ibid., p. 218.
135. Lea, *Crime and Modernity*.
136. Ibid., ch. 1, esp. p. 14.
137. Ibid., pp. 25–7.
138. Ibid., p. 31.
139. Ibid., p.32. For a full account see Mark Neocleous, *The Fabrication of Social Order*, London: Pluto, 2000.
140. Lea, *Crime and Modernity*, pp. 36–9.
141. Ibid., pp. 40–3.
142. Ibid., pp. 55–8.
143. Ibid., pp. 59–64.
144. Ibid., pp. 65–9.
145. Vladimir I. Lenin, *Imperialism, The Highest Stage of Capitalism, Selected Works*, Vol. 1. Moscow: Progress Publishers, 1970, p. 718.

146. Lea, *Crime and Modernity*, ch. 4.
147. Ibid., p. 107.
148. Ibid., pp. 110–16.
149. Ibid., pp. 117–26.
150. Ibid., p. 130.
151. Ibid., p. 136.
152. Ibid., pp. 137–8.
153. Ibid., pp. 142–3.
154. Ibid., pp. 144–7.
155. Ibid., pp. 150–1.
156. Ibid., pp. 153–4.
157. Ibid., p. 157.
158. Ibid., p. 159.
159. Ibid., pp. 183–4.
160. Ibid., p. 189.
161. Ibid., p. 190.
162. Ibid., pp. 190–1.
163. http://www.crimestatistics.org.uk/output/page54.asp
164. http://www.oecd.org/dataoecd/56/37/31613113.xls
165. House of Commons Research Paper 98/64, 4 June 1998. See: http://www.parliament.uk/commons/lib/research/rp98/rp98–064.pdf
166. http://www.labour.org.uk/health
167. See also: Castells and Himanen, *The Information Society and the Welfare State*.

6   The Lumpenproletariat as the Criminal Class?

1. This chapter is a slightly modified version of my chapter in Mark Cowling and Jim Martin (eds), *Marx's Eighteenth Brumaire: (Post)Modern Interpretations*, London: Pluto, 2002. References to the *18th Brumaire* are to the volume, which includes Terrell Carver's translation which is significantly better than that in the *Collected Works*.
2. For the best scholarly account of the lumpenproletariat in Marx see Hal Draper, 'The Concept of the Lumpenproletariat in Marx and Engels', *Economies et Sociétés*, Vol. 6, No. 12, December 1972, pp. 2285–312.
3. MECW 6, 494.
4. Karl Marx, *Class Struggle in France*, MECW 10, 62.
5. *The Eighteenth Brumaire of Louis Bonaparte*, Carver translation, pp. 77–8.
6. See Robert L. Bussard, 'The "Dangerous Class" of Marx and Engels: The Rise of the Idea of the *lumpenproletariat*', *History of European Ideas*, Vol. 8, No. 6, 1987, pp. 675–92, pp. 678–9. Stallybrass points out that Marx's exotic lists are similar to those compiled by journalists at the time – see Peter Stallybrass, ' Marx and Heterogeneity: Thinking the Lumpenproletariat', *Representations*, No. 31, Summer 1990, pp. 69–95, p. 72. For the link to generally used ideas, see Huard on the distinction between *le peuple* and *la populace*, the latter corresponding to the lumpenproletariat: Raymond Huard, 'Marx et Engels devant la marginalité: la découverte du lumpenprolétariat', *Romantisme*, Vol. 18, No. 59, 1988, pp. 4–17, p. 4.

7. For a series of references to work which shows the Mobile Guard actually comprised proletarians see Frank Bovenkerk, 'The Rehabilitation of the Rabble: How and Why Marx and Engels Wrongly Depicted the Lumpenproletariat as a Reactionary Force', *The Netherlands Journal of Sociology*, Vol. 20, No. 1, 1984, pp. 13–41, and Peter Hayes, '*Utopia* and the Lumpenproletariat: Marx's Reasoning in *The Eighteenth Brumaire of Louis Napoleon Bonaparte*', *Review of Politics*, Vol. 50, No. 3, 1988, pp. 445–65, pp. 462–3, n. 13. Huard points out Marx's own verbal ambiguity here, suggesting he was aware this move does not entirely work ('Marx et Engels devant la marginalité', p. 10.)

8. Cf. Bussard, 'The "Dangerous Class" of Marx and Engels', p. 687.

9. Karl Marx, *The Class Struggles in France*, 1848 to 1850, MECW 10, 51.

10. Hayes interprets this in terms of the dialectic of history, '*Utopia* and the Lumpenproletariat', p. 452.

11. In Cowling and Martin, (eds), *Marx's Eighteenth Brumaire*

12. Hayes, '*Utopia* and the Lumpenproletariat', p. 447; cf. Hayes on Marx and crowds, p. 460.

13. Bovenkerk, 'The Rehabilitation', p. 37.

14. For example, pp. 120–1.

15. Karl Marx, *Capital*, Vol. 1, ch. XXV, in MECW 35, 637–9.

16. Ibid., ch. XIV, Sect. 3, pp. 347–55; ch. XV, Sect. 4, pp. 420–30.

17. And, indeed, Huard suggests on the basis of one brief comment that Marx came to accept this – Huard, 'Marx et Engels devant la marginalité', p. 13.

18. Bovenkerk, 'The Rehabilitation', p. 34.

19. Mao says these elements, including Triads, can become revolutionary given proper leadership: Mao Tse Tung, 'Analysis of the Classes in Chinese Society', *Selected Works*, Peking: Foreign Languages Press, 1967, Vol. 1, p. 19.

20. Frantz Fanon, *The Wretched of the Earth*, (trans. Constance Farrington), Harmondsworth: Penguin, 1969, pp. 102–3.

21. For a careful survey of the cases where Marx and Engels attribute a political role to the lumpenproletariat, with the conclusion that they were invariably wrong about its reactionary role, see Bovenkerk, 'The Rehabilitation', pp. 22–34.

22. Charles Murray, *Charles Murray and the Underclass: The Developing Debate*, London: IEA Health and Welfare Unit in association with the Sunday Times, 1996, p. 22.

23. Ibid., p. 114.

24. Ibid., p. 111.

25. Ibid., p. 29.

26. Ibid., p. 34.

27. Ibid., p. 35. See also Charles Murray, *Underclass + 10*, London: Civitas, 2001, p. 6.

28. Murray, *Underclass*, p. 43. For further reflections in this vein see Charles Murray et al., *Does Prison Work?*, London: IEA Health and Welfare Unit, 1997.

29. More specifically: 'On the Right (Though More Libertarian Than Conservative)'. See Richard J. Herrnstein and Charles Murray, *The Bell Curve*, New York: Free Press, 1996, p. 555.

30. Murray, *Underclass*, p. 127.

31. See, for example, Ken Roberts, 'Is There an Emerging British "Underclass"'? in Robert MacDonald, (ed.), *Youth, the 'Underclass' and Social Exclusion*, London: Routledge, 1997, pp. 39–54.
32. Obviously Thatcher's New Right policies were generally paralleled by those of Reagan in the USA. For an analysis of the resulting growth in inequality see Norman Fainstein, 'A Note on Interpreting American Poverty' in Enzio Mingione (ed.), *Urban Poverty and the Underclass*, Oxford: Blackwell, 1996, pp. 152–9.
33. Les Johnston et al., *Snakes and Ladders: Young People, Transitions and Social Exclusion*, Bristol: The Policy Press/Joseph Rowntree Foundation, 2000, p. 1.
34. For a summary of the cuts in welfare provisions affecting young people at this time, see Hartley Dean, 'Young People and Social Citizenship' in MacDonald (ed.), *Youth, the 'Underclass'*, pp. 55–69, pp. 59–60.
35. Johnston et al., *Snakes and Ladders*, p. 1.
36. The most trenchant being the wonderfully titled Paul Bagguley and Kirk Mann, 'Idle Thieving Bastards? Scholarly Representations of the "Underclass"', *Work, Employment and Society*, Vol. 6, No. 1, 1992, pp. 113–26.
37. Melanie Phillips in Murray, *Underclass*, pp. 156–62. Buck points out that from 1979 to 1986 the number of inactive couple households grew by 350 per cent, far outstripping the rise in inactive single-parent households – see Nick Buck, 'Labour Market Inactivity and Polarisation' in David J. Smith (ed.), *Understanding the Underclass*, London: Policy Studies Institute, 1992, pp. 9–31, esp. p. 16.
38. Alan Walker in Murray, *Underclass*, p. 68.
39. For example, Oscar Lewis, *La Vida*, New York: Random House, 1966.
40. Johnston et al., *Snakes and Ladders*, p. 26, cf. Hartley Dean, 'Young People and Social Citizenship', p. 58, Gill Jones in MacDonald (ed.), *Youth, the 'Underclass'*, p. 112, Anthony Heath, 'The Attitudes of the Underclass', in Smith (ed.), *Understanding the Underclass*, pp. 32–47, see pp. 35–6.
41. Ibid., p. 26; cf. Rob MacDonald, 'Fiddly Jobs, Undeclared Working and the Something for Nothing Society', *Work Employment and Society*, Vol. 8, No. 4., December 1994, pp. 507–30.
42. Johnston et al., *Snakes and Ladders*, p. 29.
43. Jock Young, *The Vertigo of Late Modernity*, London: Sage, 2007, esp. chs 4 and 5.
44. Cf. ibid., p. 9.
45. Indeed, one British response to Murray has been to define the underclass as the 'socially excluded', thus including, for example, poor pensioners and the disabled in it (see, for example, Field in Murray, *Underclass*; Debbie Baldwin et al., 'The Formation of an Underclass or Disparate Processes of Social Exclusion' in Macdonald (ed.), *Youth, the 'Underclass'*, pp. 83–95). This is plainly not Murray's intent. For the idea of a link between US liberalism and the idea of an underclass on the one hand and European collectivism and the concept of social exclusion on the other, see Hilary Silver, 'National Discourses of the New Urban Poverty' in E. Mingione (ed.), *Urban Poverty*, pp. 105–38.
46. Johnston et al., *Snakes and Ladders*, pp. 27–8.

47. See, for example, Loic J. D. Wacquant and William Julius Wilson, 'The Cost of Racial and Class Exclusion in the Inner City', pp. 25–42 of William Julius Wilson (ed.), *The Ghetto Underclass*, Newbury Park, CA: Sage, 1993. Their description of what happened to the Black Belt in Chicago bears a striking resemblance to what happened in Middlesbrough, although against a background of less state intervention – see ibid., p. 30. For a more general account of the collapse of unskilled employment in US inner cities, see John D. Kasarda, 'Urban Industrial Transition and the Underclass' in Wilson (ed.), *The Ghetto Underclass*, pp. 43–64. For Murray's claim that black youth idleness has grown despite a booming economy, see Charles Murray, 'The Underclass Revisited', at: http://www.aei.org/ps/psmurray.htm

48. Murray, 'The Underclass Revisited'.

49. Charles Murray, *Losing Ground: American Social Policy, 1950–1980*, New York: Basic Books, 1984.

50. Herrnstein and Murray, *The Bell Curve*, ch. 11.

51. Charles Murray, *In Pursuit of Happiness and Good Government*, San Francisco, CA: ICS Press, 1994.

52. See, for example, the brief critique by Jock Young in Murray et al., *Does Prison Work?*, pp. 31–2.

7 Alienation

1. Marx, *Economic and Philosophic Manuscripts*, MECW 3, 275.

2. MECW 3, 275.

3. MECW 3, 275.

4. MECW 3, 296.

5. Pearson in Taylor, Walton and Young, *Critical Criminology*, p. 164.

6. Charles Fourier, *Le nouveau monde amoureux*, Oeuvres complètes de Charles Fourier, VII, Paris: Anthropos, 1967.

7. See, for example, Sheila Jeffreys, *The Idea of Prostitution*, North Melbourne, Victoria: Spinifex, 1997; Kathleen Barry, *The Prostitution of Sexuality*, New York: New York University Press, 1995.

8. MECW 24, 84–5.

9. For a detailed discussion see Ted Benton, 'Marxism and Natural Limits: An Ecological Critique and Reconstruction', *New Left Review*, No. 178, Nov-Dec 1989, pp. 51–86.

10. See: http://en.wikipedia.org/wiki/Virgin_Lands_Campaign; http://www. soviethistory.org/index.php?action=L2&SubjectID=1954tselina&Year=1954

11. See: http://en.wikipedia.org/wiki/Three_Gorges_Dam

12. See, for example, an article in *Le Monde Diplomatique*: http://mondediplo. com/2000/07/19envidisaster

13. For an interesting version of this argument see Jonathan Hughes, *Ecology and Historical Materialism*, Cambridge: Cambridge University Press, 2000, ch. 3.

14. See Benton, 'Marxism and Natural Limits', pp. 83–6.

15. This pastiche of radical feminism is put together from: Andrea Dworkin, *Intercourse*, London: Secker & Warburg, 1987 and *Pornography: Men Possessing Women*, London: Women's Press, 1981; Susan Griffin, *Woman and Nature: The Roaring Inside Her*, London: Women's Press, 1984; Mary Daly, *Gyn/ecology: The Metaethics of Radical Feminism*, London: Women's Press, 1979; Adrienne

Rich, *Compulsory Heterosexuality and the Lesbian Existence*, London: Onlywomen Press, 1981.
16. Max Stirner, *The Ego and His Own*, (trans. Steven T. Byington), New York: Benjamin R. Tucker, 1907.
17. For an account which claims to show Marx *does* have a theory of human nature, but actually demonstrates that the account in the older Marx is a thin one on the lines of that which is put forward here, see Norman Geras, *Marx and Human Nature: Refutation of a Legend*, London: Verso, 1983, pp. 72–82.

8   Crime and the Reproduction Conditions of Capitalism

1. MECW 30, 307–10.
2. The ideological backing for this approach came from two economists: R. Bacon and W. Eltis, *Britain's Economic Problem: Too Few Producers*, London: Macmillan, 1976.
3. See Louis Althusser, *Lenin and Philosophy and Other Essays*, London: New Left Books, 1970.
4. See Hall et al., *Policing the Crisis*, as discussed above in Chapter 5 and, for example, Elizabeth Wilson, *Women and the Welfare State*, London: Tavistock, 1977; Paul Corrigan and Peter Leonard, *Social Work Practice under Capitalism: A Marxist Approach*, London: Macmillan, 1978; London Edinburgh Weekend Return Group, *In and Against the State*, London: Pluto Press, 1980.
5. Michael Tonry, 'Why Aren't German Penal Policies Harsher and Imprisonment Rates Higher?', *German Law Journal*, No. 10, 1 October 2004, at: http://www.germanlawjournal.com/article.php?id=511
6. Ibid., pp. 1187–1206, especially p. 1193.
7. See Christie, *Towards GULAGS, Western Style*, p. 53.
8. See John Pratt, 'Scandinavian Exceptionalism in an Era of Penal Excess: Part 1: The Roots of Scandinavian Exceptionalism', *British Journal of Criminology*, Vol. 48, No. 2, March 2008, pp. 119–37.
9. See Garland, *Crime and Social Order in Contemporary Society*, p. 209.
10. See, for example, Peter Mandelson's comment: 'We Are Intensely Relaxed about People Getting Filthy Rich', *Financial Times*, 23 October 1998.
11. Information from company website: http://www.correctionscorp.com/aboutcca.html
12. Information from company website: http://www.thegeogroupinc.com/facts.asp
13. Information from company website: http://www.cornellcompanies.com/facilities.cfm
14. US Bureau of Justice figure for end of 2006, see: http://www.ojp.usdoj.gov/bjs/prisons.htm
15. See, particularly, Matthew Mitchell, 'The Pros of Privately Housed Cons: New Evidence on the Cost Savings of Private Prisons', 2003, available as a link from the Corrections Corporation of America at: http://www.correctionscorp.com/researchfindings2.html
16. See Joel Dyer, *The Perpetual Prisoner Machine: How America Profits from Crime*, Boulder, CO: Westview Press, 1999, ch. 9.

17. See: http://www.corrections.com/vendor
18. See: http://www.correctionalnews.com/
19. See: http://www.aca.org/Advertise/
20. Dyer, *The Perpetual Prisoner Machine*, pp. 14, 15, cf. Robert P. Weiss, '"Repatriating" Low-Wage Work: The Political Economy of Prison Labor Reprivatization in the Postindustrial United States', *Criminology*, Vol. 39, No. 2, 2001, pp. 253–91. On the other hand, Parenti offers good reasons for thinking that prison labour is, and is likely to remain, a relatively minor capitalist attraction of mass incarceration – see Parenti, *Lockdown America*, pp. 230–5.
21. Dyer, *The Perpetual Prisoner Machine*, p. 19.
22. See: http://www.swatmag.com
23. See: http://www.oletc.org/riot/
24. The lobby in favour of expanding prisons is not the exclusive preserve of capitalist corporations. In California a major influence has been the California Correctional Peace Officers Association – see Parenti, *Lockdown America*, pp. 226–7.
25. Parenti, *Lockdown America*, p. 217. Parenti also comments that prisons are not necessarily economically beneficial to areas which lobby for them, a conclusion vigorously backed by Gregory Hooks et al., 'The Prison Industry: Carceral Expansion and Employment in U.S. Counties, 1969–1994', *Social Science Quarterly*, Vol. 85, No. 1, March 2004, pp. 37–57.
26. See Dyer, *The Perpetual Prisoner Machine*, p. 260.
27. See Kyle Hopkins, 'Alaska May Lose Access to Arizona prisons', Anchorage Daily News, 2 February 2008 at: http://www.adn.com/100/story/302693.html
28. Dyer, *The Perpetual Prisoner Machine*, p. 215.
29. For details see Daniel Karpowitz and Max Kenner, 'Education as Crime Prevention: The Case for Reinstating Pell Grant Eligibility for the Incarcerated', (n. d.) at: http://www.bard.edu/bpi/pdfs/crime_report.pdf
30. Dyer, *The Perpetual Prisoner Machine*, Boulder, CO: Westview Press, 1999.
31. Ibid., p. 2.
32. Ibid., p. 62.
33. See ibid., ch. 4.
34. Ibid., p. 50, also ch. 6.
35. California, which has a particularly Draconian version of the three strikes law, was forced to slash $250 million from its university system, reducing the workforce by 8,100 people. In the meantime the Corrections Department increased its employees by 169%. The eventual cost of three strikes was estimated as $6.7 billion per year – see Dyer, *The Perpetual Prisoner Machine*, p. 256.
36. See his introductory summary, ibid., pp. 2–4, also ch. 10.
37. Ibid., ch. 2.
38. See Simon Hallsworth, 'The Case for a Postmodern Penality', *Theoretical Criminology*, Vol. 6, No. 2, 2002, pp. 145–63.
39. M. Gottschalk, *The Prison and the Gallows: The Politics of Mass Incarceration in America*, Cambridge: Cambridge University Press, 2006.
40. Ibid., ch. 3.
41. Ibid., ch. 4.
42. Ibid., chs 5 and 6.

9   Marxism and Law

1. Their writings in this area are collected in Maureen Cain and Alan Hunt, *Marx and Engels on Law*, London: Academic Press, 1979.
2. MECW 29, 263.
3. MECW 28, 26.
4. MECW 28, 35.
5. Hugh Collins, *Marxism and Law*, Oxford: Oxford University Press, 1984, p. 23.
6. Ibid., p. 25.
7. This seems the obvious implication of describing states as: 'special bodies of armed men having prisons, etc., at their command' in *The State and Revolution* (1917) – see: http://www.marxists.org/archive/lenin/works/1917/staterev/ch01.htm#s2
8. Evgeny Pashukanis, *The General Theory of Law and Marxism* in Piers Beirne and Robert Sharlet (eds), *Pashukanis: Selected Writings on Marxism and Law*, London: Academic Press, 1980, p. 44.
9. Ibid., p. 61.
10. Ibid., p. 112.
11. Ibid., pp. 113–14.
12. Ibid., p. 115.
13. Ibid., pp. 117–19.
14. Ibid., p. 120.
15. Ibid., pp. 121–2.
16. Ibid., pp. 124–5.
17. Cf. Collins, *Marxism and Law*, p. 32.
18. Garland, *Punishment and Modern Society*, p. 116.
19. Ibid., pp. 117–8.
20. Engels to Conrad Schmidt, October 27, 1890, Marxists Internet Archive, at: http://www.marxists.org/archive/marx/works/1890/letters/90_10_27.htm
21. Collins, *Marxism and Law*, pp. 64–5.
22. The ideas of Nikos Poulantzas, notably in *Political Power and Social Classes*, London: New Left Books, 1975, have been particularly influential here.
23. Paul Q. Hirst, *On Law and Ideology*, London: Macmillan, 1979, pp. 111–114.
24. Douglas Hay, 'Property, Authority and the Criminal Law' in Douglas Hay, Peter Linebaugh and Edward Thompson (eds), *Albion's Fatal Tree*, London: Allen Lane, 1975.
25. Garland, *Punishment and Modern Society*, p. 123.
26. Edward Thompson, *Whigs and Hunters*, Harmondsworth: Penguin, 1990 [1975].
27. Ibid., p. 94.
28. Ibid., p. 188, cf. p. 245.
29. Ibid., p. 190.
30. Ibid., pp. 206–7.
31. Ibid., pp. 260–1.
32. Ibid., pp. 262–3.
33. Ibid., p. 264.
34. Ibid., p. 266.

35. Edward Thompson, *The Making of the English Working Class*, Harmondsworth: Penguin, 1991 [1963], pp. 19–23.
36. See: http://www.publicinterestlawyers.co.uk/general/about.php
37. See: http://www.tridentploughshares.org/article1396

10 Marxism, Justice and Criminal Justice

1. N. Geras, 'The Controversy about Marx and Justice,' New Left Review, no. 150, Mar-Apr 1985, pp. 47–85; N. Geras, 'Bringing Marx to Justice: An Addendum and Rejoinder,' New Left Review, no. 195 Nov-Dec, 1992, pp. 37–69.
2. *Capital*, Vol. 1, MECW 35, 582.
3. *Economic Manuscript of 1861–63*, MECW 34, 234.
4. *Capital*, Vol. 1, MECW 35, 204.
5. *Capital*, Vol. 1, Harmondsworth; Penguin, 1976, p. 731. (This particular quotation comes from a passage added by Engels from the French edition which has been included in the Penguin translation but not in the *Collected Works*.)
6. MECW 24, 84.
7. MECW 42, 18.
8. MECW 24, 87.
9. MECW 20, 149.
10. *Critique of the Gotha Programme*, MECW 24, 87.
11. *Capital*, Vol. 1, MECW 35, 581.
12. Ibid., 35, 533.
13. Ibid., 35, 565.
14. Ibid., 35, 592.
15. Ibid., 35, 429, cf. p. 473. For an extensive list of similar quotations see Geras, 'Bringing Marx to Justice: An Addendum and Rejoinder,', pp. 50–1.
16. *Capital*, Vol. 1, MECW 35, 705.
17. *Capital*, Vol. 1, MECW 35, 738.
18. *Capital*, Vol. 1, MECW 35, 747, cf. 749.
19. Geras, 'The Controversy about Marx and Justice', p. 59.
20. Ibid., p. 70. Cf. G. A. Cohen, 'Review of Allen Wood, *Karl Marx*' in *Mind*, Vol. 92, 1983, p. 444.
21. Geras, 'The Controversy about Marx and Justice', p. 71.
22. Ibid., p. 85.
23. The argument of this section basically follows that of Geras, 'Bringing Marx to Justice', pp. 66–9 and G. A. Cohen, *If You're an Egalitarian, How Come You're So Rich?*, Cambridge, MA: Harvard University Press, 2000, ch. 6.
24. MECW 24, 86.
25. *Manifesto of the Communist Party*, MECW 6, 506.
26. John Rawls, *A Theory of Justice*, Oxford: Oxford University Press, 1973, pp. 575–6.
27. For a lively standard account see Hazel Croall, *Understanding White Collar Crime*, Milton Keynes: Open University Press, second edition, 2001. For arguments that white-collar criminals are punished severely see David

Weisburd et al., *Crimes of the Middle Classes: White Collar Offenders in the Federal Courts*, New Haven, CT: Yale University Press, 1994.

28. See M. J. Lynch, D. McGurrin and M. Fenwick, 'Disappearing Act: The Representation of Corporate Crime Research in Criminological Literature', *Journal of Criminal Justice*, Vol. 32, No. 5, September 2004, pp. 389–98; Steve Tombs and Dave Whyte, 'Scrutinising the Powerful: Crime, Contemporary Political Economy and Critical Social Research', in Steve Tombs and Dave Whyte (eds), *Unmasking the Crimes of the Powerful: Scrutinising States and Corporations*, New York/London: Peter Lang, 2003. The latter piece starts with a table which surveys some leading British criminology journals and finds that only 3% of the thousand or so articles appearing between 1991 and 2000 concerned corporate crime.

29. Both offerings, of course, include a fair amount of duplication and irrelevant material.

30. See Sutherland, *White Collar Crime*. (The cut version, with the names of the guilty corporations removed to protect his publisher from lawsuits, was published in 1949.)

31. Ibid., pp. 240–5.

32. Ibid., p. 9.

33. Ibid., p. 10.

34. Ibid., p. 15.

35. Ibid., pp. 56–7.

36. Ibid., pp. 233–8.

37. Donald R. Cressey, *Other People's Money: A Study of the Social Psychology of Embezzlement*, Glencoe, IL: Free Press, 1953.

38. M. B. Clinard and P. C. Yeager, *Corporate Crime*, Edison, NJ: Transaction Publishers, 2005.

39. S. Box, *Power, Crime and Mystification*, London: Routledge, 1990 (new edition).

40. F. T. Cullen and W. J. Maakestad, *Corporate Crime Under Attack: The Ford Pinto Case and Beyond*, Cincinnati, OH: Anderson Publishing, 1983.

41. J. Braithwaite, *Corporate Crime in the Pharmaceutical Industry*, London: Routledge and Kegan Paul, 1984.

42. S. Shapiro, *Wayward Capitalists: Target of the Securities and Exchange Commission*, Newhaven: Yale University Press, 1984.

43. J. Coleman, *The Criminal Elite: Understanding White-Collar Crime*, New York: St Martin's Press, 1985.

44. T. G. Poveda, *Rethinking White Collar Crime*, Westport, CT: Praeger, 1994.

45. M. Punch, *Dirty Business: Exploring Corporate Misconduct: Analysis and Cases*, Thousand Oaks, CA: Sage, 1996.

46. K. Schlegel and D. Weisburd, (eds), *White-collar Crime Reconsidered*, Boston, MA: Northeastern University Press, 1992.

47. L. Snider and F. Pearce, *Corporate Crime: Contemporary Debate*, Toronto, ON: University of Toronto, 1992.

48. K. Calavita et al., *Big Money Crime: Fraud and Politics in the Savings and Loans Crisis*, Berkeley, CA; University of California Press, 1999.

49. S. Simpson, *Corporate Crime, Law and Social Control*, Cambridge: Cambridge University Press, 2002.

50. See the review by James Williams: *Canadian Journal of Sociology Online*, May-June, 2003 at: www.cjsonline.ca/reviews/corpcrime.html
51. S. M. Rosoff, H. N. Pontell and R. Tillman, *Profit without Honour: White-Collar Crime and the Looting of America*, fourth edition, Upper Saddle River, NJ: Prentice Hall, 2006.
52. K. R. Gray, L. A. Frieder and G. W. Clark, *Corporate Scandals: The Many Faces of Greed, the Great Heist, Financial Bubbles, and the Absence of Virtue*, St Paul, MN: Paragon Press, 2005.
53. Henry N. Pontell and Gilbert L. Geis, *International Handbook of White-Collar and Corporate Crime*, New York: Springer, 2006.
54. For example, Gilbert Geis, *White Collar and Corporate Crime*, Upper Saddle River, NJ: Prentice Hall, 2006.
55. Raymond Michalowski and Ronald C. Cramer, (eds), *State-Corporate Crime: Wrongdoing at the Intersection of Business and Government*, Piscataway, NJ: Rutgers University Press, 2006.
56. J. Stiglitz and L. J. Bilmes, *The $3 Trillion War*, London: Allen Lane, 2008, pp. 13–15 and n. 36, p. 243.
57. Laureen Snider, *Bad Business: Corporate Crime in Canada*, Scarborough, ON: Nelson, 1992; Paul Palango, *Above the Law: The Crooks, the Politicians, the Mounties, and Rod Stamler: The shocking but True Story of Corporate Crime and Political Corruption in Canada*, Toronto, ON: McClelland & Stewart, 2004; Prakash Talwar (ed.), *Corporate Crime*, New Delhi: Gyan, 2006; Peter Grabosky and Adam Sutton, (eds), *Stains on a White Collar: Fourteen Studies in Corporate Crime or Corporate Harm*, Annandale, NSW: Federation Press, 1989.
58. For example Kathleen F. Brickey, *Corporate and White Collar Crime: Cases and Materials*, fourth edition, Greenvale, NY: Panel Publishers, 2006; James Gobert and Morris Punch, *Rethinking Corporate Crime*, London: Butterworth, 2003.
59. For example, Harry Glasbeek, *Wealth by Stealth: Corporate Crime, Corporate Law, and the Perversion of Democracy*, Toronto, ON: Between The Lines, 2004; Russell Mokhiber and Robert Weissman, *Corporate Predators: The Hunt for Mega-Profits and the Attack on Democracy*, Monroe, ME: Common Courage Press, 1999; Russell Mokhiber and Robert Weissman, *On the Rampage: Corporations Plundering the Global Village*, Monroe, ME: Common Courage Press, 2004.
60. G. Slapper and S. Tombs, *Corporate Crime*, London: Pearson Education, 1999.
61. Ibid., pp. 58–63.
62. Ibid., pp. 68–78. This brief argument is massively substantiated in Steve Tombs, Dave White and Hazel Croall, *Safety Crimes*, Cullompton: Willan, 2007.
63. F. Pearce and S. Tombs, *Toxic Capitalism: Corporate Crime and the Chemical Industry*, Aldershot: Dartmouth Publishing, 1998.
64. Michael Levi, *Regulating Fraud: White Collar Crime and the Criminal Process*, London: Routledge, 1988; Michael Levi, *Fraud: Organisation, Motivation and Control*, Vols 1 and 2, Aldershot: Dartmouth, 1999; Michael Levi, *The Phantom Capitalists*, second edition, Aldershot: Dartmouth, 2008; Alan Doig, *Fraud*, Cullompton: Willan, 2006.

65. Slapper and Tombs, *Corporate Crime*, p. 154.
66. Ibid., ch. 6.
67. Ibid., p,. 160.
68. Ibid., ch. 8, particularly p. 192.
69. Ibid., ch. 9.
70. E. Hobsbawm, *Primitive Rebels*, Manchester: Manchester University Press, 1974.
71. Cf. Lea, *Crime and Modernity*, pp. 142–3.
72. Adam Taylor, 'A Taxing Problem', *Guardian Unlimited*, 10 January 2007 at: http://www.guardian.co.uk/commentisfree/story/0,,1986929,00.html
73. Patrick Wintour, ' Ministers Trying to Save Cash on Benefits Take-up says Byers', *Guardian*, March 24, 2008.

11   Communism – The End of Crime?

1. Bonger, *Criminality and Economic Conditions*, p. 670.
2. Ibid., p. 671.
3. The standard contemporary view of sexual offending is that it extends across all classes and social groups; if incarcerated sexual offenders tend to be from lower social groups it is thought that this is because people from such groups tend to get caught more readily.
4. Ibid., p. 672.
5. Quinney, *Critique of Legal Order*, pp. 167, 187–91.
6. Taylor, Walton and Young, *The New Criminology*, p. 281.
7. Ibid., p. 281.
8. Ibid., p. 282, cf. Young, *Critical Criminology*, p. 90.
9. MECW 24, 87.
10. MECW 37, 807.
11. Cohen, *If You're an Egalitarian*, ch. 6.
12. http://www.eurofound.eu.int/areas/qualityoflife/eurlife/index.php?template=3&radioindic=105&idDomain=9
13. *Peoples Daily Online*, at: http://english.people.com.cn/200306/14/eng20030614_118209.shtml
14. Nicolas Stern, *Review Report on the Economics of Climate Change*, London: H. M. Treasury, 2006, p. 169, at: http://www.hm-treasury.gov.uk/independent_reviews/stern_review_economics_climate_change/stern_review_report.cfm
15. See Valerie Bryson in Georgina Blakeley and Valerie Bryson (eds), *Marx and Other Four-Letter Words*, London: Pluto Press, 2005, p. 138.
16. For what it is worth, the Cuban national revolution against Spain involved an ideology which stated that all Cubans were equal; and since the revolution which led to the introduction of communism this ideology has been very strongly reinforced. Nevertheless, to the extent that there are inequalities in Cuban society, black Cubans tend to be lower down the social scale.
17. Andy Myhill and Jonathan Allen, 'Rape and sexual assault of women: The Extent and Nature of the Problem. Findings from the British Crime Survey', Home Office Research, Development and Statistics Directorate, *Findings* 159, 2002.

18. See part 4: http://www.marxists.org/archive/lenin/works/1917/staterev/ch01.htm#s4
19. These arguments are pursued in much more detail in Collins, *Marxism and Law*, pp. 100–46.
20. Makoto Itoh, ' Marx's Economic Theory and the Prospects for Socialism' in Hiroshi Uchida (ed.), *Marx for the 21st-Century*, London: Routledge, 2006, pp. 21–35, p. 38.
21. This is extensively documented in Lydia S. Rosner, *The Soviet Way of Crime*, South Hadley, MA: Bergin and Garvey, 1986, esp. ch. 1.
22. Ibid., p. 37.
23. Ibid., p. 39.
24. For a brief explanation of the way in which Chinese statistics are compiled see Susan Trevaskes, 'Severe and Swift Justice in China', *British Journal of Criminology*, 2007, Vol. 47, No. 1, pp. 23–41, f. 2. For the Soviet Union see William E. Butler, 'Crime in the Soviet Union: Early Glimpses of the True Story', *British Journal of Criminology*, Vol. 32, No. 2, 1992, pp. 144–59.
25. Trevaskes, 'Severe and Swift Justice in China', p. 25.
26. Kam C. Wong, 'Policing in the People's Republic of China: the Road to Reform in the 1990s', *British Journal of Criminology*, Vol. 42, 2002, pp. 281–316, p. 306.
27. For example, Richard Lotspeich, 'Crime in the Transition Economies', *Europe Asia Studies*, Vol. 42, No. 4, June 1995, pp. 555–89.
28. See Butler, 'Crime in the Soviet Union'; Gennady V. Dashkov, 'Quantitative and Qualitative Changes in Crime in the Soviet Union', *British Journal of Criminology*, Vol. 32, No. 2, 1992, pp. 160–66.
29. Personal observation from Mike Teague, a Moscow resident at that period.
30. Stephen Wheatcroft, 'Victims of Stalinism and the Soviet Secret Police: The Comparability and Reliability of the Archival Data – Not the Last Word', *Europe Asia Studies*, Vol. 51, No. 2, 1999, pp. 315–45, appendix 3.
31. See Butler, 'Crime in the Soviet Union', p. 146.
32. See: http://web.amnesty.org/library/Index/ENGASA170532004?open&of=ENG-CHN; China: The Death Penalty, A Failure Of Justice at: http://asiapacific.amnesty.org/apro/APROweb.nsf/pages/appeals_ad`an_china See also Trevaskes, 'Severe and Swift Justica in China'.
33. Calum MacLeod, 'China Makes Ultimate Punishment Mobile', *USA Today*, 14 June 2006, see: http://www.usatoday.com/news/world/2006-06-14-death-van_x.htm
34. Cf. International Centre for Prison Studies, *World Prison Population List*, (seventh edition), 2007, see: http://www.prisonstudies.org

Bibliography

Althusser, L. (1970), *Lenin and Philosophy and Other Essays*, London: New Left Books.

Althusser, L. (1977), *For Marx*, London: NLB.

Amnesty International (2006), China: The Death Penalty, A Failure of Justice at: http://asiapacific.amnesty.org/apro/APROweb.nsf/pages/appeals_adpan_china

Anderson, S. (2005), 'Wal-Mart Pay Gap', Institute for Policy Studies (Washington, DC), at: http://www.ips-dc.org/projects/global_econ/Wal-mart_pay_gap.pdf

Arrigo, B. A. (1996), 'Postmodern Criminology on Race, Class, and Gender', in Schwartz, M. D. and Milovanovic, D. (eds), *Race, Gender, and Class in Criminology: The Intersections*, New York: Garland.

Arrigo, B. A. (1997), 'Dimensions of Social Justice in a Single Room Occupancy: Contributions from Chaos Theory, Policy and Practice', in Milovanovic, D. (ed.), pp. 179–94.

Arrigo, B. A. (1999), 'Constitutive Theory and the Homeless Identity: The Discourse of a Community Deviant', in Henry, S. and Milovanovic, D. (eds), pp. 67–85.

Arrigo, B. A. (2001), 'Critical Criminology, Existential Humanism, and Social Justice: Exploring the Contours of Theoretical Integration', *Critical Criminology*, Vol. 10, pp. 83–95.

Arrigo, B. A., Milovanovic, D. and Schehr, R. C. (2005), *The French Connection in Criminology: Rediscovering Crime, Law and Social Change*, Albany, NY: State University of New York Press.

Arthur, C. (1986), *Dialectic of Labour*, Oxford: Blackwell.

Bacon, R. and Eltis, W. (1976), *Britain's Economic Problem: Too Few Producers*, London: Macmillan.

Bagguley, P. and Mann, K. (1992), 'Idle Thieving Bastards? Scholarly Representations of the "Underclass"', *Work, Employment and Society*, Vol. 6, No. 1, pp. 113–26.

Baldwin, D., Coles, B. and Mitchell, W. (1997), 'The Formation of an Underclass or Disparate Processes of Social Exclusion' in MacDonald, R. (ed.), *Youth, the 'Underclass' and Social Exclusion*, London: Routledge, pp. 83–95.

Barak, G. (1999), 'Constituting O. J.: Mass Mediated Trials and Newsmaking Criminology', in Henry, S. and Milovanovic, D. (eds), pp. 87–110.

Baran, P. and Sweezy, P. (1989), *Monopoly Capital: An Essay on the American Economic and Social Order*, New York: Monthly Review Press.

Barry, K. (1995), *The Prostitution of Sexuality*, New York: New York University Press.

Bauer, O. (2000), *The Question of Nationalities and Social Democracy*, Minnesota, MN: University of Minnesota Press.

Becker, H. S. (1991), *Outsiders: Studies in the Sociology of Deviance*, New York: Free Press.

Benton, T. (1989), 'Marxism and Natural Limits: An Ecological Critique and Reconstruction', *New Left Review*, No. 178, Nov.–Dec., pp. 51–86.

Bernstein, E. (1993), *The Preconditions of Socialism*, trans. and ed. Henry Tudor, Cambridge: Cambridge University Press.

Beynon, J. and Dunkerley, D. (eds), (2000), *Globalisation: The Reader*, New York: Routledge.

Blakeley, G. and Bryson, V. (eds), (2005), *Marx and Other Four-Letter Words*, London: Pluto Press.

Böhm-Bawerk, E. von (1898), *Karl Marx and the Close of His System*, trans. Alice M. Macdonald, London: T. F. Unwin.

Bonger, W. A. (1916), *Criminality and Economic Conditions*, London: W. Heinemann.

Bonger, W. A. (1936), *Introduction to Criminology*, London: Methuen and Company.

Bonger, W. A. (1943), [1939], *Race and Crime*, New York: Columbia University Press.

Bovenkerk, F. (1984), 'The Rehabilitation of the Rabble: How and Why Marx and Engels Wrongly Depicted the Lumpenproletariat as a Reactionary Force', *The Netherlands Journal of Sociology*, Vol. 20, No. 1, pp. 13–41.

Box, S. (1983/1990), *Power, Crime and Mystification*, London: Routledge.

Braithwaite, J. (1984), *Corporate Crime in the Pharmaceutical Industry*, London: Routledge and Kegan Paul.

Brickey, K. F. (2006), *Corporate and White Collar Crime: Cases and Materials*, Fourth Edition, Greenvale, NY: Panel Publishers.

Buck, N. (1992), 'Labour Market Inactivity and Polarisation' in David J. Smith (ed.), *Understanding the Underclass*, London: Policy Studies Institute, pp. 9–31.

Burke, T. (2003), 'Warning: Drugs Cost the Earth', *New Statesman*, (Jun. 30).

Bussard, R. L. (1987), 'The "Dangerous Class" of Marx and Engels: The Rise of the Idea of the *lumpenproletariat*', *History of European Ideas*, Vol. 8, No. 6, pp. 675–92.

Butler, W. E. (1992), 'Crime in the Soviet Union: Early Glimpses of the True Story', *British Journal of Criminology*, Vol. 32, No. 2, pp. 144–59.

Calavita, K., Pontell, H. and Tillman, R. (1999), *Big Money Crime: Fraud and Politics in the Savings and Loans Crisis*, Berkeley, CA: University of California Press.

Callinicos, A. (1989), *Against Postmodernism: A Marxist Critique*, Cambridge: Polity.

Carchedi, G. (1977), *On the Economic Identification of Social Classes*, London: Routledge and Kegan Paul.

Carrington, K. (1998), 'Postmodernism and Feminist Criminologies: Fragmenting the Criminological Subject', in Walton, P. and Young, J. (eds), *The New Criminology Revisited*, Houndmills: Macmillan, pp. 76–97.

Carrington, K. and Hogg, R. (eds), (2002), *Critical Criminology: Issues, Debates, Challenges*, Cullompton: Willan.

Castells, M. (1996), *The Rise of the Network Society – The Information Age: Economy, Society and Culture*, Vol. 1, Oxford: Blackwell.

Castells, M. (2000), *End of Millennium – The Information Age: Economy, Society and Culture* , Vol. 3, Oxford: Blackwell Publishers.

Castells, M. (2004), *The Power of Identity – The Information Age: Economy, Society and Culture*, Vol. 2 (Second Edition), Oxford: Blackwell.

Castells, M. and Himanen, P. (2004), *The Information Society and the Welfare State: The Finnish Model*, Oxford: Oxford University Press.

Chambliss, W. J. (1975), 'Toward a Political Economy of Crime', *Theory and Society*, Vol. 2, pp. 149–70.

Chambliss, W. J. (1978), *On the Take: From Petty Crooks to Presidents*, London, Bloomington, IN: Indiana University Press.

Chambliss, W. J. (2001), *Power, Politics, and Crime*, Boulder, CO: Westview Press.

Chambliss, W. J. and Mankoff, M. (1976), *Whose Law, What Order? A Conflict Approach to Criminology*, New York: Wiley.

Chambliss, W. J. and Seidman, R. J. (1982), *Law, Order, and Power*, Reading, MA: Addison-Wesley Pub. Co.

Chigwada-Bailey, R. (1997), *Black Women's Experiences of Criminal Justice: A Discourse on Disadvantage*, Sherfield-on-Loddon: Waterside Press.

Christie, N. (2000), *Crime Control as Industry: Towards GULAGS, Western Style*, London: Routledge.

Christie, N. (2004), *A Suitable Amount of Crime*, London: Routledge.

Clinard, M. B. and Yeager, P. C. (1980/2005), *Corporate Crime*, Edison, NJ: Transaction Publishers.

Cloward, R. and Ohlin, L. E. (1960), *Delinquency and Opportunity: A Theory of Delinquent Gangs*, New York: Free Press.

Cohen, G. A. (1978), *Karl Marx's Theory of History: A Defence*, Oxford: Oxford University Press.

Cohen, G. A. (1983), 'Review of Allen Wood, *Karl Marx*', *Mind*, Vol. 92, p. 444.

Cohen, G. A. (2000), *If You're an Egalitarian, How Come You're So Rich?* Cambridge, MA: Harvard University Press.

Coleman, J. (1985), *The Criminal Elite: Understanding White-Collar Crime*, New York: St Martin's Press.

Colvin, M. and Pauley, J. (1983), 'A Critique of Criminology: Toward an Integrated Structural-Marxist Theory of Delinquency Production', *American Journal of Sociology*, Vol. 89, No. 3, pp. 513–51.

Cornell, D. (1991), *Beyond Accommodation: Ethical Feminism, Deconstruction, and the Law*, New York: Routledge.

Corpwatch (2006), "Corpwatch: Halliburton," at: http://www.corpwatch.org/article.php?list=type&type=15

Corrigan, P. and Leonard, P. (1978), *Social Work Practice under Capitalism: A Marxist Approach*, London: Macmillan.

Cowling, M. (1975), *The Dialectic in the Later Works of Marx and Its Relation to Hegel*, University of Manchester, PhD.

Cowling, M. (1989), 'The Case for Two Marxes, Re-stated', *Approaches to Marx*, Milton Keynes: Open University Press, pp. 1–32.

Cowling, M. (1995), 'Marx's Conceptual Framework From 1843–5: Hegelian Dialectic and Historical Necessity Versus Feuerbachian Humanistic Materialism?' *Studies in Marxism*, Vol. 2, Dec.

Cowling, M. (2002), 'Marx's Lumpenproletariat and Murray's Underclass: Concepts Best Abandoned?' in Cowling, M. and Martin, J. (eds), *Marx's Eighteenth Brumaire: (Post)Modern Interpretations*, London: Pluto Press, pp. 228–42.

Cowling, M. (2006), 'Alienation in the Older Marx', *Contemporary Political Theory*, Vol. 5, Pt. 3, August, pp. 319–39.

Cowling, M. (2006a), 'Postmodern Policies? The Erratic Interventions of Constitutive Criminology', *Internet Journal of Criminology*, pp. 1–170.

Cowling, M. and Manners, J. (1992), 'Pre-History: The Debate before Cohen' in Wetherly, P. (ed.), *Marx's Theory of History: The Contemporary Debate*, Aldershot: Avebury, pp. 9–29.

Cowling, M. and Reynolds, P. (2004), *Making Sense of Sexual Consent*, Aldershot: Ashgate.

Cressey, D. R. (1953), *Other People's Money: A Study of the Social Psychology of Embezzlement*, Glencoe, IL: Free Press.

Croall, H. (2001), *Understanding White Collar Crime*, Second Edition, Milton Keynes: Open University Press.

Cullen, F. T. and Maakestad, W. J. (1983), *Corporate Crime Under Attack: The Ford Pinto Case and Beyond*, Cincinnati, OH: Anderson Publishing.

Cutler, A., Hindess, B., Hirst, P. Q. and Hussain, A. (1977), *Marx's 'Capital' and Capitalism Today*, Vols 1 and 2, London: Routledge and Kegan Paul.

Daly, M. (1979), *Gyn/ecology: The Metaethics of Radical Feminism*, London: Women's Press.

Dashkov, G. V. (1992), 'Quantitative and Qualitative Changes in Crime in the Soviet Union', *British Journal of Criminology*, Vol. 32, No. 2, pp. 160–66.

Davis, H. B. (1978), *Toward A Marxist Theory of Nationalism*, New York: Monthly Review Press.

Dean, H. (1997), 'Young People and Social Citizenship' in MacDonald, R. (ed.), *Youth, the 'Underclass' and Social Exclusion*, London: Routledge, pp. 55–69.

Doig, A. (2006), *Fraud*, Cullompton: Willan.

Dorling, D. (2005), 'Prime Suspect: Murder in Britain' in Hillyard, P., Pantazis, C., Tombs, S., Gordon, D. and Dorling, D. (eds), *Criminal Obsessions: Why Harm Matters More Than Crime*, London: Crime and Justice Foundation, pp. 23–38.

Downes, D. and Rock, P. (1998), *Understanding Deviance: A Guide to the Sociology of Crime and Rule Breaking*, Oxford: Oxford University Press.

Draper, H. (1972), 'The Concept of the Lumpenproletariat in Marx and Engels', *Economies et Sociétés*, Vol. 6, No. 12, December, pp. 2285–312.

Durkheim, E. (1984), *The Division of Labour in Society*, Basingstoke: Macmillan.

Dworkin, A. (1987), *Intercourse*, London: Secker & Warburg.

Dworkin, A. (1981), *Pornography: Men Possessing Women*, London: Women's Press.

Dyer, J. (1999), *The Perpetual Prisoner Machine: How America Profits from Crime*, Boulder, CO: Westview Press.

Ericson, R. V. and Doyle, A. (2004), 'Criminalization in Private: The Case of Insurance Fraud' in Law Commission of Canada (ed.), *What is a Crime?* Vancouver, BC: University of British Columbia Press, pp. 99–124.

Evans, E. J. (2004), *Thatcher and Thatcherism*, (Second Edition), London: Routledge.

Fainstein, N. (1996), 'A Note on Interpreting American Poverty' in Mingione, E. (ed.), *Urban Poverty and the Underclass*, Oxford: Blackwell, pp. 152–9.

Fanon, F. (1969), *The Wretched of the Earth*, trans. Constance Farrington, Harmondsworth: Penguin.

Ferrell, J. A., Hayward J. K., Morrison, W. and Presdee, M. (eds), (2004), *Cultural Criminology Unleashed*, London: Glasshouse.

Ferrell, J. and Saunders, C. R. (eds), (1995), *Cultural Criminology*, Boston, MA: Northeastern University Press.

Fourier, C. (1967), *Le nouveau monde amoureux*, Oeuvres Complètes de Charles Fourier, VII, Paris: Anthropos.

Freeman, A. (2002), 'Marx after Marx after Sraffa', at: http://ideas.repec.org/p/pra/mprapa/2619.html

Freire, P. (1972), *The Pedagogy of the Oppressed*, Harmondsworth: Penguin.

Garland, D. (1990), *Punishment and Modern Society: A Study in Social Theory*, Oxford: Clarendon Press.

Garland, D. (2001), *The Culture of Control: Crime and Social Order in Contemporary Society*, Oxford: Oxford University Press.

Gay, P. (1979), *The Dilemma of Democratic Socialism: Eduard Bernstein's Challenge to Marx*, New York: Octagon Books.

Geis, G. (2006), *White Collar and Corporate Crime*, Upper Saddle River, NJ: Prentice Hall.

Geras, N. (1983), *Marx and Human Nature: Refutation of a Legend*, London: Verso.

Geras, N. (1985), 'The Controversy about Marx and Justice', *New Left Review*, No. 150, Mar.–Apr., pp. 47–85.

Geras, N. (1990), *Discourses of Extremity: Radical Ethics and Post-Marxist Extravagances*, London: Verso.

Geras, N. (1992), 'Bringing Marx to Justice: An Addendum and Rejoinder', *New Left Review*, No. 195 (Nov.–Dec.), pp. 37–69.

Gill, S. (1995), 'Globalisation, Market Globalisation and Disciplinary Neo-Liberalism', *Millennium, Journal of International Studies*, Vol. 24, Pt. 3, pp. 399–423.

Glasbeek, H. (2004), *Wealth by Stealth: Corporate Crime, Corporate Law, and the Perversion of Democracy*, Toronto, ON: Between The Lines.

Glaser, D. and Walker, D. (eds), (2007), *Twentieth Century Marxism: A Global Introduction*, London: Routledge.

Gobert, J. and Punch, M. (2003), *Rethinking Corporate Crime*, London: Butterworth.

Gottschalk, M. (2006), *The Prison and the Gallows: The Politics of Mass Incarceration in America*, Cambridge: Cambridge University Press.

Grabosky, P. and Sutton, A. (eds), (1989), *Stains on a White Collar: Fourteen Studies in Corporate Crime or Corporate Harm*, Annandale, NSW: Federation Press.

Gray, J. (2004), 'Blair's Project in Retrospect', *International Affairs*, Vol. 80, 1, January, pp. 39–48.

Gray, K. R., Frieder, L. A. and Clark, G. W. (2005), *Corporate Scandals: The Many Faces of Greed, the Great Heist, Financial Bubbles, and the Absence of Virtue*, St Paul, MN: Paragon Press.

Gregerson, H. and Sailer, L. (1993), 'Chaos Theory and Its Implications for Social Science Research', *Human Relations*, Vol. 46, pp. 777–802.

Griffin, S. (1984), *Woman and Nature : The Roaring Inside Her*, London: Women's Press.

Gross, R. and Levitt, N. (1994), *Higher Superstition: The Academic Left and Its Quarrels with Science*, Baltimore and London: Johns Hopkins University Press.

Hagen, J. (1994), *Crime and Disrepute*, Thousand Oaks, CA: Pine Forge Press.

Hall, S. M. and Jefferson, T. (1976), *Resistance through Rituals*, London: Hutchinson University Library.

Hall, S. M., Critcher, C., Jefferson, T., Clarke, J. and Roberts, B. (1978), *Policing the Crisis : Mugging, the State, and Law and Order*, London: Macmillan.

Hall, S. M. and Jacques, M. (1990), *New Times: The Changing Face of Politics in the 1990s*, London: Lawrence and Wishart.

Hallsworth, S. (2002), 'The Case for a Postmodern Penality', *Theoretical Criminology*, Vol. 6, No. 2, pp. 145–63.

Harding, N. (1977/1981), *Lenin's Political Thought*, Vols 1 and 2, London: Macmillan.

Harding, N. (1996), *Leninism*, Basingstoke: Macmillan.

Harman, C. (1999), *Explaining the Crisis – A Marxist Re-Appraisal*, London: Bookmarks.

Hayes, P. (1988), '*Utopia* and the Lumpenproletariat: Marx's Reasoning in *The Eighteenth Brumaire of Louis Napoleon Bonaparte*', *Review of Politics*, Vol. 50, No. 3, pp. 445–65.

Heath, A. (1997), 'The Attitudes of the Underclass', in David J. Smith (ed.), *Understanding the Underclass*, London: Policy Studies Institute, pp. 32–47.

Heidensohn, F. (1995), *Women and Crime*, Houndmills: Macmillan Press.

Held, D. and McGrew, A. (eds), (2001), *The Global Transformation Reader*, Cambridge: Polity, Cambridge.

Henry, S. and Milovanovic, D. (1996), *Constitutive Criminology: Beyond Postmodernism*, London: Sage.

Henry, S. and Milovanovic, D. (eds), (1999), *Constitutive Criminology at Work: Applications to Crime and Justice*, New York: State University of New York Press.

Henry, S. and Milovanovic, D. (2000), 'Constitutive Criminology: Origins, Core Concepts, and Evaluation', *Social Justice*, Vol. 27, No. 2, 268. Questia. 9 November 2006, at: http://www.questia.com/PM.qst?a=o&d=5001793345

Henry, S. and Milovanovic, D. (2001), 'Constitutive Definition of Crime: Power as Harm' in Henry, S. and Lanier, M. M. (eds), *What is Crime? Controversies over the Nature of Crime and What to Do about It*, Lanham, MA: Rowman and Littlefield, pp. 165–78.

Herrnstein, R. J. and Murray, C. (1996), *The Bell Curve*, New York: Free Press.

Hillyard, P. and Tombs, S. (2005), 'Beyond Criminology?' in Hillyard, P., Pantazis, C., Tombs, S., Gordon, D. and Dorling, D. (eds), *Criminal Obsessions: Why Harm Matters More Than Crime*, pp. 5–22.

Hindess, B. and Hirst, P. Q. (1975), *Pre-Capitalist Modes of Production*, London: Routledge.

Hindess, B. and Hirst, P. Q. (1976), *Mode of Production and Social Formation*, London: Routledge.

Hirst, P. Q. (1975), 'Marx and Engels on Law, Crime and Morality' in Taylor, I., Walton, P. and Young, J. (eds), *Critical Criminology*, London: Routledge and Kegan Paul, pp. 203–32.

Hobsbawm, E. (1974/1959), *Primitive Rebels*, Manchester: Manchester University Press.

Hodgson, G. (1982), *Capital, Value and Exploitation*, Oxford: Blackwell.

Home Office, 'What is the British Crime Survey?' at: http://www.homeoffice.gov.uk/rds/bcs1.html

Hooks, G., Mosher, C., Rotolo, T. and Lobao, L. (2004), 'The Prison Industry: Carceral Expansion and Employment in U.S. Counties, 1969–1994', *Social Science Quarterly*, Vol. 85, No. 1, March, pp. 37–57.

Hopkins, K. (2008), 'Alaska May Lose Access to Arizona Prisons', *Anchorage Daily News*, February 2, at: http://www.adn.com/100/story/302693.html

House of Commons Research Paper 98/64. (1998), June 4. at: http://www.parliament.uk/commons/lib/research/rp98/rp98–064.pdf

Huard, R. (1988), 'Marx et Engels devant la marginalité: la découverte du lumpenprolétariat', *Romantisme*, Vol. 18, No. 59, pp. 4–17.

Hughes, J. (2000), *Ecology and Historical Materialism*, Cambridge: Cambridge University Press.

Hunt, A. (1993), *Explorations in Law and Society: Toward a Constitutive Theory of Law*, New York: Routledge.

Itoh, M. (2006), 'Marx's Economic Theory and the Prospects For Socialism' in Hiroshi Uchida (ed.), *Marx for the 21st-Century*, London: Routledge, pp. 21–35.

International Centre for Prison Studies, (2007), *World Prison Population List*, (Seventh Edition), at: http://www.prisonstudies.org

Jeffreys, S. (1997), *The Idea of Prostitution*, North Melbourne, Victoria: Spinifex.

Jessop, B. (1990), *State Theory: Putting the Capitalist State in Its Place*, Cambridge: Polity Press.

Johnston, L., MacDonald, R., Mason, P., Ridley, L. and Webster, C. (2000), *Snakes and Ladders: Young People, Transitions and Social Exclusion*, Bristol: The Policy Press/Joseph Rowntree Foundation.

Karpowitz, D. and Kenner, M. (n. d.), 'Education as Crime Prevention: The Case for Reinstating Pell Grant Eligibility for the Incarcerated', at: http://www.bard.edu/bpi/pdfs/crime_report.pdf

Kasarda, J. D. (1993), 'Urban Industrial Transition and the Underclass' in Wilson, W. J. (ed.), *The Ghetto Underclass*, Newbury Park, CA: Sage, pp. 43–64.

Kavanagh, D. (1987), *Thatcherism and British Politics: The End of Consensus*, Oxford: Oxford University Press.

Kidron, M. (1970), *Western Capitalism Since the War*, Harmondsworth: Penguin Books.

Kliman, A. (2007), *Reclaiming Marx's 'Capital': A Refutation of the Myth of Inconsistency*, Lanham, MD: Lexington Books.

Konings, M. (2007), 'Simon Clarke's Theory of Crisis: A Critique', *Studies in Marxism*, Vol. 11, pp. 5–20.

Lacan, J. (1961), *The Seminar of Jacques Lacan: Book IX: Identification 1961–1962*, trans. Cormac Gallageur (unpublished).

Laffargue, B. and Godefroy, T. (1989), 'Economic Cycles and Punishment: Unemployment and Imprisonment, A Time-Series Study: France, 1920–1985', *Contemporary Crises*, Vol. 13, pp. 371–404.

Lea, J. (2002), *Crime and Modernity: Continuities in Left Realist Criminology*, London: Sage.

Lenin, V. I. (1970), *Imperialism, The Highest Stage of Capitalism, Selected Works*, Vol. 1, Moscow: Progress Publishers.

Lenin, V. I. (1972), *The Right of Nations to Self Determination* (1914), in *Collected Works*, Moscow: Progress Publishers, Vol. 20, pp. 393–454.

Levi, M. (1988), *Regulating Fraud: White Collar Crime and the Criminal Process*, London: Routledge.

Levi, M. (1999), *Fraud: Organisation, Motivation and Control*, Vols 1 and 2, Aldershot: Dartmouth.

Levi, M. (2008), *The Phantom Capitalists*, Second Edition, Aldershot: Dartmouth.

Lewis, O. (1966), *La Vida*, New York: Random House.

London Edinburgh Weekend Return Group (1980), *In and Against the State*, London: Pluto Press.

Lotspeich, R. (1995), 'Crime in the Transition Economies', *Europe Asia Studies*, Vol. 42, No. 4, June, pp. 555–89.

Luhmann, N. A. (1992), 'Operational Closure and Structural Coupling: The Differentiation of the Legal System', *Cardozo Law Review* Vol. 13, pp. 1419–41.

Luxemburg, R. (1951), *The Accumulation of Capital*, London: Routledge and Kegan Paul.

Lynch, M. J., McGurrin, D. and Fenwick, M. (2004), 'Disappearing Act: The Representation of Corporate Crime Research in Criminological Literature', *Journal of Criminal Justice*, Vol. 32, No. 5, September, pp. 389–98.

Lyotard, J. F. (1984), *The Postmodern Condition*, Manchester: Manchester University Press.

McCarney, J. (1980), *The Real World of Ideology*, Brighton: Harvester.

MacDonald, R. (1994), 'Fiddly Jobs, Undeclared Working and the Something for Nothing Society', *Work Employment and Society*, Vol. 8, No. 4, December, pp. 507–30.

McGrew, A. (1997), *The Transformation of Democracy*, Cambridge: Polity.

MacLeod, C. (2006), 'China Makes Ultimate Punishment Mobile', *USA Today*, June 14, at: http://www.usatoday.com/news/world/2006–06-14-death-van_x.htm

Mandel, E. 'Marx's Theory of Crises' at: http://www.isg-fi.org.uk/spip.php?article140

Mandelbrot, B. (1983), *The Fractal Geometry of Nature*, New York: W. H. Freeman.

Mao, T. T. (1967), 'Analysis of the Classes in Chinese Society', *Selected Works*, Peking: Foreign Languages Press, Vol. 1.

Marcuse, H. (1972), *One Dimensional Man*, New York: Sphere.

Marcuse, H. (1986), *Reason and Revolution*, London: Routledge.

Marx, K. (1976), *Capital*, Vol. 1, Harmondsworth: Penguin.

Marx, K. and Engels, F. E. (1956–62), *Werke*, Berlin: Dietz Verlag.

Marx, K. and Engels, F. E. (1975–), *Collected Works*, London: Lawrence and Wishart (referenced as MECW).

Mathiesen, T. (2000), *Prison on Trial*, Winchester: Waterside.

Matsuda, M. J., Larence, C. R., Delgado, R. and Crenshaw, K. W. (eds), (1993), *Words That Wound*, San Francisco, CA: Westview Press.

Mead, G. H. (1967), *Mind, Self and Society from the Standpoint of a Social Behaviorist*, Chicago, IL: Chicago University Press.

Merton, R. K. (1938), 'Social Structure and Anomie', *American Sociological Review*, Vol. 3, pp. 672–82.

Messner, S. F. and Rosenfeld, R. (1997), *Crime and the American Dream*, Belmont, CA: Wadsworth Publishing Company.

Michalowski, R. J. and Carlson, S. M. (1999), 'Unemployment, Imprisonment, and Social Structures of Accumulation: Historical Contingency in the Rusche-Kirchheimer Hypothesis', *Criminology*, Vol. 37, No. 2, pp. 217–49.

Michalowski, R. and Cramer, R. C. (eds), (2006), *State-Corporate Crime: Wrongdoing at the Intersection of Business and Government*, Piscataway, NJ: Rutgers University Press.

Milovanovic, D. (1994), 'Law, Ideology, and Subjectivity: A Symbiotic Perspective on Crime and Justice', in Barak, G. (ed.), *Varieties of Criminology: Readings from a Dynamic Discipline*, Westport, CT: Praeger, pp. 231–51.

Milovanovic, D. (1996), 'Postmodern Criminology', *Justice Quarterly* 13: 567–610.

Milovanovic, D. (1997), *Postmodern Criminology*, New York: Garland Publishing.

Milovanovic, D. (2002), *Critical Criminology at the Edge: Postmodern Perspectives, Integration, and Applications*, Westport, CT: Praeger.

Milovanovic, D. (ed.), (1997a), *Chaos, Criminology, and Social Justice: The New Orderly (Dis)Order*, Westport, CT: Praeger.

Milovanovic, D. and Ragland, E. (eds), (2001), *Topologically Speaking*, New York: Other Press.

Mitchell, M. (2003), 'The Pros of Privately Housed Cons: New Evidence on the Cost Savings of Private Prisons', available as a link from the Corrections Corporation of America at: http://www.correctionscorp.com/researchfindings2.html

Mokhiber, R. and Weissman, R. (1999), *Corporate Predators: The Hunt for Mega-Profits and the Attack on Democracy*, Monroe, ME: Common Courage Press.

Mokhiber, R. and Weissman, R. (2004), *On the Rampage: Corporations Plundering the Global Village*, Monroe, ME: Common Courage Press.

Muncie J. (2001), 'The Construction and Deconstruction of Crime' in Muncie, J. and McLaughlin, E. (eds), *The Problem of Crime*, London: Sage.

Murray, C. (1984), *Losing Ground: American Social Policy, 1950–1980*, New York: Basic Books.

Murray, C. (1994), *In Pursuit of Happiness and Good Government*, San Francisco, CA: ICS Press.

Murray, C. (1996), *Charles Murray and the Underclass: The Developing Debate*, London: IEA Health and Welfare Unit in association with the Sunday Times.

Murray, C. (2000), 'The Underclass Revisited', American Enterprise Institute Short Publications at: http://www.aei.org/publications/pubID.14891/pub_detail.asp

Murray, C. (2001), *Underclass + 10*, London: Civitas.

Murray, C., Young, J., Rutherford, A. and Davies, M. (1997), *Does Prison Work?* London: IEA Health and Welfare Unit.

Musto, M. (2007), 'The Rediscovery of Karl Marx', *International Review of Social History*, Vol. 52, 2007, pp. 477–98.

Myhill A. and Allen J. (2002), 'Rape and Sexual Assault of Women: The Extent and Nature of the Problem. Findings from the British Crime Survey', Home Office Research Report 237, available at: http://www.homeoffice.gov.uk/rds/pdfs2/r159.pdf

Neocleous, M. (2000), *The Fabrication of Social Order*, London: Pluto.

Norris, C. (1990), *What's Wrong with Postmodernism: Critical Theory and the Ends of Philosophy*, London: Harvester Wheatsheaf.

Obaid, T. A. (2005), *Statement, Panel on International Migration and the Millennium Development Goals*, 2005, available at: http://www.unfpa.org/news/news. cfm?ID=685

Packard, V. (1959), *Status Seekers*, London: Longman.

Palango, P. (2004), *Above the Law: The Crooks, the Politicians, the Mounties, and Rod Stamler: The Shocking But True Story of Corporate Crime and Political Corruption in Canada*, Toronto, ON: McClelland & Stewart.

Parenti, C. (1999), *Lockdown America: Police and Prisons in the Age of Crisis*, London: Verso.

Pashukanis, E. B. (1980), *Pashukanis: Selected Writings on Marxism and Law*, London: Academic Press.

Pearce, F. (1978), [1976], *Crimes of the Powerful*, London: Pluto.

Pearce, F. and Tombs, S. (1998), *Toxic Capitalism: Corporate Crime and the Chemical Industry*, Aldershot: Dartmouth Publishing.

Penna, S. and Yar, M. (2003), 'From Modern To Postmodern Penality? A Response to Hallsworth', *Theoretical Criminology*, Vol. 7, No. 4, pp. 469–82.

Penney, S. (2004), 'Crime, Copyright, and the Digital Age' in Law Commission of Canada (ed.). *What is a Crime?* Vancouver, BC: University of British Columbia, pp. 61–98.

Pickover, C. (1988), 'Pattern Formation and Chaos in Networks', *Communication of the ACM*, Vol. 31, pp. 136–51.

Pontell, H. N. and Geis, G. L. (2006), *International Handbook of White-Collar and Corporate Crime*, New York: Springer.

Poulantzas, N. (1975), *Classes in Contemporary Capitalism*, London: New Left Books.

Poveda, T. G. (1994), *Rethinking White Collar Crime*, Westport, CT: Praeger.

Pratt, J. (2008), 'Scandinavian Exceptionalism in an Era of Penal Excess: Part 1: The Roots of Scandinavian Exceptionalism', *British Journal of Criminology*, Vol. 48, No. 2, March, pp. 119–37.

Presdee, M. (2000), *Cultural Criminology and the Carnival of Crime*, London: Routledge.

Punch, M. (1996), *Dirty Business: Exploring Corporate Misconduct: Analysis and Cases*, Thousand Oaks, CA: Sage.

Quinney, R. (1970), *The Social Reality of Crime*, Boston, MA: Little, Brown and Co.

Quinney, R. (1970a), *Crime and Justice in Society, The Problem of Crime*, New York: Dodd, Mead.

Quinney, R. (1974), *Criminal Justice in America: A Critical Understanding*, Boston, MA: Little, Brown and Company.

Quinney, R. (1977), *Class, State and Crime*, New York: David McKay.

Quinney, R. (2002), [1974], *Critique of Legal Order*, New Brunswick, NJ and London. (Originally Boston: Little, Brown and Company).

Rawls, J. (1973), *A Theory of Justice*, Oxford: Oxford University Press.

Reiman, J. (1998), *The Rich Get Richer and the Poor Get Prison: Ideology, Class, and Criminal Justice*, Boston, MA: Allyn and Bacon.

Reiman, J. (2004), 'The Rich (Still), Get Richer...Understanding Ideology, Outrage and Economic Bias' at: http://paulsjusticepage.com/elite-deviance/ reiman.htm

Rich, A. (1981), *Compulsory Heterosexuality and the Lesbian Existence*, London: Onlywomen Press.

Roberts, K. (1997), 'Is There an Emerging British "Underclass"?' in MacDonald, R. (ed.), *Youth, the 'Underclass' and Social Exclusion*, London: Routledge, pp. 39–54.

Rosner, L. S. (1986), *The Soviet Way of Crime*, South Hadley, MA: Bergin and Garvey.

Rosoff, S. M., Pontell, H. N. and Tillman, R. (2006), *Profit without Honour: White-Collar Crime and the Looting of America*, Fourth Edition, Upper Saddle River, NJ: Prentice Hall.

Rusche, G. and Kirchheimer, O. (1939), *Punishment and Social Structure*, New York: Columbia University Press.

Sanders, T. (2004), *Sex Work: A Risky Business*, Cullompton: Willan.

Särlvik, B. and Crewe, I. (1983), *Decade of Dealignment*, Cambridge: Cambridge University Press.

Sayer, D. (1979), *Marx's Method*, New York: Humanities Press.

Schehr, R. C. (1999), 'Intentional Communities, the Fourth Way: A Constitutive Integration' in Henry, S. and Milovanovic, D. (eds), pp. 249–74.

Schlegel, K. and Weisburd, D. (eds), (1992), *White-Collar Crime Reconsidered*, Boston, MA: Northeastern University Press.

Schwendinger, H. and J. (1975), 'Defenders of Order or Guardians of Human Rights?' in Taylor, I., Walton, P. and Young, J. (eds), *Critical Criminology*, London: Routledge, pp. 113–46.

Shapiro, S. (1984), *Wayward Capitalists: Target of the Securities and Exchange Commission*, Newhaven: Yale University Press.

Shaw, W. (1978), *Marx's Theory of History*, Hutchinson: London.

Silver, H. (1997), 'National Discourses of the New Urban Poverty' in Mingione, E. (ed.), *Urban Poverty and the Underclass*, Oxford: Blackwell, pp. 105–38.

Simpson, S. (2002), *Corporate Crime, Law and Social Control*, Cambridge: Cambridge University Press.

Slapper, G. and Tombs, S. (1999), *Corporate Crime*, Harlow: Longman.

Snider, L. (1992), *Bad Business: Corporate Crime in Canada*, Scarborough, ON: Nelson.

Snider, L. and Pearce, F. (1992), *Corporate Crime: Contemporary Debate*, Toronto, ON: University of Toronto.

Sokal, A. and Bricmont, J. (1999), *Intellectual Impostures*, London, Profile Books.

Spitzer, S. (1975), 'Toward a Marxian Theory of Deviance', *Social Problems*, Vol. 22, June, pp. 638–51.

Spivak, G. (1988), 'Can the Subaltern Speak?' in Nelson, C. and Grossberg, L. (eds), *Marxisms and the Interpretation of Culture*, London: Macmillan.

Stalin, J. V. (1913), *Marxism and the National Question*, at: http://www.marxists.org/reference/archive/stalin/works/1913/03.htm

Stalin, J. V. (1976), *Foundations of Leninism*, Peking: Foreign Languages Press, at: http://www.marx2mao.com/Stalin/FL24.html

Stallybrass, P. (1990), 'Marx and Heterogeneity: Thinking the Lumpenproletariat', *Representations*, No. 31, Summer, pp. 69–95.

Steedman, I. (1977), *Marx after Sraffa*, London: New Left Books.

Steele, J. and Goldberg, S. (2008), 'What is the Real Death Toll in Iraq?' *Guardian*, March 19.

Stern, N. (2006), *Review Report on the Economics of Climate Change*, London: H. M. Treasury, available at: http://www.hm-treasury.gov.uk/independent_ reviews/stern_review_economics_climate_change/stern_review_report.cfm

Stiglitz, J. and Bilmes, L. J. (2008), *The $3 Trillion War*, London: Allen Lane.

Stirner, M. (1907), *The Ego and His Own*, trans. Steven T. Byington, New York: Benjamin R. Tucker.

Sumner, C. (1994), *The Sociology of Deviance: An Obituary*, Buckingham: Open University Press.

Sutherland, E. (1945), 'Is "White-collar Crime" Crime?' *American Sociological Review*, Vol. 10, pp. 132–9.

Sutherland, E. (1985), *White Collar Crime: The Uncut Version*, London: Yale University Press.

Sykes, G. M. and Matza, D. (1957), 'Techniques of Neutralization', *American Sociological Review*, Vol. 22, pp. 664–70.

Talwar, P. (ed.), (2006), *Corporate Crime*, New Delhi: Gyan.

Tappan, P. W. (1947), 'Who is the Criminal?', *American Sociological Review*, Vol. 12, pp. 96–102.

Taylor, A. (2007), 'A Taxing Problem', *Guardian Unlimited*, January 10, at: http://www.guardian.co.uk/commentisfree/story/0,,1986929,00.html

Taylor, I. (1999), *Crime in Context: A Critical Criminology of Market Societies*, Cambridge: Polity.

Taylor, I., Walton, P. and Young, J. (1973), *The New Criminology: For a Social Theory of Deviance*, London: Routledge and Kegan Paul.

Taylor, I., Walton, P. and Young, J. (1973a), 'Rejoinder to the Reviewers', *British Journal of Criminology*, Vol. 13, No. 4, 1973, pp. 401–3.

Taylor, I., Walton, P. and Young, J. (1975), *Critical Criminology*, London: Routledge and Kegan Paul.

Teubner, G. (1988), *Autopoietic Law: A New Approach to Law and Society*, New York: Walter de Gruyter.

Teubner, G. (1992), 'The Two Faces of Janus: Rethinking Legal Pluralism', *Cardozo Law Review*, Vol. 13, pp. 1443–62.

Teubner, G. (1993), *Law as an Autopoietic System*, Oxford: Blackwell.

Thomas, J. and Milovanovic, D. (1999), 'Revisiting Jailhouse Lawyers: An Excursion into Constitutive Criminology' in Henry, S. and Milovanovic, D. (eds), pp. 227–46.

Thompson, K. (1998), *Moral Panics*, London: Routledge.

Tierney, J. (1996), *Criminology, Theory and Context*, London: Prentice Hall.

Tillman, R. and Indergaard, M. (2005), *Pump and Dump: The Rancid Rules of the New Economy*, New Brunswick, NJ; London: Rutgers University Press.

Tombs, S. and Whyte, D. (2003), 'Scrutinising the Powerful: Crime, Contemporary Political Economy and Critical Social Research', in Tombs, S. and Whyte, D. (eds), *Unmasking the Crimes of the Powerful: Scrutinising States and Corporations*, New York/London: Peter Lang.

Tombs, S., White, D. and Croall, H. (2007), *Safety Crimes*, Cullompton: Willan.

Tonry, M. (2004), 'Why Aren't German Penal Policies Harsher and Imprisonment Rates Higher?', *German Law Journal*, No. 10, 1 October.

Trevaskes, S. (2007), 'Severe and Swift Justice in China', *British Journal of Criminology*, Vol. 47, No. 1, pp. 23–41.

Trotsky, L. D. (1936), *The Revolution Betrayed*, at: http://www.marxists.org/archive/trotsky/1936/revbet/index.htm

Unger, T. (1987), *False Necessity*, New York: Cambridge University Press.

United Nations Office on Drugs and Crime (2005), 'United Nations World Drugs Report, Executive Summary', United Nations, at: http://www.unodc.org/pdf/WDR_2005/volume_1_ex_summary.pdf

Van Bemmelen, J. M. (1955), 'Pioneers in Criminology: VIII Willem Bonger', *The Journal of Criminal Law, Criminology, and Police Science*, Vol. 46, 1955, pp. 293–302.

Veblen, T. (1925), [1899], *The Theory of the Leisure Class*, London: Allen and Unwin.

Virgin Lands (2007), at: http://en.wikipedia.org/wiki/Virgin_Lands_Campaign; http://www.soviethistory.org/index.php?action=L2&SubjectID=1954tselina&Year=1954

Wacquant, L. J. D. and Wilson, W. J. (1993), 'The Cost of Racial and Class Exclusion in the Inner City' in Wilson, W. J. (ed.), *The Ghetto Underclass*, Newbury Park, CA: Sage, pp. 25–42.

Walton, P. and Young, J. (eds), (1998), *The New Criminology Revisited*, Basingstoke: Macmillan.

Weisburd, D., Wheeler, S., Waring, E. and Bode, N. (1994), *Crimes of the Middle Classes: White Collar Offenders in the Federal Courts*, New Haven, CT: Yale University Press.

Weiss, R. P. (2001), '"Repatriating" Low-wage Work: The Political Economy of Prison Labor Reprivatization in the Postindustrial United States', *Criminology*, Vol. 39, No. 2, pp. 253–91.

Wheatcroft, S. (1999), 'Victims of Stalinism and the Soviet Secret Police: The Comparability and Reliability of the Archival Data – Not the Last Word', *Europe Asia Studies*, Vol. 51, No. 2, pp. 315–45.

Wigmore, J. H. (1941), 'Willem Bonger', *Journal of Criminal Law and Criminology*, Vol. 31, Pt. 5, p. 657.

Williams, C. R. and Arrigo, B. A. (2004), *Theory, Justice and Social Change: Theoretical Integrations and Critical Applications*, New York: Kluwer.

Williams, J. (2003), Review of Susan Simpson, *Corporate Crime, Law and Social Control* in *Canadian Journal of Sociology Online*, May–Jun, at: www.cjsonline.ca/reviews/corpcrime.html

Wilson, E. (1977), *Women and the Welfare State*, London: Tavistock.

Wilson, J. Q. (1985), *Thinking About Crime*, New York: Vintage Books.

Wintour, P. (2008), 'Ministers Trying to Save Cash on Benefits Take-up Says Byers', *Guardian*, March 24.

Wong, K. C. (2002), 'Policing in the People's Republic of China: The Road to Reform in the 1990s', *British Journal of Criminology*, Vol. 42, pp. 281–316.

Wright, E. O. (1975), *Class, Crisis and the State*, London: New Left Books.

Wright, E. O. (1985), *Classes*, London: Verso.

Young, J. (1997), 'Breaking Windows: Situating the New Criminology' in Walton and Young (eds), pp. 14–46.

Young, J. (1997a), 'Left Realist Criminology' in Maguire et al. (eds), *The Oxford Handbook of Criminology*, Oxford: Oxford University Press, pp. 473–95.

Young, J. (1997), *The Vertigo of Late Modernity*, London: Sage.

Young, J. (1999), 'The Failure of Criminology: The Need for a Radical Realism' in Muncie, J. et al. (eds), *Criminological Perspectives*, ch. 40. London: Sage.

Young, J. (2002), 'Critical Criminology in the Twenty First Century: Critique, Irony and the Always Unfinished', in Carrington and Hogg, R. (eds), pp. 251–74.

Young, J. and Matthews, R. (eds), (1992), *Rethinking Criminology: The Realist Debate*, London: Sage.

Index

Note: the index does not include the endnotes or the bibliography. Entries in **bold** are the main place where the entry is discussed. Book titles are included only if the book is discussed rather than simply mentioned.

LaVergne, TN USA
26 September 2010
198444LV00001B/79/P